An Exemplary Man

An Exemplary Man

Cornelius and Characterization in Acts 10

BONNIE J. FLESSEN

◈PICKWICK *Publications* · Eugene, Oregon

AN EXEMPLARY MAN
Cornelius and Characterization in Acts 10

Copyright © 2011 Bonnie J. Flessen. All rights reserved. Except for brief quotations in critical publications or reviews, no part of this book may be reproduced in any manner without prior written permission from the publisher. Write: Permissions, Wipf and Stock Publishers, 199 W. 8th Ave., Suite 3, Eugene, OR 97401.

Unless otherwise noted, all Scripture quotations in English are from the New Revised Standard Version Bible, copyright © 1989, Division of Christian Education of the National Council of the Churches of Christ in the United States of America. Used by permission. All rights reserved.

Pickwick Publications
An Imprint of Wipf and Stock Publishers
199 W. 8th Ave., Suite 3
Eugene, OR 97401

www.wipfandstock.com

ISBN 13: 978-1-61097-294-9

Cataloging-in-Publication data:

Flessen, Bonnie J.

    An exemplary man : Cornelius and characterization in Acts 10 / Bonnie J. Flessen

    p. ; 23 cm. Includes bibliographical references and indexes.

    ISBN 13: 978-1-61097-294-9

    1. Bible. N.T. Acts X—Criticism, Narrative. 2. Masculinity. I. Title.

BS2625.2 F5 2011

Manufactured in the U.S.A.

Contents

Acknowledgments / vii
Abbreviations / viii

   Introduction / 1
1 Method and Hermeneutic / 7
2 Scholarly Perspectives on Masculinity / 37
3 Cornelius and the Virtue of Piety / 68
4 Cornelius the Centurion: Masculinity and Empire / 114
   Conclusion / 157

Bibliography / 173
Subject and Name Index / 185
Ancient Documents Index / 191

Acknowledgments

Many people have helped bring this project to fruition. I am thankful for the vision and support of my teachers and colleagues at Carthage College and the Lutheran School of Theology at Chicago. David Rhoads, Barbara Rossing, and Ray Pickett guided my research and clarified my writing. David Rhoads also served as my advisor; I am grateful for his patience and wisdom. Finally, I want to thank my husband, Soren, and our daughters, Maren and Ivy. Their persistent graciousness and humor have been invaluable.

Abbreviations

Ag. Ap.	*Against Apion*
Ann.	*Annals*
ANRW	*Aufstieg und Niedergang der Römischen Welt: Geschichte und Kultur Roms im Spiegel der Neueren Forschung.*
Ant.	*The Antiquities of the Jews*
Ant. rom.	*The Roman Antiquities*
Aug.	*The Deified Augustus*
BDAG	Bauer, Danker, Arndt, and Gingrich. *Greek-English Lexicon of the New Testament and Other Early Christian Literature.*
Brag.	*The Braggart Warrior*
BIS	Biblical Interpretation Series
BibInt	*Biblical Interpretation*
BTB	*Biblical Theology Bulletin*
CBQ	*Catholic Biblical Quarterly*
CIL	*Corpus Inscriptionum Latinarum*
CBQ	*Catholic Biblical Quarterly*
Conc. Apam.	*On Concord with Apamea*
Dom.	*Domitian*
Dreams	*On Dreams*
Embassy	*Embassy to Gaius*
Ep.	*Moral Essays*
Eth. nic.	*Nicomachean Ethics*
HTR	*Harvard Theological Review*
Hist.	*Histories*, Livy
Histor.	*Histories*, Tacitus

ILS	*Inscriptiones Latinae Selectae*
JBL	*Journal of Biblical Literature*
JRS	*Journal of Roman Studies*
JSNT	*Journal for the Study of the New Testament*
JSNTSS	*Journal for the Study of the New Testament: Supplement Series*
Jul.	*The Deified Julius*
Leg.	*Laws*
LCL	*Loeb Classical Library*
Life	*The Life*
Mem.	*Memorable Sayings and Doings*
Moses	*On the Life of Moses*
Nat.	*Natural History*
NRSV	New Revised Standard Version
OCD	*Oxford Classical Dictionary*
OGIS	*Orientis Graeci Inscriptiones Selectae*
Peri.	*Perikeiromene: The Girl with her Hair Cut Short*
Poet.	*Poetics*
QE	*Questions and Answers on Exodus*
Res. gest. divi Aug.	*The Deeds of the Divine Augustus*
Rom. hist.	*Roman History*
Sat.	*Satire*
Satyr.	*Satyricon*
SCJ	Studies in Christianity and Judaism
Sib. Or.	*Sibylline Oracles*
SIG	*Sylloge Inscriptionum Graecarum*
TDNT	*Theological Dictionary of the New Testament*
Tib.	*Tiberius*
Tumult.	*Protest against Mistreatment*
Vesp.	*Vespasian*
War	*The Jewish War*

Introduction

A GALLERY OF MEN

ENTERING INTO THE STORY of Acts of the Apostles may be compared to entering into an exhibit in an art gallery. The exhibit brims with portraits of bold and gallant men. Each portrait features a different man, each with his own unique and appealing features. As one walks through the exhibit, one can also discern patterns in these portraits. Most portraits convey a strategic interest in men who represent their gender in positive ways. The arrangement of portraits and the patterns therein communicate to the viewer the positive potential of men as well as the realization of that potential.

At the far end of this exhibit is a mural that features each man and his role in the overarching theme of the exhibit. This grand mural presents a collection of models of masculinity for the viewer to study and absorb. From the portraits and the mural, characteristics of the ideal man emerge. A man with these characteristics persuades the masses, receives and obeys divine direction, and shows a willingness to change when God demands it. This exhibit also highlights patterns concerning rhetorical skill, obedience, and generosity. These men look up to God in prayer, and they look out to the crowds, conveying the power of God to guide and shape the lives of both men and women.

Much like an exhibit in an art gallery, the story of the Acts of the Apostles presents several different exemplary models. Acting as a painter and a docent, the narrator guides the audience through a number of positive exemplars of masculinity and proposes a composite that could function as a model for men in the emerging church. Each portrait proposes its own aspects of masculinity. Some individual portraits show audiences how an exemplary man prays, or what he does with his money, or how to respond to the Holy Spirit. Other portraits, especially of military men, show how one can be affiliated with the Roman military and yet live out one's faith in the God of Israel.[1] As a whole, the story of Acts offers male audiences an alternative way of being masculine in a world that valued and perpetuated male domination.

AIMS OF THIS STUDY

Some New Testament scholars highlight the pattern of gender in Acts, recognizing that Acts presents a series of men who skillfully evangelize and defend the developing church in adverse circumstances. However, most scholars do not fully identify the significance of this gender pattern, nor do they investigate the gender-related rhetorical strategies inherent in each portrait and the narrative as a whole. In an effort to exegete Acts 10 as a turning point for the mission to the Gentiles, most scholars do not recognize that Cornelius is, as a man, an exemplar of masculinity as well as a representative of the Gentiles. Although Cornelius plays an important role in the plot of Acts and the ethnic expansion of the emerging church, the characterization of Cornelius is more complex than most scholars suggest. Gender is an important feature of his characterization. Because gender contributes to rhetorical impact, the masculinity of Cornelius deserves to be further explored.

Another relevant feature of the portrait of Cornelius is related to his affiliation with the Roman military. In Acts 10, Luke presents us with a military man whose piety toward the God of the Judeans is exemplary. While some have investigated Cornelius as a character who may have some role in Luke's overall strategy with regard to empire, most scholars do not add issues of masculinity to their analysis. Cornelius is a man, a Roman, and a God-fearer, and it is possible that Luke is speaking to all of these realities in Acts 10. Here we can envision Luke's multilayered approach; issues of masculinity, empire, piety, Judaism, and sovereignty all come into view. The portrait of Cornelius thus deserves further study

---

1. This study uses the phrases "God of Israel" and "God of the Judeans" interchangeably.

that integrates these issues and takes into account what kind of man Luke is presenting to us.

This study will assess the portrait of Cornelius and analyze the details and purposes for his portrait. Using the method of narrative criticism, the lens of masculinity studies, and literary and material remains from antiquity, this study will investigate the gender-related strategies of the implied author of Acts that appear in the characterization of Cornelius.[2] The method of narrative criticism is an appropriate tool to interpret the story of Acts. The method also allows for an in-depth analysis of his characterization. Historical remains from the Mediterranean world will provide a foundation from which to view Luke's persuasive goals in the episode, but narrative analysis will take precedence. The burgeoning subfield of masculinity studies will function as an interpretive lens through which we can view characterization, rhetoric, and gender in Acts 10.

Using the method of narrative criticism and a hermeneutic of masculinity, I will argue that Cornelius is an exemplary man in Luke's story. In the characterization of Cornelius, Luke presents his audience with a model man. From an historical perspective, Cornelius does not exemplify all the features of elite Greco-Roman, military, and Jewish masculinities. However, in Luke's story, Cornelius stands out as a model of masculinity in several specific ways. The portrait of Cornelius brings three key features to the mural of masculinity in Acts: piety toward the God of Israel, generous almsgiving, and the relinquishment of control over Judean subjects. These traits of piety, generosity, and submission illustrate Luke's vision of masculinity, as well as Luke's rhetorical strategies concerning sovereignty and the Roman Empire. Cornelius' role as a centurion in the Roman military associates him with the dominance and power of Rome, yet Cornelius falls to the feet of Peter, a Judean subject. This surprising gesture points the audience toward the God of Israel and proposes submission, rather than dominance, as a key trait of masculinity. In Acts 10, Luke shows his audience that good men give up their power and recognize the God of Israel as the ultimate sovereign.

---

2. While the primary focus of this study is to investigate Luke's strategies with regard to masculinity, other dynamics are involved. The complex nature of masculinity in antiquity, as well as its rhetorical presentation, complicates historical research and narrative analysis. Other dynamics that are related to masculinity include political and religious sovereignty, ethnicity, class, and rhetoric.

This study is informed by a variety of primary and secondary sources. Primary sources include the writings of Josephus, Philo, Tacitus, and Suetonius. Material remains such as monuments, inscriptions, images, and coinage add historical evidence with which to compare and contrast the portrait of Cornelius. Luke's Gospel also serves as an important informant in the analysis of Acts 10. Secondary sources include the works of Colleen Conway and Stephen Moore, both of whom present literary readings that are sensitive toward characterization, rhetoric, and gender. Scholars of Roman history, including Karl Galinsky and Yann Le Bohec, shed some light on imperial Roman rule and the military that supported it. Finally, scholars of Jewish history help flesh out the political and religious dynamics between Romans and Judeans in the first and second centuries CE. These scholars include Martin Goodman and Shaye Cohen.

OVERVIEW OF ARGUMENT

In Chapter 1, I will discuss secondary scholarship regarding the interaction of characterization, rhetoric, and gender in Acts 10. I will discuss how scholars assess characterization in general and how literary critics who work with Luke-Acts do not fully explore the implications of the characterization of Cornelius. I will provide an overview and rationale for the lens of masculinity studies, the method of narrative criticism, and the ways that these two approaches can fuse effectively. The fusion of narrative criticism and a hermeneutic of masculinity productively investigates the gender-related rhetorical strategies inherent in the characterization of Cornelius. Finally, I will describe the characterization of positive examples of masculinity in Acts 1–9, along with their similarities and differences in relationship to one another. These forerunners of Cornelius begin to establish the audience's standards of judgment and they affect the audience's experience of Cornelius.

In Chapter 2, I will review secondary scholarship on the topic of masculinity among classicists and New Testament scholars. Three classicists are featured in this chapter: Maud Gleason, Carlin Barton, and Craig Williams. Each of these scholars illuminates aspects of elite Greco-Roman masculinity, especially the aspect of control over oneself and others. New Testament scholars have built on the works of these classicists and other scholars. The book entitled *Behold the Man: Jesus and Greco-Roman Masculinity* by Colleen Conway and the anthology entitled *New Testament Masculinities*, edited by Stephen Moore, come to center stage at this point. These scholars consider elite masculinity as well as alternative masculinities that take shape among non-elites and under colonizing powers like Rome. More work needs to be done, however, on the topic of military masculinity. While scholarship in this area is not extensive, it is possible to interpret the characterizations of military men in New Testament texts in light of the historical representations of military men in literary and material remains.

In Chapter 3, I investigate the specific words and phrases that Luke uses to describe the piety of Cornelius. One way to explore constructs of masculinity in antiquity is to study the virtues of men. Through these virtues, we see a glimpse of "the good man." Here I build on Colleen Conway's conclusion that piety and masculinity were intertwined. Language about piety appears in a variety of literary and material remains that refer to elite Greco-Roman men such as emperors and to Jewish patriarchs such as Moses. These references include εὐσέβεια (piety and reverence), δικαιοσύνη (righteousness and fairness), and generosity with one's financial resources. Similar language also appears in the characterization of Cornelius in Acts 10. Luke uses words about piety that his audience is likely to understand, repeats them for emphasis, and reconfigures them so that they point away from personal honor and toward the God of Israel. As a God-fearer, Cornelius is a model of how Gentiles, especially military men, could exemplify piety toward Yahweh.

In Chapter 4, I explore the literary and material remains concerning military men in general and centurions in particular. I attempt here to give priority to evidence from the first- and second-centuries CE, although evidence from outside these parameters is sometimes considered. These remains provide historical background with which to compare and contrast the portrayal of Cornelius. Also relevant here is the possibility of military masculinity and its embrace of physical combat and the use of force to coerce subjects into submission. Cornelius is similar to extrabiblical portrayals of centurions in that he interacts with civilians and occasionally gives orders that people are to follow. However, Cornelius differs from extrabiblical portrayals in that he follows the orders of the God of Israel and kneels before a Judean subject. The προσκυνεῖν gesture will be discussed here, as a way in which Luke brings down the mighty Romans from their thrones.[3] In addition to the ramifications of this gesture, I will also review the portrayals of angry Roman rulers, like Pilate and Herod, who act violently and insist on personal glory. In the narrative, these characters reveal the vices of Roman administration and function as foils for Cornelius.

Finally, in the conclusion, I ask the question, "What kind of man is this?" Luke presents us with a multifaceted role model whose features are not easily summarized or isolated from one another, yet all the facets reveal something about Luke's strategies in Acts 10. I also ask how the methods and sources that are used to interpret New Testament texts can develop so that the male characters in texts can be seen in terms of their masculinity.

---

3. In Luke 1:52, Mary states that God has "brought down the mighty from their thrones." In this study, unless otherwise noted, all Bible quotations in English are from the NRSV.

Method and Hermeneutic

CORNELIUS COMES TO US in the form of a story. Luke crafts his account in narrative form so that the audience experiences the characters and events in a literary context. This chapter focuses on the literary nature of the book of Acts and the literary methods with which Luke-Acts has been studied. I will review different scholarly perspectives on ancient characterization and characterization among modern literary critics. Here the work of Schlomith Rimmon-Kenan and David Gowler will take precedence. I will also review works written by John Darr, who has studied characterization in Luke-Acts. While this study does not wholly adopt the perspectives of these scholars, I will suggest that characterization, rhetoric, and gender can form a prism through which we can view the masculinity of Cornelius. I will define key terms and suggest that a hermeneutic of masculinity can be fused with narrative criticism in order to gauge what kind of man Cornelius is. Finally, I will review the sequence of male characters leading up to Cornelius in Acts 10, identifying how Luke characterizes each of them.

CHARACTERIZATION AS AN AREA OF SCHOLARLY DEBATE

Since literary criticism of the New Testament began to appear on the scholarly scene, literary critics have studied how narrators of New Testament texts describe and reveal the characters that appear in New Testament narratives. In this section, I will summarize the scholarly debates regarding ancient characterization. Since New Testament narratives are ancient, some scholars insist on discussing how the ancients revealed and described their characters. Rather than focus on how modern authors build characters, these scholars study biblical stories for clues about ancient techniques of characterization. These studies have produced four insights: a preference for indirect characterization rather than direct description of characters, a focus on the outward activities of a character rather than the psychological makeup of a character's mind, a tendency toward characters that do not change, and an emphasis on how a character is embedded in society. I will also summarize modern debates about characterization in literature, including issues of plot and narration. This summary will set the stage for an assessment of the secondary scholarship surrounding characterization in Luke-Acts.

Critical studies of ancient characterization have provided biblical scholars with four main insights about the ways in which the ancients developed and revealed their characters. First, studies point out a preference for indirect characterization rather than direct description of ancient characters. Indirect or implicit characterization relies on the audience to infer character traits. Rather than telling the audience directly about the character, the narrator describes the actions or speech of a character, and the audience extracts and infers traits from those actions. Richard Thompson states that in Greco-Roman literature, "the typical way to present a character is by implicit description, in which the narrative focuses on the character's actions rather than one's ἦθος."[1] This implicit method is far from incomplete, however. According to Aristotle, to know one's *praxis* is to know one's *ethos*.[2] The description of the activities of Cornelius (his prayer and almsgiving, for example) focuses on his *praxis*; from these actions, the audience infers that Cornelius is pious.[3]

Second, ancient narratives tend to describe the outward activities of a character rather than his or her inward thoughts and reflections. Ancient narrators rarely reflect on the psychological makeup of a character; thus the audience sometimes remains unaware about a character's

---

1. Thompson, "Believers and Religious Leaders," 330; Burnett, "Characterization and Reader Construction."

2. Aristotle, *Poetics* 15:2: "the character will be good, if the choice is good" (Fyfe, LCL).

3. In this specific instance, the narrator reinforces the traits of piety with the direct descriptions εὐσεβὴς and δικαῖος.

motivations.⁴ These ancient narratives do not address psychological questions, and according to some critics, do not allow for individuality among ancient characters.⁵ To ask why Cornelius became affiliated with Judaism is to ask a question that the narrator will not answer; instead the narrator brings his outward activities to the fore without explaining the reasons for or complications of Cornelius' religious choice.

Third, in ancient narratives, some scholars consider ancient characters to be "unchanging and predictable."⁶ These predictable characters model certain traits or behavior that the audience can evaluate.⁷ In regard to classical literature such as Homer, Fred Burnett argues that "characters were presented as types, that is, either as ideal representation or as an example of the characteristics of a species or group."⁸ For example, the narrator of Acts portrays Cornelius as an ideal God-fearer and faithful representative of Gentiles who can be incorporated into the Way. Because of the direction of the Holy Spirit, Cornelius changes, but he continues to appear faithful as he joins the emerging church and becomes baptized as a follower of Jesus.

Fourth, ancient characterization places emphasis on the relationships that a character has with larger families or groups. Ancient characters and people were embedded in layers of biological and fictive kin, religious groups, patron-client networks, and other political and social strata. This embeddedness appears even in one's personality; the phrase "dyadic personality" refers to the ways that one person was intimately connected with another. As a result, even one's view of self reflects others. In his book *Portraits of Paul*, Bruce Malina studies ancient rhetorical handbooks and texts as "native informants" in order to learn

4. Burnett, "Characterization and Reader Construction," 11.

5. Ibid., 14. Burnett argues that ancient narratives do allow for some degree of individuality and character development. For more on the spectrum of characterization and the poles of plot agent and autonomous individual, see the section on modern debates about characterization below.

6. Rhoads et al., *Mark as Story*, 100.

7. M. Thompson, "'God's Voice,'" 179. Marianne Meye Thompson argues that most ancient narratives "illustrate an ethical ideal or virtue," while biblical characters do not. Thompson suggests that biblical characters "may be held up as models for certain exemplary behaviors." However, the distinction between the illustration of an ethical ideal or virtue and the modeling of certain exemplary behaviors is not immediately clear. Cornelius illustrates ethical ideals and virtues, and the narrator of Acts holds him up as a model of exemplary behaviors such as prayer and almsgiving.

8. Burnett, "Characterization and Reader Construction," 6.

how ancient people described and understood the self and one another.⁹ According to Malina, ancient rhetorical texts such as encomiums, progymnasmata, and forensic speeches reveal a high regard for individuals who are deeply embedded in society. Encomiums included references to a person's origin and birth, education, accomplishments, and a comparison to other persons; these references linked a person to others and compared that person to others who did not measure up.¹⁰ Although Malina's approach is not without problems, his argument draws attention to the tightly woven nature of Greco-Roman society and the individuals who maneuvered within that society.¹¹ As a character that is embedded in Roman political structure, Judaism, friendship, and the emerging church, Cornelius illustrates the way in which a man could be integrated into multiple groups at one time.

Characterization continues to generate debate among modern literary critics and critics of New Testament texts. While some New Testament scholars put more emphasis on comparison with ancient characterization, others consult scholars who do not limit their inquiry to ancient narratives. Critics of modern literature such as Schlomith Rimmon-Kenan figure into the current scholarly landscape about how to understand characterization in biblical literature. Biblical scholars such as Gowler see debates revolving around the theories of characterization.¹² I will summarize Gowler's analysis and include two other literary issues: telling versus showing, and the reliability or unreliability of a narrator.

Robert Fowler detects a common theme in the general debate about characterization when he states "The theory of characterization is underdeveloped and underutilized, both in literary studies generally and in biblical literary criticism in particular."¹³ Neither literary studies in general nor biblical criticism in particular resolves the issues. First, as with the discussion of ancient characterization, the issue of indirect

---

9. Malina and Neyrey, *Portraits of Paul*, 5.

10. Ibid., 23–24.

11. Although Malina provides a plethora of primary sources as evidence for an ancient understanding of dyadic or modal personality, his approach to those sources could more fully recognize the political nature of oratory and rhetoric in general. Encomiums may be a means to discover what was important to ancient people, but orators often praised individuals who held influential political positions.

12. Gowler, *Host, Guest, Enemy, and Friend*, 29.

13. Fowler, "Characterizing Character in Biblical Narrative," 97.

or implicit presentation (showing) versus direct description (telling) appears in scholarly arguments about modern literature. Modern literary critics such as Schlomith Rimmon-Kenan have become authority figures in this debate. According to Rimmon-Kenan, direct description refers to the description of a character by an adjective (εὐσεβής for Cornelius in Acts 10:2) or possibly some other kind of noun or part of speech.[14] Indirect presentation, however, "does not mention the trait but displays and exemplifies it in various ways, leaving to the reader the task of inferring the quality they imply."[15] Rimmon-Kenan suggests that direct description carries the most weight in a narrative; when a narrator describes a character directly, that description is "voiced by the most authoritative voice in the text."[16] Rimmon-Kenan also adds to the discussion the issue of comparison and contrast, a technique that places characters next to one another for "reciprocal characterization."[17] Because of the proximity of characters, the audience begins to note similarities and differences between them, and both characters grow and develop in light of that comparison and contrast. For example, the narrator of Acts compares and contrasts Peter and Cornelius in Acts 10; this technique is particularly effective because it places Cornelius, an authoritative Roman centurion, at the feet of Peter, "an unlettered and ordinary man" (Acts 4:13).

David Gowler analyzes the current discussion about characterization when he discusses characters as merely words on a page or as autonomous individuals who seem more like real persons. On one end of the spectrum is Aristotle, who considers characters as agents of plot only. From this perspective, characters are more like words on a page. This view of character is sometimes called "textual" in that they are generated by words.[18] Characterization serves the development of the plot and characters keep the plot moving. Characters are "important because of what they do, not because of who they are."[19] On the other end of the spectrum, characters are autonomous individuals whose features stand

14. Rimmon-Kenan, *Narrative Fiction*, 59.
15. Ibid.
16. Ibid., 60.
17. Ibid., 70.
18. Gowler, *Host, Guest, Enemy, and Friend*, 35
19. Ibid., 43. Here Gowler notes that Aristotle, formalists, and structuralists would agree with this view of characters.

out as unique. Characters are not only agents; they are people who have qualities that do not necessarily move the plot forward.[20] As I will show below, scholars have too often placed Cornelius in the category of plot agent. Although Acts 10 functions as a fulcrum in the plot of Acts, the characterization of Cornelius contributes to the gender-related rhetorical purposes of the narrative. This approach has not yet been fully discussed in secondary scholarship about the characterization of Cornelius.

The degree of reliability of a narrator has also arisen among scholars who discuss characterization in biblical literature. A narrator is someone created by the implied author to convey standards of judgment, values, and beliefs. The narrator communicates the ideology of the implied author. "Reliability" is a technical term that denotes the narrator's ability to create a consistent storyworld and establish consistent standards of judgment. A reliable narrator tells a story in such a way that the audience can enter into the storyworld, believe the events contained therein, and be persuaded by the rhetoric of the narrative. Wayne Booth has suggested that a reliable narrator "speaks or acts in accordance with the work (which is to say, the implied author's norms, unreliable when he does not."[21] The most common opinion among literary critics of biblical literature is expressed by John Darr, who states that the narrator of biblical narratives is reliable.[22] When a narrator describes a character, the audience should believe what the narrator is saying. For Darr, a reliable narrator is an essential element in a biblical narrative, and the narrator "fully and faithfully represents the implied author."[23]

Alice Bach, on the other hand, considers the narrator of a biblical story unreliable and encourages audiences to distance themselves, for the narrator is "a fictive henchman of the author."[24] "Too often," she states, "biblical critics have been ideal readers, allied with the patriarchal narrator, and have not recognized that he was telling it slant."[25] For Bach, resisting the narrator allows the audience to "peel away" the

---

20. Merenlahti, "Characters in the Making," 59.
21. Booth, *Rhetoric of Fiction*, 158–59.
22. "Luke-Acts has a single, omniscient, (usually) third person reliable narrator." Darr, *Herod the Fox*, 61; Darr, *On Character Building*, 51.
23. Darr, *Herod the Fox*, 80n53.
24. Bach, "Signs of the Flesh," 64.
25. Ibid., 63.

ideology of a text, "a necessary task for the feminist critic."[26] While Bach is correct in thinking critically about the ideology of a text, she confuses resisting the ideology of a text with resisting the narrator as construct. The narrator *is* "a fictive henchman of the author," and by studying the role of the narrator, we discover the ideology that we can (or must) then resist. The modern biblical critic studies the role of the narrator as a means to communicate the ideology. The critic may disagree with the rhetoric or ideology of a narrative without questioning the narrator's role as representative of the implied author. For instance, when one questions the narrator's direct description of the piety of Cornelius in Acts 10, the plot of Acts breaks down.[27] Cornelius is no longer a worthy character (or man) to carry the emerging church into a new era. One then questions the patterns of characterization and does not recognize the rhetorical devices inherent in those patterns. Darr correctly surmises the role of narrator as part of the rhetoric or ideology of a text; Like Darr, I suggest that considering the narrator reliable is to allow oneself to view the entire vista of rhetorical impact. The characterization of Cornelius is a reliable representation of the narrator's standards of judgment regarding masculinity.

CHARACTERIZATION IN LUKE-ACTS

Not only have scholars discussed theories of characterization, but they have also discussed characterization in Luke-Acts. In this section, I will summarize the discussions of scholars who treat the issues of characterization in Luke-Acts, including the aforementioned David Gowler and John Darr. These scholars focus their attention on the characterization of Jews and Judaism in Luke-Acts, while narrative critics such as Robert Tannehill, Beverly Roberts Gaventa, and Ronald Witherup address the characterization of Cornelius in Acts 10. These scholars, however, do not combine characterization, rhetoric, and gender to the necessary extent. I will state how I can build on their arguments for the benefit of the present study.

---

26. Ibid., 68.

27. Darr states that seeing the narrator as unreliable "destabilizes the entire narrative." Darr, "Narrator as Character," 54.

David Gowler studies the characterization of the Pharisees in Luke-Acts with a socio-narratological approach that combines narrative insights with an assessment of the "cultural scripts" that manifest themselves along with the Pharisees in selected episodes.[28] Gowler asks literary questions about selected episodes, but also asks questions about social dynamics drawn from anthropological models, such as patron/client, honor/shame, and limited good. "A dialogue is necessary," Gowler writes, "between literary analyses and analyses of the cultural contexts in which the narratives were created."[29] Of the most relevance to this study is Gowler's treatment of Acts 15, in which he sees a combination of direct and indirect characterization of the Jews present at the Apostolic Council. However, this section of Gowler's argument is brief, and he does not fully assess Cornelius as a gendered character.

Through his publications, John Darr expresses a clear interest in characterization and rhetoric in Luke-Acts, but despite his methodological precision, he does not consider the characterization of Cornelius. Instead, he focuses on recurring characters[30] and the portrayals of Jews.[31] His method differs from that of the present study as well. In *Herod the Fox* and *On Character Building*, Darr employs the method of reader-response criticism to characterization and rhetoric in Luke-Acts.[32] While this approach is literary and combines two important facets of literary analysis, reader-response criticism differs significantly from and should be distinguished from narrative criticism.[33] Narrative criticism is a bet-

---

28. Gowler studies twelve episodes from Luke's Gospel and three episodes from Acts.

29. Gowler, *Host, Guest, Enemy, and Friend*, 9.

30. Particularly in *On Character Building*, Darr look at recurring characters. These include John the Baptist, the Pharisees, and Herod.

31. About Gamaliel, Darr wrote the essay "Irenic or Ironic?"

32. Darr employs reader-response criticism in "'Watch How You Listen'" and "Narrator as Character," noted above.

33. Narrative criticism and reader-response criticism have some features in common. Both belong under the aegis of literary criticism, and as colleagues under that umbrella, both pay attention to characterization. Both narrative and reader-response criticisms have to determine how to relate to history, and both include historical settings and backgrounds as interpretive factors. In addition, Darr suggests that "literary works achieve certain effects—aesthetic, emotional, moral, ideological—in an audience by means of rhetorical strategies" Darr, *Herod the Fox*, 20. Narrative criticism shares this critical premise, but the two methods part ways when one asks how those rhetorical effects are produced. For reader response critics, rhetorical effects are gener-

ter fit for the study of the characterization of Cornelius; narrative critics do not need to reconstruct a specific reader and his or her extratext, a difficult task when dealing with the dating and place of composition for Acts. The narrative method also promotes an interest in repetition and patterns, which allows for recognition of gender patterns. Darr's work contributes to this study by combination of characterization and rhetoric, but he does not draw his reader's attention to gender.[34]

Acts 10 garners more attention among narrative critics, but even in these scholarly circles, the pattern of gender does not receive its due. I begin with Robert Tannehill. In both volumes of *The Narrative Unity of Luke-Acts*, Tannehill perceives common theological threads, such as a loyalty to Israel, the tragedy of Jewish rejection, and the activity of the Holy Spirit.[35] According to Tannehill, these theological threads take shape in a unified narrative that connects events and individuals together for the purpose of mission. Tannehill's sensitivity to the plot of Acts leads him to chapters 10–11. Most of his treatment of this episode

---

ated by the interaction of two distinct parties: the text and the extratext, defined as a cultural repertoire of language, social norms, literary conventions, and commonly known historical and geographical facts. Darr, *On Character Building*, 22. In order to reconstruct a specific reader and his or her interpretive moves, reader response critics must then identify as carefully as possible the time and place in which a document was written and the accompanying cultural scripts. That reader will look for consistency in the text and fill in gaps with his or her extratext. For narrative critics, however, the implied author builds rhetorical effects into in the narrative, and the reconstruction of the reader's interpretive moves becomes less important. Nevertheless, narrative critics do attempt to identify the rhetorical effects of a narrative on an implied audience, and some attention toward the location and dating of a story helps a narrative critic in this regard. On this issue, Rhoads states, "narrative criticism affirms that a Gospel narrative is a historical artifact, a first-century contextual document fully conditioned by its time and place and representing one person's (or one community's) conception of the world." Rhoads, *Reading Mark*, 27–28. It is possible that both reader response criticism and narrative criticism will need to adjust their approaches as other methods move onto the interpretive scene, particularly performance criticism and other readings that are based on an oral, instead of literary, paradigm. Stephen Moore predicts this problem when he differentiates reading from hearing. Moore, *Literary Criticism*, 85. Darr uses a different quote from the same work by Moore and suggests that reading and hearing are essentially the same thing. Darr, *On Character Building*, 28. For more on an oral paradigm for interpretation of New Testament texts as well as the foundations of performance criticism, see Rhoads, "Performance Criticism."

34. Other authors use reader response criticism to study characterization of Jews in Luke-Acts: Thompson, "Subtlety as a Literary Technique"; Thompson, "Believers and Religious Leaders in Jerusalem"; Carroll, "Luke's Portrayal of the Pharisees."

35. Tannehill, *Narrative Unity*, 2:2–3.

centers on a debate with Haenchen, who argues that Cornelius passively accepts the will of God and contributes little else to the story.[36] According to Haenchen, Cornelius is a passive character. Tannehill counters that the visions and directions of the Holy Spirit are only "divine promptings" that require "human action or reflection."[37] The characterization of Cornelius figures prominently in both analyses, and Tannehill notes the indirect and direct characterization of Cornelius as well as his piety, which "parallels that of a devout Jew."[38] Tannehill also asserts the importance of narrative rhetoric: "The narrator is always seeking to weave a spell over us, so the reader must beware. On the other hand, those who are so suspicious that they cannot play the game lose their chance for excitement."[39] For Tannehill, "playing the game" requires a critical interpretation that detects the power of the narrator's persuasive skills without discounting the narrator altogether.[40] However, Tannehill focuses on the role of Cornelius in the plot of Acts, and relates Acts 10 to the overall theological themes in Luke-Acts in general. He writes, "It is more difficult for Jewish Christians to reject the divine promptings by declaring Cornelius unclean and unacceptable to God when they recognize so much of what they honor and emphasize in this man."[41] The characterization of Cornelius then serves both the plot and the tension between Jews and Gentiles. While Acts 10–11 does address these issues, Cornelius is more than a conduit for mission. The narrator of Acts presents him as an ideal man and exemplar of masculinity as well as faithfulness. Tannehill does not take this interpretive route.

Beverly Roberts Gaventa uses the narrative method to interpret Acts 10 in *From Darkness to Light: Aspects of Conversion in the New Testament*. Gaventa's holistic, literary point of view and insights regarding the integrity of Acts 10–11 reveal her assumption that the narrative was composed by one hand rather than multiple redactors.[42] To employ an art-related metaphor, the portrait of Cornelius is in its original

36. Haenchen, *Acts of the Apostles*, 362.
37. Tannehill, *Narrative Unity*, 2:131.
38. Ibid., 2:133.
39. Ibid., 2:4.
40. See above for my critique of Bach on this issue.
41. Tannehill, *Narrative Unity*, 2:133.
42. Gaventa tackles the redaction-critical approach of Martin Dibelius. Gaventa, *Darkness to Light*, 110.

frame. By naming literary precedents for double visions, noting the series of conversions in this section of Acts, and focusing on the theme of hospitality, Gaventa highlights Cornelius as a centerpiece of the narrative. She compares and contrasts Cornelius with the Ethiopian eunuch (Acts 8: 26–40) and considers Cornelius the pattern for the incorporation of Gentiles into the emerging church.[43] Like Tannehill, however, her analysis is oriented toward criticism of another scholar (Dibelius, in this case). She aims to argue for the "whole-cloth" nature of Acts 10–11 rather than examine the details of the characterization of Cornelius. Her analysis also does not approach the issue of gender patterns and the ways in which the narrator presents masculinity.[44]

From the summaries of these scholarly arguments, one can discern a need in secondary scholarship among literary and narrative critics of Acts 10. Some studies combine characterization and rhetoric, but use a different method and do not discuss Cornelius. Other studies use narrative criticism but subsume Cornelius into plot analysis. All of these scholars discussed here tend not to see gender patterns and the portrayals of exemplary men as significant elements of Acts 10. We move now to a brief assessment of masculinity studies in relationship to the characterization of men in Acts.

A HERMENEUTIC OF MASCULINITY FOR NEW TESTAMENT STUDIES

Exegeting a biblical text with literary criticism and a gendered lens is not a new endeavor. Feminist scholars began the process many years ago

43. Ibid., 105–6.

44. In an article published in *JSNT*, "Cornelius Over and Over," Ronald Witherup uses literary criticism to examine redundancy in Acts 10–11. His attention toward structure puts the narrator's use of repetition into bold print. At the outset, Witherup appears to intend to study the characterization of Cornelius when he states, "The importance of characterization has often been overlooked in the study of the Cornelius story" (47). However, in the course of Witherup's argument, the details about Cornelius as well as his masculinity become subsumed in yet another analysis of plot. This careful study of structure leads toward his conclusion that "characterization serves the development of the plot . . . the figures of Ananias and Cornelius respectively fade out of the story as its redundant features take shape, while simultaneously the figures of Paul and Peter come to the fore for purposes of witnessing to the gospel" (63). While the article helps critics discern repetition as an important element of an episode, this conclusion does not take the next step toward the analysis of gender patterns.

and continue their important work today. Some feminist scholars would consider the study of masculinity and New Testament texts as similar enterprises. From the perspective of those feminist scholars, all New Testament texts overtly or covertly reinforce masculinity as the status quo. However, in the last five years, the study of masculinity has broken new ground among New Testament interpreters. The complexity of ancient masculinity is now a high-profile issue. Across disciplinary lines, gender is now a complex, socially constructed phenomenon consisting not only of biology but also of social roles and responsibilities assigned to a person because of his or her biological sex. Concepts of masculine behavior fluctuate with time, culture, and geography. Our modern concepts of gender do not necessarily correspond to the concepts of gender in the Mediterranean during the early centuries of the Roman Empire. Thus it is helpful for New Testament interpreters to learn the challenges and expectations specific to each gender during the time of the New Testament writings. While ancient women were under pressure to be feminine, it is likely that ancient men were under pressure to be masculine. Determining what that meant, precisely, is the task not only of historians but also of biblical scholars. This study will contribute to the ancient understandings of gender by exploring how masculinity—especially upper-class masculinity—plays a role in Acts 10.[45]

Seeing a New Testament text in light of characterization, rhetoric, and gender allows us to ponder how ancient authors reflected and challenged the concepts of gender in the text's original audience. Such a perspective gained scholarly attention with the recent publication of *New Testament Masculinities*, edited by Stephen Moore and Janice Capel Anderson. The essays in this anthology approach ancient masculinity and New Testament interpretation from a multiplicity of angles.[46] The essay by Mary Rose D'Angelo treats issues of masculinity in Luke-Acts. In the essay she contends that "in the late first and early second century, early Christian texts begin to express explicit interest in an anxiety about

---

45. For a review of literature on masculinity studies and New Testament interpretation, see chapter 2 below.

46. The essays include a social-scientific approach to Matthew (Neyrey, "Jesus, Gender"), a postcolonial reading of the man Jesus (Thurman, "Looking for a Few Good Men"), an investigation of Stoicism and effemination (Swancutt, "'Disease of Effemination'"), and a study of the pastorals as masculine protocols (Glancy, "Protocols of Masculinity").

the confirmation of a masculine role."[47] Although masculinity during this time period "was by no means monolithic,"[48] D'Angelo recognizes in the Pastorals, *The Shepherd of Hermas* and Luke-Acts the trademarks of traditional imperial patriarchy and the requirements of a *paterfamilias* (self-control and authority).[49] For D'Angelo, the narrator of Luke-Acts directs his story to Theophilus, an elite male, and grounds his story in elite masculinity.[50] According to classicists such as Maud Gleason, "public speaking . . . was the hallmark of the socially privileged male."[51] D'Angelo builds on this statement and highlights the host of men in Acts who speak in public. Perhaps because of her (over)emphasis on public speaking, D'Angelo does not include Cornelius in her study of upper-class men in Acts. However, as a Roman centurion and most likely an upper-class man, Cornelius needs to be considered. Like Peter and Paul, Cornelius plays a role in the construction of masculinity within the storyworld of Acts.

Intriguingly, a book about women in early Judaism and Christianity comes close to the method and lens of this study. In *First Converts: Rich Pagan Women and the Rhetoric of Mission in Early Judaism and Christianity*, Shelly Matthews argues that Hellenistic Jewish women, particularly wealthy women, were attracted to and actively propagated early Christianity. Matthews takes note of high-standing women in Josephus and Acts, studying each example from the angles of characterization, rhetoric, and gender, in addition to historical background.[52] Relevant primary sources and the secondary work of classicists help build her argument that the repeated mention of high-standing women in Josephus and Acts has positive rhetorical effects.[53] Though written about female characters, key features of this book speak to masculinity and male exemplars in Acts. Matthews combines characterization, rhetoric, gender, and class sensitivities to create an original reading of wealthy women in Josephus and Acts. This study will also feature such

---

47. D'Angelo, "'Knowing How to Preside,'" 265.

48. Ibid., 270.

49. Ibid.

50. D'Angelo asserts that Theophilus is most likely of the equestrian order.

51. Gleason, "Elite Male Identity," 67.

52. Matthews describes rhetorical analysis as the study of historical narratives that attempt to create their own reality and persuade their readers.

53. Matthews, *First Converts*, 29.

a combination, but will approach the evidence from the perspective of a hermeneutic of masculinity.

THE MASCULINITY OF CORNELIUS

Both literary criticism and masculinity studies do not fully explore Cornelius as a contributor to the overall rhetorical and gender-related strategies of Acts. I will now suggest some possible reasons for this. Scholars may subordinate some details of his portrait and neglect his masculinity because they cannot resist comment on his pivotal role in the plot. The recognition of Cornelius as a man, and therefore a gendered character, may reflect the relatively new status of masculinity studies in general.

While it may seem obvious that Cornelius is male, even scholars who are sensitive to gender issues have not fully addressed this element in his characterization. In recent decades, scholars who wished to explore gender as an interpretive lens looked to the portrayals of women in New Testament texts. Frequently asked questions included, "What does it mean to be a woman in the first century CE? How did women live, how they did they rebel, and how were they remembered?" Feminists asked questions about the religious lives of women, the fundamental differences and inequalities in their social roles, and the effects of class on both of these issues. Feminists scoured the New Testament for female characters, looking to reconstruct their historical contexts, to place a spotlight on their roles in narratives, or to interpret inscriptions or other material remains upon which their messages and images survive. The feminist hermeneutic remains vital to our understanding of the world and cultures of the early imperial period and to our interpretation of New Testament texts.

Some feminists may be reluctant to study ancient masculinity and male characters based on a concern that masculinity studies could undermine their work. Feminists have fought not only on theoretical grounds—to include gender as an important element in biblical interpretation—but they have also fought to bring submerged female voices to the surface when New Testament texts are appropriated in modern and postmodern settings. A focus on masculinity and men may erode foundations laid by feminists who have labored to gain credibility among traditional biblical criticism. These concerns should be taken into account when anyone steps toward a hermeneutic of masculinity.

Probably because of those concerns, feminists have not asked the kinds of questions about male characters that we have asked about female characters. These inquiries might include: Who determines the standards of masculinity? How do class, ethnicity, and other features of social location affect the construction, performance, and judgment of masculinity? Given the androcentric nature of New Testament texts, female characters are bound to be exceptional. While the study of exceptions to the rule is valuable, the study of the rule may be valuable as well. We have not taken the next step toward the critical assessment of ancient masculinity and the portrayals of men in the New Testament in light of that assessment. The examination of ancient masculinity will not reinforce male dominance. Instead, we should study masculinity precisely *because of* male dominance. Through the understanding of the theme and variations of ancient masculinity, we will comprehend not only the complicated nature of women's lives but also the lives of men who do not conform to elite standards.[54] This recovery resonates with the feminist definition of patriarchy as the rulership of some men over other men, women, and children.

Because of its awareness of power imbalances, a hermeneutic of masculinity reveals more than gender. In primary sources from the first and second centuries CE, and in New Testament texts themselves, issues of gender and empire are often intertwined. It is likely that issues of gender and empire illuminate one another. In her book *Apostle to the Conquered: Reimagining Paul's Mission*, Davina Lopez proposes an approach that is both "gender-critical" and "empire-critical."[55] Lopez demonstrates how Roman imperial images communicate not only male dominance, but also Roman dominance. A key image in her argument comes from the *Sebasteion* at Aphrodisias.[56] This image, dated to the middle of the first century CE, shows the emperor Claudius violently subduing the nation of Britannia, who is personified as a woman whose shirt has been torn open. This image has layers of meaning, so that a

---

54. To understand ancient women and women's roles, one must understand men and men's roles in antiquity. Maybe we will even learn about the lives of some men who do conform to elite standards.

55. Lopez, *Apostle to the Conquered*, 7.

56. Ibid., 2, and front cover.

gendered lens does not entirely encompass it. The military might of Claudius reigns victorious over the effeminized Britannia, who lies helpless before him. This study suggests that the portrait of Cornelius the man, who is also Roman centurion, reveals Luke's rhetorical strategies about both masculinity and empire. As Luke reshapes masculinity, he also reshapes empire, so that a good Roman man humbles himself before a Judean subject.

HOW TO ILLUMINATE THE PORTRAIT OF CORNELIUS

I have posed some possibilities as to why the portrait of Cornelius the man has been neglected, and described some of the concerns associated with a hermeneutic of masculinity. In order to clarify important definitions, theoretical premises, and methodological foundations, I will describe the approach that this study will take as it addresses the scholarship surrounding Cornelius in Acts 10.

A definition is in order. A hermeneutic of masculinity is a way of reading ancient texts. This way of reading incorporates several important tenets. First, the interpreter who uses this lens maintains the feminist assertion that masculinity and femininity were not equally constructed. Because of power imbalances, elite men determined the social influence of other men, all women, and all children, as well as the standards by which they were judged. While there may be some correlation between the concerns of ancient men and women, the two genders did not exist side by side. Gender roles were constructed in relationship to one another, but in a hierarchical relationship. Much like patriarchy, ancient masculinity depended upon and thrived on the submission of other men, women, and children. Second, the interpreter remains suspicious regarding the problem of dominance. Being a man does not necessarily imply being dominant. Approaching masculinity as a spectrum allows for different ways in which masculinity could be performed. Both masculinity and femininity were heterogeneous. This tenet disallows binary constructions of gender and avoids gender stereotypes.[57] Third, the interpreter perceives and yet resists narrative rhetoric,

---

57. In *The New Testament World: Insights from Cultural Anthropology*, Bruce Malina argues that ancient gender can be described with a binary model. While some commonalities existed among men and among women, the binary model places gender on opposite sides of the same coin. This model falls short of the complexity necessary to

so that we understand what the author wants to convey about gender and yet maintain enough distance to view the rhetoric of a text critically. This tenet makes masculinity explicit by exposing it to literary criticism and rhetorical examination. We aim to explore and expose the ancient conceptions and understandings of masculinity, which we then critically assess. No longer will masculinity be "everywhere and nowhere in the discipline."[58] Male characters in the New Testament will be analyzed and interpreted *as men* in addition to other roles that they play in their respective narratives.

Acts of the Apostles is particularly well suited for a hermeneutic of masculinity. The narrator of Acts puts forth a parade of persuasive and confident men who make dangerous decisions and lead others into uncertain territory. Few women appear in Acts, and even fewer women speak. Moreover, the portrait of Cornelius reveals several important characteristics of men in the Roman era. He is an ideal candidate for narrative analysis with regard to ancient masculinity. His authority, piety, and generosity communicate the narrator's rhetorical interest in exemplary men who could bear the title of "Christian" with a blend of obedience, flexibility, and service.[59] His identification as a Roman centurion also provides fodder for Luke's strategies regarding the Roman Empire.

In order to address these issues, this study will fuse a hermeneutic of masculinity with narrative criticism. The two approaches will work together to discover how the narrator of Acts shapes masculinity and presents models for men in the emerging church. I will now provide an overview of the elements of narrative criticism and how it will collaborate with a hermeneutic of masculinity.

---

study ancient gender. This model too quickly stereotypes women as passive and men as active, and it does not take into account class differences. See ibid., 46–52.

58. Moore, "'O Man Who Art Thou,'" 1.

59. The term "Christian" appears in Acts 11:26; 26:28; 1 Pet 4:16. Some caution should be exercised when using this term in regard to the followers of Jesus in the Gospels and especially in regard to the communities that Paul established. It is likely that the term was not in use when Paul wrote his letters, and its relative infrequence in canonical New Testament texts indicates its rarity when those texts were written. However, the term does appear in Acts; thus it is appropriate here.

Brief Overview of Narrative Criticism

The first rumblings of narrative criticism began in secular literary criticism and in form criticism of biblical texts.[60] An emphasis on text-centered biblical interpretation developed in response to the dominance of historical critical scholarship and diachronic readings that splintered narratives. Several scholars began to interpret the Gospels in particular as coherent, unified narratives instead of a collection of once-scattered sayings and events. These scholars include Alan Culpepper,[61] Robert Tannehill,[62] and the team of David Rhoads, Joanna Dewey, and Donald Michie, whose *Mark as Story: An Introduction to the Narrative of a Gospel* marked a new stage in the development of the narrative method. According to Stephen Moore, "this systematic and relatively comprehensive account of the narrative mechanics of the gospel has no real precursors in literary exegesis..."[63] Likewise, *New Testament Masculinities* has few predecessors in its method and scope. A study of the masculinity of Cornelius will build upon previous scholarship in narrative criticism and masculinity studies, but it will present an original contribution to the exegesis of Acts.

From the beginning, narrative critics have fielded questions from scholars who favor the historical critical method. These scholars asked how one's narrative interpretation should relate to the history in which the story is immersed. Narrative critics consider narratives to be historical artifacts from a specific time and place rather than windows to history. While historical evidence provides a backdrop to the narrative, the primary focus of interpretation is the story itself. Narrative critics stay focused on the text and interpret the story at the textual level. Their goals are to understand the storyworld and to read as an implied reader, who will detect and be persuaded by the rhetoric of the story. However, some scholars argue that narrative criticism needs to at least interact with "factors which are *outside* the text itself, and which can in some way render our interpretations more objective."[64] Francis Moloney argues

---

60. Narrative critics often rely on secular literary critics such as Chatman, *Story and Discourse*.

61. Culpepper, *Anatomy of the Fourth Gospel*.

62. Tannehill, *Narrative Unity of Luke-Acts*.

63. Moore, *Literary Criticism*, 43. For a concise summary of the origins of narrative criticism, see Merenlahti and Hakola, "Reconceiving Narrative Criticism."

64. Moloney, "Narrative Criticism," 184. Italics his.

that while objectivity can never be fully reached, diachronic approaches guard against subjectivism and "personal reaction."[65] He suggests that narrative critics heed both the world behind the text and the world in front of the text, from which the critics read.[66] "No single interpretation of any narrative should ever claim to have produced the final word," Moloney correctly asserts.[67] He also makes a wise point when he states that neither the historical-critical method nor the narrative method will produce "greater control over the objective meaning of a text."[68]

The goal of narrative criticism, however, is not to produce a final interpretation or to gain control over the meaning of a text. Instead, narrative critics attempt to contribute to the scholarly landscape about a narrative and to understand the story and discourse that flow out of a text. As an artifact from a distant time and place, narratives are rooted in history, and therefore narrative critics study "history, society, and cultures of the first-century Mediterranean world *as a means to help us understand the story better."*[69] In narrative criticism, the goal is not to rebuild the set but comprehend the power of the drama as it unfolds in front of the set. While I will examine historical evidence from the first and second centuries of the Mediterranean world, the purpose of that examination will be to understand the characterization of Cornelius: as Roman centurion, as God-fearer, and as almsgiver. This study will discuss ancient literary and material remains about men in order to grasp the power of an ancient story about an exemplary man.

Narrative criticism consists of the examination of several elements that make up a story. Narrator, character, and rhetoric are most important for this study.[70] First, we consider the narrator and four facets of the narrator's role: point of view, standards of judgment, repetition, and

---

65. Ibid., 185. Moloney critiques the narrative method without mentioning David Rhoads, whose *Mark as Story* had been published nine years before in 1982. Moloney refers to Culpepper, Tannehill, and Talbert, but not Rhoads.

66. Moloney, Narrative Critcism," 187.

67. Ibid.

68. Ibid.

69. Rhoads, "Narrative Criticism," 268. Italics his.

70. Other elements include settings and plot. For more on settings, see Powell, *What Is Narrative Criticism?*, 70; Rhoads et al., *Mark as Story*, 63–70; Resseguie, *Narrative Criticism*, 87, 94, 113–20. Settings will be discussed to some extent in chapter 4 below. For more on plot, see Powell, *What Is Narrative Criticism?*, 35–50; Rhoads et al., *Mark as Story*, 73–97; Resseguie, *Narrative Criticism*, 197–98.

tempo. "The narrator is the literary term for the storyteller of a narrative," writes David Rhoads.[71] "The narrator is not the author but the teller that is embedded in the narrative itself."[72] Narrators can tell a story in the first person, third person, or they may tell from an omniscient perspective.[73] Not a neutral or objective teller, the narrator has a point of view. Moore defines point of view well: "a narrator's encompassing attempt to impose a story-world upon a reader (or hearer)."[74] All characters "are judged from the point of view of the narrator," states Resseguie.[75] From this peculiar point of view, a narrator can describe a character so that the audience is persuaded to share the narrator's point of view. As a result, characterization is not neutral or objective; characterization becomes a means of persuasion and a tool for employment of a rhetorical strategy. By drawing the audience toward the positive (like Cornelius) and away from the negative (Simon Magus, for example), the narrator creates standards in the narrative. Called "standards of judgment" by narrative critics, these inherent standards or measuring rods represent not only the narrator's point of view but also the conclusion of the ideal audience. Standards of judgment accumulate over time; as the story progresses, the narrator guides the audience to compare one character to another. Some characters "measure up" to those standards, while others fall short. In Acts, the narrator presents man after man whom the audience can evaluate as positive. Events can also meet or fall short of the standards of judgment. In Acts, the incorporation of Gentiles is a positive event.[76]

---

71. Rhoads et al., *Mark as Story*, 39.

72. Ibid.

73. The degree of omniscience is a matter of debate. Darr states that "Luke has a single, omniscient, (usually) third person, reliable narrator." Darr, *Herod the Fox*, 61. However, Rimmon-Kenan states, "'Omniscience' is perhaps an exaggerated term . . . the characteristics connoted by it are still relevant, namely familiarity, in principle, with the characters' innermost thoughts and feelings, knowledge of past, present, and future, presence in locations where characters are supposed to be unaccompanied . . . and knowledge of what happens in several places at the same time." Rimmon-Kenan, *Narrative Fiction*, 95.

74. Moore, *Literary Criticism*, 56.

75. Resseguie, *Narrative Criticism*, 169.

76. The story of the successful mission to Gentiles in Acts is told from the point of view of a narrator who views the mission as a reflection of God's goals for the emerging church. The narrator downplays the conflict with Judaism by limiting direct discourse about the conflict and by giving one of the most conservative Jews (James) the role of agreeing to the change (Acts 15:14–21). Jewish Christians paid a higher cost for the

With the leadership of the Holy Spirit, Peter and Cornelius usher in a new phase of mission and an alternative way of being masculine, both of which are positive in the narrative.

Narrators also employ repetition, and repetition and tempo can work together to build standards of judgment. Narrators repeat words, phrases, events, characters, or gender of characters, in the case of men in Acts.[77] Repetition indicates a strategic interest on the part of the narrator to convey an important point. In Acts, the Holy Spirit speaks to and directs male characters in Acts thirteen times in ten pericopes.[78] The Holy Spirit speaks only to men in Acts.[79] The repetition of these dynamics establishes a connection between the Holy Spirit and men, a connection that the ideal audience should perceive and embrace. Narrators also have a tempo or pace of storytelling. This pace enables the narrator to speed up or slow down in order to draw the attention of the audience toward certain characters or events and away from others. In Acts 10–11, Peter's speeches slow down the pace of the story and place the audience into "real-time" experience of an event.[80] Time speeds up, however, as Peter travels to and from the house of Cornelius (Acts 10:23–24; 11:1–3). The tempo of a narrative can highlight the ways that a narrator employs repetition. For example, in the telling of the double visions of Peter and Cornelius, the Holy Spirit acts repeatedly in a short stretch of narrative time. Because of concentrated appearances and activities of divine authorities, the ideal audience will not miss the point that God organized the event, and that the event was a step in the right direction.

The second element of narrative criticism crucial for this study is characterization. Simply stated, "characters are the actors in a story."[81]

---

integration of the Gentiles because they gave up both circumcision and dietary laws. This loss, however, does not receive full treatment in Acts.

77. For repetition in Mark's Gospel, see Rhoads et al., *Mark as Story*, 47–55.

78. Acts 8:29; 10:19; 11:12, 28; 13:2,4; 16:6,7; 19:21; 20:22, 23; 21:11; 28:25.

79. One young woman has a "python spirit," but Paul angrily casts it out (Acts 16:16–18). The daughters of Philip, described in Acts as having the gift of prophecy (παρθένοι προφητεύουσαι), have no discourse whatsoever (Acts 21:7–14). The prophet Agabus (11:27–30) takes over the scene and gives his own prophecy, which forecasts difficulty for Paul. Despite protests by his companions, they "got ready and started to go up to Jerusalem" (21:15).

80. For more on the acceleration and deceleration of time in a narrative, see Rimmon-Kenan, *Narrative Fiction*, 52–53.

81. Powell, *What Is Narrative Criticism?*, 51.

According to Rhoads, "characterization refers to the way a narrator brings characters to life in a narrative."[82] Narrators bring characters to life by direct description (comments by the narrator) or by indirect presentation (what characters say, how they act, their gestures or clothing, or by what other characters say about them).[83] Events in the plot of a story reveal characters, and characters contribute to events in the plot.[84] While scholars have discussed the role of Cornelius in the plot of Acts at length, scholars have not studied the details of the portrait of Cornelius from a perspective of masculinity. Because the gender of characters can be repeated and patterns of gender can be formed, this study will include gender as an important facet of characterization.

This third and final element of narrative criticism relevant to this study is rhetoric. "Narrative is inescapably rhetorical," states Stephen Moore.[85] Narrative is rhetorical not only because of the point of view and standards of the judgment of the narrator, but also because the narrator determines what and how the audience learns about characters. Tannehill affirms this view when he writes, "We see and hear only what the narrator wants us to see and hear, and in the way that the narrator wants us to see and hear it."[86] In an essay about characterization and persuasion in Luke 16, Outi Lehtipuu argues that Luke "uses characterization to persuade his readers to share his ideological program."[87] For Lehtipuu, characterization guides the reader to choose the right ways of reading and to reject false ways. "Building credible characters and showing how they respond to what they have seen and heard, instead of just telling the reader how one should act, is a more powerful means to get the reader attached to the story."[88] This study will employ such a

---

82. Rhoads et al., *Mark as Story*, 98.

83. As described above, scholars usually refer to this distinction between direct description and indirect presentation as "telling" and "showing," respectively. Resseguie, *Narrative Criticism*, 121–28.

84. "Characters are agents in a plot . . . " and yet "the actions of the plot are expressions of the characters and they reveal the characters for who they are." Rhoads et al., *Mark as Story*, 98. For the interaction of character and plot, see Rimmon-Kenan, *Narrative Fiction*, 35. For an application of this interaction, see Darr, "Irenic or Ironic?," 120.

85. Moore, *Literary Criticism*, 66–67.

86. Tannehill, *Narrative Unity of Luke-Acts*, 1:4.

87. Lehtipuu, "Characterization and Persuasion," 82.

88. Ibid.

combination of characterization and rhetoric, but will add the element of gender as a means to persuade. Rhetoric accumulates during the telling of a story, and the cumulative effect of that rhetoric persuades and transforms the audience to think, feel, or do something in response. The cumulative rhetoric of the repetition of exemplary male characters in Acts encourages men in the original audience to relinquish authority, obey the Holy Spirit, pray, and speak persuasively on behalf of God's panoramic mission. While Peter and Paul model public and persuasive speech, the rhetorical impact of the characterization of Cornelius, in particular, coaxes men to be obedient to the Spirit, to pray, and to give generously. The rhetoric of the story transforms the ideal reader into an obedient, prayerful, and generous man.[89]

While narrative criticism is the primary method, this study also makes use of reader-response criticism to the extent that I discuss the rhetorical effects of the narrative on the people who experienced the story. It is important for interpreters to be aware of what the audience may have brought to the story, how they may have understood it, and how they may have been transformed by the experience of reading (or hearing) it. Investigating the historical background of Acts and attempting to discern the major social, political, and religious dynamics in the Roman Empire provide a glimpse of the historical audience of Acts. Primary sources from the first and second centuries CE help us determine what the audience of Acts may have known or experienced, as well as how Acts may have confirmed or challenged their ways of understanding the world.[90] While Luke-Acts has proved challenging with regard to its dating and place of composition, careful historical investigation of the overall time period helps the interpreter discern the rhetorical potential of the story.

---

89. Rhoads, Dewey, and Michie define the ideal reader as "the mirror image of the narrator. The ideal reader is the reader that the author creates (has in mind to shape) in the course of telling the story—an imaginary reader with all the ideal responses *implied* by the narrative itself." Rhoads et al., *Mark as Story*, 138.

90. Establishing the expectations of the historical audience of Acts should be done with caution. In the fourth chapter, I suggest that primary sources from the period can lend insight into how ancient people may have perceived or understood centurions and their activities as representatives of Roman military power.

ENTERING THE STORYWORLD: ACTS 1–9

Cornelius appears in the tenth chapter of Acts, and several other positive models of masculinity appear in Acts 1–9. The narrator of Acts guides the audience through the gallery of portraits and presents models as the story progresses. With each portrait, the narrator erects another pillar in the story's standards of judgment and beckons the reader toward male characters who boldly go where the Spirit bids them. Because the experience of a text is sequential, I will briefly sketch some of the positive models of masculinity in Acts 1–9. I will describe these portraits in the order that they appear: Peter, Barnabas, Stephen, the Ethiopian eunuch, Paul, and then Cornelius. I will delineate some of their common features and distinguish each portrait for its unique contributions. This sequential approach will highlight the pattern in which Cornelius participates. Not all masculine traits appear in the characterization of Cornelius, but Cornelius nonetheless emerges as a model of authority, piety, and generosity.

It is fitting to study the portrait of Peter in Acts first. He is the first disciple named (Acts 1:13), the first to speak after Pentecost (Acts 2:14), and the first to speak about the gift of the Holy Spirit, one of the main themes in the story (Acts 2:38). He performs the first miracle (Acts 3:10), is the first to be arrested (Acts 4:7), and the first disciple to be directly described as filled with the Holy Spirit (Acts 4:8). Peter is involved in the first "negative miracle story," in which Ananias and Sapphira die (Acts 5:3, 9), and he is the first and only disciple to raise anyone from the dead (Acts 9:32–43). While Peter is not the first to have a vision, he does receive one, and the vision leads him to reconsider dietary laws. Using passages from his own Scriptures (the Hebrew Bible), he demonstrates an ability to interpret events that take place around him. The coming of the Spirit at Pentecost, the healing of a lame man, and the second coming of the Spirit in the house of Cornelius all lead Peter to interpret these events as signs of the power and leadership of the Holy Spirit. Most often, the narrator characterizes Peter through indirect presentation, focusing on Peter's actions, speech, and interactions with divine and human characters. Therefore the direct description of Peter as "an unlettered and ordinary man" stands out (Acts 4:13). He is nonetheless bold (Acts 4:29, 31, μετὰ παρρησίας πάσης) and forges new trails with the guidance of the Holy Spirit. In Acts 1–9, Peter demonstrates the obedience, flexibility, and boldness that he will also demonstrate in Acts 10.

Although Barnabas is not mentioned in the list of disciples in Acts 1:13, he is the first and only named man in Acts 1–9 who carries out the ethic of selling and giving away for the common good (Acts 4:35–37). He enters the narrative at a time of concord, and his portrait reinforces the ethic of sharing shown among the disciples (Acts 2:43–47; 4:32–35).[91] The narrator directly describes Barnabas immediately upon his entry into the narrative, giving his name, his nickname, his religious affiliation, and his country of origin. After this brief and direct introduction, the narrator does not mention Barnabas by name again until chapter 9, where Barnabas acts as a liaison between the Jerusalem disciples and the newly converted Saul.[92] Although the role of Barnabas develops after chapter 10, his gift of money prefigures the generous almsgiving of Cornelius.

Stephen appears in the story during a rare internal conflict among the disciples (Acts 6:1–6).[93] The narrator identifies by name Stephen, Philip, and others who are chosen to preside over the distribution of food to widows. Stephen is first on the list of "men of good standing, full of the Spirit and of wisdom" (Acts 6:3). Implicitly characterized with these traits, the narrator directly singles Stephen out as "a man full of faith and the Holy Spirit" (Acts 6:5) and "full of grace and power" (Acts 6:8). As with Barnabas, the narrator "front-loads" his characterization and directly describes Stephen immediately and efficiently. Within six verses, the narrator notes the Spirit's relationship with Stephen twice. This employment of repetition signals an economy with words and narrative time, and an emphasis on the Spirit's role in leading men.[94] After

---

91. Immediately after Barnabas presents a positive example of giving one's goods away, the narrator focuses on an example of greed and deception (Acts 5:1–11).

92. One could infer the presence of Barnabas in Acts 6:7, where priests become obedient to the faith. After Acts 10, the role of Barnabas takes on added importance. Barnabas is filled with the Holy Spirit (11:24) and set apart by the Holy Spirit in 13:2–3. The narrator also associates him with boldness (14:3) and he is the only man in Acts whom the narrator describes as "ἦν ἀνὴρ ἀγαθός" (11:24). Unless he speaks with Paul, he has no direct discourse (13:46; 14:15–17). He is "a good man" who never speaks independently. This may be due to his partnership with Paul; the narrator may want to give Paul as much attention and direct discourse as possible. Barnabas is close to but not quite Paul's equal.

93. If the story were being performed, only moments before would the audience have heard of Ananias and Sapphira, another example of internal conflict.

94. Stephen is the only man or woman in Acts whose face "was like the face of an angel." This direct description is intensified by the fact that even his opponents see him that way (6:15).

his powerful speech, Stephen is filled with the Holy Spirit once again (Acts 7:55), receives a vision of the Son of Man, and dies with forgiveness of his enemies on his lips (Acts 7:60). The portrait of Stephen communicates a willingness to follow the direction of the Spirit even if that obedience leads to death. This kind of man gives up control to the very end.[95] Like Cornelius, Stephen demonstrates how a man can be led by the Spirit and how a man can still be masculine.

The narrator introduces the Ethiopian eunuch in much the same way as he introduces Barnabas and Stephen: with direct and immediate description. The narrator supplies details instantly: where the eunuch came from, whom he serves, what he does, where he is traveling, how he is traveling, why he came to Jerusalem, and the name of his reading material (Acts 8:26–28). This direct method of characterization is balanced by indirect presentation of the eunuch's interest in learning Isaiah and his apparent attempt to read Isaiah aloud (Acts 8:30).[96] By inference, the audience determines that the eunuch is inquisitive, committed to learning about the God of Israel, and willing to be baptized. The pericope about the Ethiopian eunuch represents mission to the Gentiles on the frontier.[97] While the home of Cornelius is located in Caesarea—a center of empire-related activity and architecture—and the eunuch's home is far from Rome, both the eunuch and Cornelius show a high level of commitment to the Way and an ability to adhere to religious practice. These men go to great lengths to participate in the movement.

Acts 1–9 belongs to Peter's narrative realm of activity; thus the influence of Saul/Paul does not bloom until chapter 13.[98] In contrast

---

95. The death of Stephen does not prevent his reappearance in the narrative. Stephen's name surfaces in the narrator's reference to persecution (ἀπὸ τῆς θλίψεως, 11:19) and in Paul's defense speech (ὅτε ἐξεχύννετο τὸ αἷμα Στεφάνου τοῦ μάρτυρός σου, 22:20).

96. While the narrator of Acts does not identify a specific passage in Isaiah, Isa 56:4–8 seems relevant.

97. Not only is the Ethiopian eunuch on the geographical frontier, but he is also on the frontier of masculinity. As a eunuch, he does not possess the biological markers of masculinity, and he does not conform to upper-class Roman standards of masculinity.

98. There is a brief period in the story where both Peter and Paul are in the lead, although in opposite directions at first (Acts 8). In Acts 15, they are both in the same place at the same time, but Peter seems to take over the event; he says, "My brothers, you know that in the early days God made a choice among you that I should be the one through whom the Gentiles would hear the message of the good news and become believers" (15:7). Paul has no direct discourse during the debate in Acts 15.

to the introduction of what might be called secondary characters, the narrator introduces Paul with very little direct description. From Acts 7:58 and 8:1–3, the audience infers that Paul cooperates with and even spearheads the persecution of members of the Way.[99] The narrator shifts the audience's attention back to Saul in 9:1. In this episode, Jesus speaks first, and Paul alone hears the voice. As with Acts 10, a double vision takes place; God works on both sides to ensure that two individuals meet. The powerful prosecutor is humbled by a vision that forces him to the ground and blinds him for 3 days. He must be led by the hand to the home of Ananias, a disciple in Damascus (Acts 9:10). Through the intervention of God, Ananias meets Paul and enables him to regain his sight, be filled with the Holy Spirit, and be baptized (Acts 9:17–19).[100]

This transformation of Saul the antagonist to a protagonist signals dramatic change for the narrative and a significant achievement for the narrator. The vision of Jesus brings about transformation for Paul and for the narrative. A destructive character makes a surprising change but the audience accepts this change because such powerful divine forces are involved. Other characters show resistance (Acts 9:26–9) and his former colleagues plot to kill him (Acts 9:19b–25). Because of the omniscient narrator, however, the audience is privy to the vision, while the characters hear about it secondhand. The standards of judgment in the narrative must expand at this point in the story to include a reliable character with a questionable past. Paul's dramatic change amplifies the power and potency of God's intervention, intensifies the conflict with some Jewish authorities, and celebrates change as a sign of God's activity. Moreover, the narrative's standards of judgment for masculinity evolve. As a result of the rhetorical slant of this episode, Paul is not a wishy-washy character or indecisive man. He appears obedient, courageous, and willing to shoulder the risks of following Jesus, even if it means alienation from his kin.

---

99. The only direct description of Paul in this section is that he is "young" (7:58).

100. In Acts 1–9, Paul's character is defined by transformation, while Peter's preaching and activities have remained constant in the narrative up to this point. When Cornelius comes on the scene in Acts 10, Peter is the natural choice for the incorporation of the Gentiles. After Acts 11 and beginning in Acts 13, Paul takes the reins of the narrative, speaking frequently, publicly, and with great influence. Paul continues to obey the direction of the Holy Spirit (13:1–3; 16:6; 19:21; 20:22–23) and to be filled with the Holy Spirit (13:9).

Like the introduction of other secondary characters noted above, the characterization of Cornelius is immediate and direct. Through direct description, the audience learns of the location of his home, his name, his profession, his cohort, his religious affiliation, and the ways in which he demonstrates his religious affiliation (Acts 10:1–2). A vision quickly follows the description, and the voice of an angel repeats the emphasis on his prayers and alms (Acts 10:4). This repetition spoken by a reliable character reinforces the piety of Cornelius. Although his introduction is also "front-loaded," the portrait of Cornelius is also fleshed out by indirect presentation. He has slaves, ranks of soldiers, and one devout soldier (Acts 10:7–8). An obedient man, Cornelius did as the angel bid him (Acts 10:7–8) and the slaves' description of Cornelius adds the phrase "well-spoken of by the whole Jewish nation" to his portrait (Acts 10:22). Cornelius clearly expects that the slaves' mission to retrieve Peter would be successful (Acts 10:24); this expectation is a result of his authority. He is accustomed to being obeyed. He has "many" friends (Acts 10:27), relatives (Acts 10:24), and perhaps a home big enough to accommodate them all. Yet Cornelius the authoritative centurion falls at Peter's feet in a demonstration of εὐσεβής, and obeys when Peter tells him to get up (Acts 10:27).[101] Along with his relatives and friends, Cornelius receives the Holy Spirit, speaks in tongues, and extols God (Acts 10:46). Peter, not Cornelius, orders their baptism, and they do not resist (Acts 10:48). In return, Cornelius extends hospitality to Peter and his visit lasts several days (Acts 10:48).

In Acts 10, the narrator employs comparison and contrast in order to further characterize Peter and Cornelius. Both men pray, Peter in Acts 10:9 and Cornelius in Acts 10:30. During their prayers, divine visions materialize. Like Peter before him (Acts 10:23), Cornelius shows hospitality (Acts 10:48). Both men have entourages or followers (Acts 10:23; 11:12, and 10:7–8, 24, 27, respectively). Peter employs his own authority by ordering baptism (Acts 10:48) and Cornelius by sending emissaries (Acts 10:7–8). Both show a willingness to relinquish authority and control, and both are apparently unaware that the Holy Spirit will appear "just as it had upon us in the beginning" (Acts 11:15). The portraits of Peter and Cornelius contrast with one another as well, though not to the same degree. Peter is Jewish, while Cornelius is a Gentile. This

---

101. Cornelius is the first centurion to appear in Acts, but not the last (22:25; 24:23; 27:1).

is the most striking contrast, and perhaps the only one.[102] By heaping up comparisons and limiting contrasts, the narrator paints these portraits so that they have much in common. The narrator emphasizes the commonalities between the men, and guides the audience through a scene in which they interact with each other and with the Spirit. The proximity of the two characters and the numerous comparisons unite the two men and corroborate their shared masculinity.

When all these characters appear in the mural of masculinity in Acts 1–10, similarities and differences emerge. In these ten chapters, some patterns become clear. These patterns include a close connection or relationship with the Holy Spirit, obedience to the Spirit, a willingness to change, and for primary characters such as Peter and Paul, an ability to persuade individuals and groups. Each character also adds to the mural a specific element of masculinity. Peter is "uneducated and ordinary," Barnabas gives money away, and Stephen witnesses to the God of Israel with grave consequences. Paul changes dramatically, and the Ethiopian eunuch deviates from the biological standard of masculinity. To this mural Cornelius adds direct connections to the empire. His Roman authority is unparalleled up to this point, and he is the most obedient and responsive centurion in the story. His piety is also unparalleled in Acts 1–9; the Ethiopian eunuch foreshadows the affiliation of Gentiles to the Way but only the centurion is "well-spoken of by the whole Jewish nation" (Acts 10:22). Barnabas sold a field and gave the money to the apostles, but only Cornelius gives almost generously (ποιῶν ἐλεημοσύνας πολλὰς, Acts 10:2). The characterization of Cornelius includes features of previous male characters but carries them to new heights. He sets a new standard for authority, piety, and generosity. Gentile by birth, God-fearer by choice, and Christian by baptism, Cornelius is a hybrid man and a paradigm of complete devotion to God.

CONCLUSION

This chapter has introduced the need for the present study, its methodological foundations, and reviewed some secondary scholarship surrounding characterization, masculinity studies, and narrative criticism. I have described the characterizations of positive examples of masculin-

---

102. Though Luke tells us about the education of Peter (Acts 4:13), the education of Cornelius is less clear.

ity that line the walls of the narrative exhibit as well as the rhetorical impacts of their portrayals. With this tour of Acts 1–9, I have set the stage for the analysis of Cornelius as an authoritative, pious, and generous man. Before that analysis begins, however, it is necessary to review in greater detail the subfield of masculinity studies and the secondary scholarship that has contributed to its growth.

2

Scholarly Perspectives on Masculinity

INTRODUCTION

"THE PROBLEM WITH MEN'S history is that there is too much of it," writes Mathew Kuefler, whose study on masculinity and Christian ideology tackles the abundance of male-oriented literature in antiquity.[1] While Kuefler's work focuses on late antiquity, the same can be said of the early imperial period.[2] Many androcentric writings and other types of remains survive from the first and second centuries CE. Classicists and biblical scholars have begun to organize these materials in an effort to understand the principles and standards of masculinity during that time, as well as how an upper-class man demonstrated his masculinity

---

1. Kuefler, *Manly Eunuch*, 1. Although Kuefler's study is located in a later era than this one, Kuefler shows how an alternative masculinity took shape under traditional Roman understandings of masculinity. He shows how that alternative or subordinate masculinity took on a position of power and the gradual process by which the Christian understandings of masculinity became institutionalized and powerful during after the era of Constantine. It is possible that the transformation of alternative masculine ideals began at an earlier time, perhaps during the first century CE, but the later scope of Kuefler's study does not allow him to easily speculate on this possibility.

2. The primary and secondary sources will focus on the first and second centuries CE.

in public and private arenas.³ As one aspect of honor and a central component of Greek and Roman society, masculinity merits further study.

This chapter addresses the abundance of androcentric sources by summarizing what classicists and New Testament scholars have done with those sources. This chapter discusses the published works of three classicists who have contributed to our understanding of masculinity and honor in the first and second centuries CE: Maud Gleason, Carlin Barton, and Craig Williams. All of these scholars emphasize the need for control over oneself and others as a primary characteristic of elite masculinity. Each scholar identifies key ways that elite Greek and Roman men showed themselves to be men. Gleason opens a door to the intensely competitive world of public speaking and physiognomy among elite men. Barton traces the political shifts from republic to empire and notes how the most powerful men exercised their prerogative to redefine masculinity. Williams interprets the sexual behavior of powerful men as a means to convey and perpetuate domination.

This chapter then summarizes how New Testament scholars have relied upon the works of classicists in order to interpret masculinity as it is constructed in biblical texts. New Testament scholars have built upon and added to the work of Gleason and Williams so that research from the field of classics can enrich and enlighten New Testament interpretation.⁴ D'Angelo and Liew will be featured in this portion of the chapter, as well as Colleen Conway and Stephen Moore. A book by Colleen Conway will be discussed in greater detail. Each of these scholars takes masculinity studies and New Testament interpretation in his or her own direction.

This chapter concludes with a discussion of what will be called "alternative masculinities" and a recognition of need. More research is necessary regarding masculinity among military men and non-elites. Although scholars have taken strides in this direction,⁵ most scholarship centers on elite Greek and Roman masculinity. New Testament texts do not arise solely from elite settings, and the men in New Testament narratives are not always elite. Therefore some New Testament scholars have begun to assemble our knowledge of masculinities beyond elite circles.

---

3. I use "elite" and "upper-class" interchangeably.
4. Other classicists will be included in this chapter as well.
5. Military masculinity will be featured in chapter 4.

RESEARCH FROM THE FIELD OF CLASSICS: MASCULINITY, CONTROL, AND HONOR

According to classicists such as Carlin Barton, masculinity is one component of the larger framework of honor in the Greco-Roman world during the first and second centuries CE. When collated and integrated, the works of Gleason, Barton, Williams, and others form a map of masculinity for New Testament scholars who are interested in exploring masculinity during that era.[6] Like a topographical map, this survey includes elevation; since most extant sources originated in upper-class contexts, classicists are more able to map the high elevations. First, I will delineate three criteria that influence a man's eligibility for reaching the summit of manhood. The scholarship of Martin, Richlin, and others guide us into this territory.[7] These criteria are somewhat beyond a man's control. However, an elite man did have some control over himself and others. Building on the scholarship of Gleason, Barton, and Williams, I will describe the ways that an elite man demonstrated his self-control and control over others, thereby acting out his manliness for all to see. I will then review other relevant scholarship in order to propose the ultimate goal of a Roman man's displays of masculine behavior: honor among other elite men.

Any attempt at mapping masculinity in antiquity is accompanied by some degree of caution. The ancient sources do not always agree. Most often we encounter primary sources that tell of men who failed to achieve masculinity and who became the object of debate and critique.[8] Scholars must then infer from these sources a positive example of masculinity. Gleason has shown this strategy to be fruitful. In addition to conflicting sources, classicists themselves sometimes disagree about important aspects of masculinity. For example, while sexual behavior is the key to understanding masculinity for Craig Williams, others argue that this is not the case. Moreover, studies of masculinity during the

---

6. The idea of mapping gender is not new. Burrus writes that mapping gender "is a process that manifests within ancient religious discourses, as gender is produced iteratively at multiple sites and according to large unpredictable (even chaotic) orders of causality." Burrus, "Mapping as Metamorphoses," 1.

7. Some New Testament scholars have also researched ancient masculinity using primary sources and attempted to understand masculinity in the New Testament period. They are included in this section because of their contributions to historical research.

8. Gleason, "Semiotics of Gender," 392.

Roman Empire appear mostly in essay form rather than monographs or reference works. These essays argue for specific components of masculinity operant during a precisely defined era, using a limited number of sources. The curious exegete is then forced to connect the dots, make caveats, and forge ahead in dimly lit conditions. Despite these disagreements, I suggest that guiding principles of masculinity can be carefully mapped with the help of classicists. The map in this study is a result of allegiance to both complication and conclusion. I propose not a tidy system to decode masculinity but a possible framework for New Testament scholars to use as they ask new questions of old texts.

Beyond a Man's Control: Biology, Ethnicity, and Class

Elite masculinity entailed competition. Men competed with one another to be considered masculine by their peers and to epitomize masculine behavior. Not all males were able to compete, however. The boundaries of eligibility corresponded with the boundaries of class; only free, wealthy, and educated men could play the game. Although issues of class are the most influential, two other criteria affect a man's eligibility for full manhood: biology and ethnicity. To some extent, these criteria were beyond a man's control. For example, a man was often born into an elite status. We begin with the issue of biological issues involved in masculinity.

The first criterion for elite masculinity and honor was related to biology. By "biology," I refer to a man's physical anatomy and the body with which he was born. Although an elite man could manage and maintain this body, he was nonetheless born with it, and to some extent its features were beyond his control. In an essay about masculinity and sexuality, Dale Martin states, "The male was secure, but men were not."[9] The presence of male genitalia did not alone determine eligibility, although the biological markers of manhood should be intact. The male was by nature (or naturally) superior. Using Aristotle, Galen, and Herophilus, Diana Swancutt argues that ancient physicians and other writers constructed a one-body anatomical model for both men and women. Women were imperfect, "inside-out" men. The ideological matrix of gender could be drawn in a vertical line, with elite men at the top

---

9. Martin, "Contradictions," 105.

and others at the bottom, including women.[10] On this vertical spectrum, men were naturally warmer and drier than women.[11] In addition to his biological or natural superiority, in order to be masculine, a man must properly manage this bodily temperature and moisture. Men needed to pay attention to their bodily fluids and ensure a proper balance. This achievement of balance, as well as the genitalia with which a man was born, would be visible to others in the bath because men bathed in the nude.[12] Gleason writes, "Since the price of admission was fixed very low, the baths were one place where a gentleman would be expected to mingle with his social inferiors in the buff. Here the extent of one's paunch advertised the extent of one's wealth (or self-control)."[13] Baths gave elite men opportunity to advertise their biological superiority as well as an opportunity to consult professionals on the management of their temperature and moisture levels. Martin notes the relationship between biological factors and class: "So by making masculinity something that requires the regular care of a physician, the medical writers, products of the higher class and servants of its interests, assume for themselves the power of assigning, maintaining, certifying, and restoring masculinity—at least by the standards of the upper class."[14] By maintaining their bodies, elite men also maintain their class boundaries and promote their own eligibility for masculinity.

The second criterion for elite masculinity and honor relates to a man's ethnicity. Not only did biology affect one's ability to be considered fully masculine, but ethnicity was also a criterion. A man was born with a specific ethnicity or combination of ethnicities, and therefore his ethnicity was out of his control.[15] Elite discourse from the first and second centuries CE reveals a tension regarding ethnicity. Although the Romans depended upon and preserved some Greek cultural traditions, Romans asserted their superiority over Greeks through discourse. Diana Swancutt notes the identification of the penetrating phallus with the Roman Empire; this symbol signaled the pervasive power of the Romans as well as propaganda against the

10. Swancutt, "'Disease of Effemination,'" 197; Swancutt "Still before Sexuality."
11. Martin, "Contradictions," 82.
12. Gleason, "Elite Male Identity," 73.
13. Ibid.
14. Martin, "Contradictions," 107.
15. In this study, I will concentrate on the ethnicities of Greek, Roman, and Jewish.

Greeks.[16] Language, clothing, or one's style of writing or speech could reveal ethnicity. Amy Richlin suggests that although the "Asianist" style of rhetorical performance appealed to the young Seneca,[17] the Greek East and "the Orient, in Roman thought, was associated with luxury and a concomitant deviant sexuality—effeminacy, even self-castration."[18] According to Brigette Russell, Mark Antony's reputation was in danger when he associated so closely with Cleopatra and "the Greco-Egyptian East."[19] Plutarch described Antony as a Roman man whom Cleopatra dominated and feminized; the relationship between Antony and Cleopatra troubled Plutarch because Cleopatra was both foreign and a woman. Such submission to foreign and female powers put Antony in a woman's place and threatened to destabilize Roman dominance over other ethnic groups. Roman views about the Greeks were not monolithic; Gleason notes that some Romans preferred Greek culture. As Gleason demonstrates, some of the most prominent public speakers in the second century CE were Greek.[20] Yet other Romans felt a "puritanical abhorrence" for Greek culture.[21] Anti-Greek sentiments do survive in Roman discourse in a number worth consideration. Greek men developed their own ways of evaluating masculinity, but at the same time some Roman men considered them inferior.[22]

The third factor that influenced a man's eligibility for masculinity and honor was the man's social class. Biology, ethnicity, and class weave themselves together, but it is difficult to overestimate the influence of class. "Health requires autonomy," writes Gleason.[23] To be autonomous, men must be free and wealthy enough to afford medical care, education, proper attire, and an ability to associate well with other autonomous men. As far back as the fourth century BCE, it was "not labour

---

16. Swancutt, "Still before Sexuality," 32–33.

17. Richlin, "Gender and Rhetoric," 94–95.

18. Ibid.,106.

19. Russell, "Emasculation of Antony," 122.

20. See below for more about Polemo, a Greek eunuch and physiognomist, and Gleason's treatment of his performances in her book.

21. Gleason, "Elite Male Identity," 75–76. The Roman emperor Hadrian displayed an enduring interest in all in things Greek.

22. According to Gleason, "Quintilian's attitude exemplifies a certain Roman squeamishness toward Greek culture and the arts in general." Gleason, *Making Men*, 116.

23. Ibid.

but leisure" that associated men with being masculine.[24] While this distinction appeared during the classical era in Greece, it became even more demanding in Roman gender ideology, particularly with regard to sexual behavior. Although Greeks "might openly engage in romantic and sexual relationships with free-born adolescent males," this behavior was *stuprum* to Romans, or "disgraceful or illicit."[25] To elite Romans, males who would become or were already citizens were not to be penetrated; thus Romans increased the stipulations regarding sexual behavior and reinforced the importance and privileges of citizenship. In sum, class issues determined both who could be eligible to be considered masculine and how one could participate in the competition for it. Although some aspects of masculinity were largely beyond their control—biology, ethnicity, and class—elite men must tend to what they could control.

Within a Man's Control: Oratory and Physiognomy

We turn now to a discussion of how elite men demonstrated their masculinity and honor in public.[26] This discussion concentrates on the ways that elite men showed that they were in control of themselves and others. We begin with public speaking and the performances that took place in the forum, as elite men acted out their manliness through speech and gesture.

The first classicist featured in this section is Maud Gleason. Her book *Making Men* and her subsequent essays take center stage among some New Testament scholars who investigate masculinity. To our map of masculinity, Gleason contributes several fundamental principles. Masculinity is performed and acted out in the forum, where orators communicate manliness both verbally and nonverbally.[27] One's body, voice, and style of speech are all means to convey one's elite status and one's self control. Because elite men were trained from youth to perform in publicly acceptable ways, masculinity became an achievement. If achieved, masculinity was only temporary; it was "always under construction and

---

24. Osborne, "Sculpted Men of Athens," 29.
25. Williams, *Roman Homosexuality*, 62.
26. See Richlin, "Gender and Rhetoric," 91–93, about the Roman forum as gendered space.
27. In this study, I use "manliness" and "masculinity" interchangeably.

constantly open to scrutiny..."[28] Masculinity was something that people *did*, rather than something that people *were*.

Gleason's works complicate our understanding of elite Greek and Roman masculinity. They also provide depth to our portrait of an upper-class masculinity and physiognomy that appeared homogenous but was in fact streaked with contradictions. First, I briefly summarize here Gleason's work with elite, highly controlled Greek orators. Her book *Making Men* discusses two popular orators from the second century CE, Favorinus of Ephesus and Polemo of Laodicea. These orators embodied "competing paradigms of masculinity" among elite men.[29] Both men had fans in the Greek East and Roman West, and each man scrutinized the body, voice, and style in order to criticize the other.[30] A Greek-speaking "virtuoso"[31] who was born without testicles,[32] Favorinus used his high-pitched voice to embrace a singing style of performance and to critique the emperor.[33] From Gleason's description, one perceives the possibility that Favorinus espoused this paradigm of masculinity flagrantly and yet skillfully.[34] Like Favorinus, Polemo was also Greek, but his opinions were more consistent with traditional moralism. A descendant of Hellenistic kings, "the citizens of Smyrna chose him to represent them in their dealings with a philhellenic emperor [Hadrian], who found it politic to present Rome's political domination as cultural patronage."[35] Polemo studied other orators closely for signs of effeminacy; as a flagrant deviant, Favorinus provided Polemo with many opportunities.

Polemo codified his perspective on physiognomy, which Gleason defines as a "merciless discipline"[36] that "specialized in spotting males who were not real men at all."[37] Physiognomy, writes Gleason, is "the art

---

28. Gleason, *Making Men*, xxii.
29. Ibid., xxviii.
30. Ibid.
31. Ibid., 17.
32. Ibid., 3.
33. Ibid., xxvii–viii.
34. "People thought there were two kinds of effeminates, the flagrant ones, whose deportment plainly showed their deviance, and the hidden ones, who might be anywhere." Gleason, "Elite Male Identity," 77.
35. Gleason, *Making Men*, 22.
36. Ibid., 28. Gleason translated Greek and Arabic versions of Polemo's treatises.
37. Gleason, "Semiotics of Gender," 389–90.

of reading character from face and gesture."[38] For Polemo and other critics of rhetorical performance, a man's physical appearance determined his inner character. According to Polemo and other writers, effeminacy and other faults made themselves known in a man's eyes, gestures, voice, and style of speaking. A man's eyelids are not to droop, nor are the pupils of the eye to be restless.[39] The voice was to be dignified, calm, and low-pitched, without conveying the impression of singing.[40] The gestures should not be soft or delicate, and they should not appear similar to dancing.[41] Improper rhetorical style was distasteful to Seneca the Elder, who warned against singing and dancing as behaviors that "impair, rather than develop, one's masculine dignity."[42] Seneca the Younger "eagerly scans his subject's grooming and deportment for signs of rot."[43] For Quintilian, improper rhetorical style can be likened to wearing women's jewelry.[44] With these and other references, Gleason demonstrates that elite Greek and Roman physiognomy, regardless of source, relied on fear and fed on prejudice. Elite writers and orators throughout the empire traded barbs and accused one another of being feminine. These rivalries and accusations were part of the elite experience, reinforced the boundaries of class, and placed emphasis on the control of the body during public speech.

Within a Man's Control: Physical Appearance

The second classicist featured in this discussion takes a slightly different approach to masculinity among elite men. Carlin Barton contributes to our understanding of masculinity and honor through a nuanced discussion of men who were even more elite than Gleason's Favorinus and Polemo.[45] According to Barton, imperial men such as Julius Caesar and

---

38. Gleason, "Elite Male Identity," 75.
39. Gleason, *Making Men*, 32.
40. Ibid., 106.
41. Ibid., 107.
42. Ibid., 109.
43. Ibid., 113. Seneca found such rot in the behavior of Maecenas, associate of Augustus; see Graver's "Manhandling of Maecenas."
44. Gleason, *Making Men*, 114.
45. Barton suggests that honor concerned all Romans, not only elite men: "But emotionally the slave was every bit as sensitive to insult as his or her master. The plebeian was as preoccupied with honor as the patrician, the client as the patron, the woman

Augustus demonstrated that they were not only in control of themselves but also in control of masculinity itself.

Barton makes these points in an essay entitled "All Things Beseem the Victor: Paradoxes of Masculinity in Early Imperial Rome." Barton consults a suite of primary Latin sources in order to flesh out our understanding of masculinity among the most powerful at a time of flux in government.[46] Barton defines pre-war masculinity as a value system focused on the concept of *gravitas*, defined as "exceptional self-control" and "the basis of the Roman idea of *fides* (faithfulness, predictability), the cement of all contractual relations, the bond of society."[47] Men were to embody these virtues and demonstrate physically and publicly that they were conforming to the conventional elite Roman standards of masculinity. Behavior other than *gravitas* and *fides* belonged to Greeks and women, who embodied softness and levity.[48]

Barton writes that while some elite Romans valued self-control, conformity, and dignity, these values were nonetheless able to change as the republic shifted to principate and then to autocracy. Among imperial men during the civil war and the age of Augustus, contradictions in masculinity made themselves known in physical appearance, including clothing and hairstyles. Victors such as Julius Caesar and Augustus exercised their prerogative to resist decorum and defy social convention with regard to clothing and hair. In contrast to previous leading men, Caesar shaved his head and face, and even "plucked his body hair," habits usually attributed to effeminate men.[49] According to Macrobius, Caesar wore a toga with fringes and let it drape loosely around him. This style of garment was at best innovative among traditionally dressed Romans, and at worst a sign of effeminacy.[50] Barton suggests that Caesar

---

as the man, the child as the adult." Barton, *Roman Honor*, 11.

46. Barton, "All Things." For more on Roman honor and how Roman honor plays its out through the physical body of a man, see Barton, *Roman Honor*, 7.

47. Barton, *Roman Honor*, 86–87. Barton asserts that during the Republic, "the values of the ancient Romans . . . were overwhelmingly those of a warrior culture." As evidence, Barton refers to the writings of Valerius Maximus, in which Roman soldiers yearn for glory. Ibid., 13.

48. Ibid., 87. The public nature of masculine behavior leads Barton to conclude that "being a man was a mannerism." Ibid. 41.

49. Barton quotes Suetonius on this issue, especially *Dei. Jul.* 45:2–3.

50. Barton, "All Things," 88. Gamel concurs: "Caesar, Antony, Maecenas, Nero . . . defied, in their self-presentation, the sanctions against effeminacy. They dressed with

was "peevish and fretful about his person," and his attention toward such matters solicited some critique.[51] Despite the presence of critique, Caesar's behavior was an employment of the ultimate power and control; he could change even gender standards because "standards only apply to the defeated."[52]

Two other classicists, Jonathan Walters and Craig Williams, have found similar concerns about the relationship between physical appearance and masculinity in different locales. Walters studies the Latin narrative entitled *Metamorphoses*, also known as *The Golden Ass*, written by Apuleius in the second century CE. In this ancient text he finds that the lack of a manly appearance can be a sexual liability.[53] In the narrative, a male character who is "no more than a boy" takes advantage of a woman while her husband is away; Apuleius signals that the young man is indeed a boy because of his "smooth cheeks."[54] The absence of facial hair indicates youth, and to the jealous husband, a sexual partner. In this narrative, the presence of body hair was the mark of an adult man. By this standard, Caesar, who depilated, associated himself with the absence of masculinity rather than the abundance of it. According to Craig Williams, the plucking of facial hair and preference for lavish clothing challenged the Roman standard of grooming and gave the impression of effeminacy.[55] These behaviors were akin to a fondness for perfume and delicate walking, sure signs of gender deviance.[56] Although even the most powerful men such as Caesar and Augustus could be ridiculed for their apparent lack of self-control and non-conformity, they paved new ways for men to be masculine. They showed that they could control and change the standards of masculinity.

Within a Man's Control: Sexual Behavior

I have discussed two ways in which men demonstrated their masculinity and honor: oratory and physical appearance. Both emphasize the importance of self-control and control over others and underscore the

---

care, but unconventionally." Gamel, "Reading as a Man," 91.

51. Barton, "All Things," 88.
52. Ibid., 89.
53. Walters, "'No More Than a Boy.'"
54. Ibid., 28.
55. Williams, *Roman Homosexuality*, 129.
56. Ibid.

public nature of elite masculinity. In the following section, I will discuss how elite men performed their masculinity through sexual behavior. Like oratory and physical appearance, sexual behavior emphasized control over oneself and others. The works of two classicists come to the fore in this section: Craig Williams and Jonathan Walters.

Treatments of sexual behavior, control, and masculinity during the early imperial period among classical scholars have reached a fever pitch. Classicist Marilyn Skinner traces the progress of what she calls "sexuality wars" among classicists. The key issue of the war is not whether sexuality is important for gender history. Instead, the war rages over how to use the trilogy of historical works written by Foucault.[57] While this study will not enter into that controversy, classicists have identified Roman sexual behavior as a means to convey control, power, and domination.

In what Stephen Moore calls "the best one-volume entrée to this proliferating subfield, perhaps—certainly the most encyclopedic,"[58] Craig Williams uses primary sources from the second century BCE to the second century CE to unveil the "basic organizing principles of Roman scripts for masculinity."[59] These principles include "an opposition between freeborn Romans and everyone else," "an opposition between masculine and effeminate traits of behaviors that . . . relied . . . on the association of masculinity of dominion and control," and "a conceptual system concerned with the role played in sexual acts . . ."[60] Although Williams' protocols are more general in scope, he also suggests that Roman sexuality had its own organizing principles. Using a distinction that New Testament scholars later adopt, Williams separates Roman men from "un-men," including inferior men and women.[61] Modern understandings of sexual orientation do not appear in ancient literary sources. Instead, Roman sexual behavior was bifurcated into active and passive categories. Either one penetrates (men) or is penetrated (un-men). In addition, one must exercise one's dominion over threats, including the threat of sexual passivity.[62]

57. Skinner, "Zeus and Leda."
58. Moore, "'O Man Where Art Thou,'" 20.
59. Williams, *Roman Homosexuality*, 14.
60. Ibid.
61. Ibid., 7.
62. Ibid., 133.

The second scholar who contributes to our understanding of masculinity and honor demonstrated through sexual behavior is Jonathan Walters. Like Craig Williams, he investigates sexual behavior among Romans but links sexual behavior and bodily boundaries to the boundaries of the empire. Using Latin texts from the first century BCE to the third century CE, Williams addresses only hegemonic masculinity but finds interesting parallels to modern sexuality there.[63] Like Williams, Walters suggests that active and passive categories do exist in Roman sexual behavior, but social class plays a role. Noting Seneca's definition of *vir*, Williams defines *viri* as "adult males who are freeborn Roman citizens in good standing."[64] Roman discourse characterizes these men as "sexually impenetrable penetrators" who manifest their self-control and control over others by penetrating others.[65] Because they were not penetrated, these dominant men showed that they were able to protect the boundaries of their own bodies, which was a sign of masculinity among the elite.[66] Men like this held positions of power over an empire that sought to protect the boundaries of its body from violation. Invaders from other countries threatened not only the superiority of Roman men but also had implications for the masculinity of the empire's leaders. While some classicists do not consider sexual behavior as the most prominent key to understanding Roman masculinity,[67] Walters and Williams have shown that sexual behavior is at least a symbolic location for men to take control and to perform their masculinity.

This attention paid toward oratory, appearance, and sexual behavior reveals the pursuit of masculinity during the Roman era, however difficult it may have been to reach. In any venue, a successful performance of one's masculinity conveys the achievement of self-control and control over others. Elite men worked to achieve these goals. Ultimately, if a man was able to demonstrate his masculinity well, he would win

---

63. Walters, "Invading the Roman Body," 29.

64. Ibid., 32.

65. Ibid.

66. Gleason addresses the control over one's bodily boundaries as well. She writes, "What Jesus clearly did not control was the boundaries of his own body." Gleason, "By Whose Gender Standards," 325–27.

67. Matthew Fox suggests that although sexual behavior may have been the key to gender for Foucault, "the idea that the secret of identity will be revealed if we look for sex is a very modern notion." Fox, "Constrained Man," 9–10.

approval and honor from his peers, at least temporarily fit the exacting paradigm established by them, and gain honor in the society as a whole.

Self-Control and Control over Others: A Means to an End

The criteria for elite Greco-Roman masculinity indicate an interest in control. While some biological factors, ethnicity, and class were beyond a man's control, he was nonetheless to exercise a great deal of control over his speech, body, physical appearance, and sexual behavior. Perhaps most importantly, elite standing indicates and preserves control over social inferiors and reinforced the importance of class as a feature of true masculinity. These factors feed into and off of one another, so that each factor cannot be isolated from the other. Nonetheless, control is a means to an end; an elite man's self-control and control over others demonstrates his masculinity, which in turn leads to honor among other elite men.

With regard to oratory and physiognomy, Gleason discussed how public speaking gave elite men an opportunity to perform their manliness in the forum, and the goal of that training was to communicate control of one's body, voice, and rhetorical style. The whole self—body, voice, style—was to be trained for that purpose. Physical appearance could indicate control as well, so that one's appearance gave the impression of dignity and conformity. Gleason sees such dignity in statues of men and women from modern Turkey and Italy. While her method of interpreting statues could be more clearly identified, using images as a means for discerning gender is a helpful development in the study of ancient masculinity. About a statue of a priest from Aphrodisias, she sees "the dignified authority of a leading citizen accustomed to unquestioning respect."[68] The priest wears a heavy toga and poses in a calm manner; he gives the impression of weight and stability. Sexual behavior could also be controlled so that a man only penetrates, rather than be penetrated. Moreover, when a manly, elite man made his sexual advance, he approached only suitable persons who were not citizens nor would

---

68. Gleason, "Elite Male Identity," 69. Likewise, a statue of "the ideal woman" found in Italy "reveals some of the same characteristics representative of the ideal man: dignity, authority, and self-control." Ibid., 71. Images provided lasting models of masculinity. As Hanson points out, living models of masculinity were in short supply because of the limited life expectancy of men during that time. Stone endures; life does not. About life expectancy and its effects on fathers and sons, see Hanson, "Roman Family" 27, 46.

they become citizens. Moreover, his sexual activity was limited to a certain amount; too much sexual activity was dangerous to his health.[69] In this regard, Martin states, "All people *might* be encouraged to control their sexual activities, but that encouragement was always understood within a larger structure in which self-control was basically a male characteristic."[70]

Although self-control was a tantalizing goal for elite men who wished to be considered masculine among their peers, some ancient writers seem to be fascinated with a moment when self-control was not complete. This brief lapse was made visible by an involuntary blush of the face. The moment in which men revealed their lack of total control over their bodies garnered some attention from Roman writers such as Catullus and Cicero.[71] The blush could not be overcome by sheer force of will; in fact, the blush was a mark of sincerity. Barton writes, "while the Romans yearned for and idealized autonomy and self-mastery, mild shaming was one of the most important socializing mechanisms in ancient Rome *precisely because it was involuntary.*"[72] For Seneca, this involuntary coloring of the face separated sincere men from actors, whose behaviors were to be avoided.[73] Even Pompey, "the great warlord of the dying republic,"[74] blushed; according to Seneca, "Nothing was more tender than the face of Pompey; he blushed whenever he was in public, especially in assemblies." [75] As discussed above, one's external appearance gave the public a glimpse into inner character. Men who blushed involuntarily could be trusted. At the same time, too much blushing could be considered a pretense. One should blush at the right moments, and only to a degree that indicates sincerity. The blush was only valued when it occurred at appropriate times. Self-control was a goal of the performance of masculinity and honor, but self-control could go too far;

---

69. The fluids involved in sexual activity drained a man and threatened his moisture levels.
70. Martin, "Contradictions," 90. Italics his.
71. Barton, "Roman Blush."
72. Ibid., 214. Italics his.
73. Ibid.
74. Ibid.
75. Ibid.

"the deliberate blush," as an extreme manifestation of self-control, was to be avoided.[76]

Control over self does not necessarily lead to control over others, but both were important facets of masculinity and honor. Control over others begins at the most basic level, in the household.[77] The household was a private and yet essential place to reach for masculine identity. A *paterfamilias* had power over his wife, children, family wealth and property, slaves, and freed dependents.[78] The power of the father (*patria potestas*)[79] sanctioned by Roman law gave the man of the house "supreme authority" and the "highest respect."[80] An elite man was to demonstrate his control and authority over his own household in public and in private. Control over the household and one's dependents was a microcosm of the control over empire that an elite man shared with his peers. He must keep his household in order and show that he was qualified to keep the empire in order.[81]

Ultimately, the pursuit of control and masculinity led to honor. Elite Greek and Roman men in the first and second centuries CE were trained to communicate so that they could preserve self-control and control over others. This expansive (and expensive) pursuit led to the achievement of masculinity. Masculinity, in turn, led to honor among one's peers; masculinity was one aspect of honor as a whole. Elite men wanted to be considered manly and therefore worthy of inclusion in the "club" of rulers and other privileged men. Ironically, they set their own high standards and critiqued each other, sometimes harshly, when someone failed to achieve those standards. A great deal of energy and effort went into the scrutiny of one another, ferreting out secret feminine traits, and fostering suspicion. The work of classicists in this area gives the impression of a relentless pressure to speak, dress, and move like

---

76. Ibid., 222.

77. Penner and Vander Stichele suggest that control over home and then over others is a sequence: "Control of one's household is thus the first stage in the public performance of the elite male in this cultural context." Penner and Vander Stichele, "All the World's a Stage,'" 388.

78. Hanson, "Roman Family," 21–22.

79. Ibid., 26.

80. Ibid., 28.

81. See Williams, *Roman Homosexuality*, 127: "I suggest that the various manifestations of effeminacy are symptoms of an underlying failure to live up to the central imperative of masculinity, control and dominion, both of others and of oneself."

a man, even when being buffeted by involuntary bodily reactions such as blushing.[82] Where could a man let his guard down? Did men have a safe space in which they could blush without suspicion? Even inside one's home, a man must demonstrate his authority and control over others. Clearly these men have the education and leisure to invest in their masculinity.

However, as Martin and others have pointed out, elite gender ideology has gaps and fissures. One must avoid extremes of singing, dancing, and acting, and yet figures such as Polemo, who lacked the biological markers of maleness and who openly embraced his idiosyncrasies, was popular among second-century audiences. One's clothing and hairstyle should conform to the dignity of old Rome, yet Caesar could redefine masculinity and still maintain his power. One's sexual behavior should focus on penetration, but too many encounters with women could effeminize a man. The involuntary blush revealed a lack of self-control, yet confirmed a man's trustworthiness. Martin has noted these contradictions and argued that the uncertainty of masculinity made it all the more precious. The contradictions allowed the ideology to function and increased its allure.[83] A masculinity that difficult to reach must be valuable. The primary and secondary sources consulted for this study indicate that, according to their own discourse, very few men were able to demonstrate the right balance of self-control, control, and masculinity at the right times.

However, the elevated standards for elite masculinity did not stop men from attempting to reach the summit. An excellent performance on the stage, in the forum, or in the home could lead to more public recognition, awards, or accolades. While these rewards may not result only from laudable masculine behavior, it is likely that a man would not be able to achieve public recognition without acting like a man.[84] Specific rewards may be inscriptions which recognize the ἀρετή (excellence or virtue) of a man.[85] Other inscriptions may name someone as "a good

---

82. Martin writes that even a scratch of the head or a certain type of sneeze indicated effeminacy. Martin, "Contradictions," 81.

83. Ibid., 81–82.

84. The orator Polemo, as described by Gleason, would be a notable exception.

85. Danker, *Benefactor*, 318.

man."[86] Other forms of recognition may include crowns,[87] statues, and commendation in public speeches. These rewards reinforced the pursuit of masculinity as one facet of honor and underscored the complicated nature of honor itself.

As some men attempted to appear masculine and to earn the approval of their elite peers, other men failed to reach those goals. The absence of manly behavior among elite men could lead to ridicule and shame. Barton states that in Rome, "a sense of shame functioned as a deterrent. And so Roman punishments, when they did occur, tended to be theatrical, designed to mortify the transgressor. A man's statue might be torn down and broken into pieces. He might be publicly displayed or forced to perambulate carrying the conspicuous weight of odd and ugly bonds and impediments."[88] Manly behavior may even include one's style of writing. A man could be shamed for a poorly written speech or letter. For example, Seneca criticized Maecenas of *mollitia* (softness, effeminacy, excess pleasure) because Seneca thought Maecenas' writing style was too emotional, lacked self-discipline, and was therefore effeminate.[89] Nearly every facet of an elite man's life and body could be subjected to public view, but nonetheless, elite men sought public honor and acted like men in order to get it.

RESEARCH FROM THE FIELD OF NEW TESTAMENT: MASCULINITY AMONG ELITE MEN

We shift now from a review of literature written by classicists to a review of literature written by New Testament scholars. Overall, New Testament scholars are in the beginning stages of the search for clues to

---

86. Ibid., 318–19.

87. Barton refers to the writing of Pliny the Elder, who describes the different kinds of crowns given to Romans for glorious deeds. Barton, *Roman Honor*, 52; Pliny the Elder, *Nat.* 22.4. Soldiers, who were not always elite, also received crowns as a form of public recognition. For example, a centurion who saved the "life of a fellow citizen in great danger" received the "civic crown of oak leaves." Webster, *Roman Imperial Army*, 133.

88. According to Barton, a man who defaulted on a loan might see his name posted on a column. More grave consequences might occur as well: "He might be stripped naked and flogged" or "torn into bits by a crowd." "His corpse might be dragged by a hook to the Tiber." Barton, *Roman Honor*, 22.

89. Graver, "Manhandling of Maecenas," 609.

the components of masculinity during the first and second centuries CE. New Testament scholarship on masculinity occurs mostly in essay form. These essays signal the development of a hermeneutic of masculinity that depends on classicists such as Gleason, Williams, and others.[90] Like some classicists, some New Testament scholars emphasize oratory and sexual behavior as ways for men to demonstrate their masculinity.[91] Of all the classics scholars featured by New Testament scholarship, Gleason appears the most often.

This section will explore how New Testament scholars Mary Rose D'Angelo and Tat-Siong Benny Liew have used classics to interpret specific New Testament texts. While issues of control come to the fore in classical scholarship, neither D'Angelo nor Liew summon those issues as such. However, they do survey issues of power in New Testament texts, specifically how a male character's class and power manifest themselves in the rhetoric of a narrative. In their respective works, D'Angelo and Liew each take masculinity as defined by classicists in a different direction: D'Angelo toward Jewish sources and themes and Liew toward the issue of sexual behavior. I will discuss the contributions of each New Testament scholar, but it is important to note that the approaches of these scholars do not fit into neat methodological columbaria. For example, Liew's approach could be associated with both sexuality studies and postcolonial studies. I offer one possible way to organize New Testament interpretations while noting their dependence on works by classicists.

The first set of works we will explore are written by Mary Rose D'Angelo. Author of incisive and influential works about both women and men in the early imperial period, D'Angelo appeared in the first chapter of this study, where I suggested that her work could more fully assess the characterization of Cornelius as a man in Acts. Here the focus will be on D'Angelo's sources. Her scholarship cannot be reduced to masculinity studies because it alludes to much more: Roman political intrigue, piety for the conqueror and the conquered, and propaganda that reached as far as Egypt. However, in general, Gleason's work is a

90. Some New Testament scholars prefer to base their gender-related insights on models from cultural anthropology. However, this study focuses on primary sources rather than anthropological models. For more on cultural anthropology and masculinity in New Testament texts, see Moxnes, "Conventional Values."

91. Issues of the personal appearance of biblical characters rarely figure into New Testament scholarship.

springboard for D'Angelo. D'Angelo uses Gleason to shed light on the characters in Luke-Acts who speak publicly like elite Roman men. D'Angelo builds on Gleason's research on public speaking and applies that scholarship to the interpretation of leading men in Luke-Acts.

One essay by D'Angelo especially relies on Gleason's work. Published in 2001, the essay D'Angelo focuses more overtly on masculinity than any of her essays consulted for this study.[92] Here she establishes elite male status and gender-related ideology relevant issues in Luke-Acts. She uses Gleason's "Elite Male Identity" essay to illuminate the descriptions of the apostles, noting that "public speaking is the hallmark of the elite male."[93] For example, Paul formally addresses crowds in Acts; these and other formal addresses in Acts indicate Luke's interest in portraying the leaders of the early church as powerful, elite men who can stand on an imperial stage.[94] According to D'Angelo, Luke "manifestly seeks to present at least some early Christians as possessing Roman citizenship, and all believers as worthy of it."[95] Powerful apostles such as Paul could compete with elite men because of his ability as a public speaker. Both men and women in Luke-Acts conform to Roman standards of "gendered behavior" and thus contribute "to the stability of the imperial order."[96] In this way, D'Angelo utilizes research on gendered behavior in order to discern the rhetorical contours of Luke-Acts regarding the empire.[97]

D'Angelo's interest in masculinity has since developed into what she calls "family values." In more recent essays, she focuses on Jewish sources and themes. In a thorough word study on εὐσεβεία, she investigates Roman propaganda and compares its use in primary sources to its use in 4 Maccabees and the Pastorals. Like the Roman concept of *pietas*, εὐσεβεία was exemplified by imperial men such as Trajan and

---

92. D'Angelo, "ANHP Question."
93. Ibid., 52; Gleason, "Elite Male Identity," 79.
94. D'Angelo, "ANHP Question," 56.
95. Ibid., 66.
96. Ibid.
97. In a 2003 essay, "'Knowing How to Preside,'" D'Angelo does not use Gleason but she does, however, discuss control over family and empire and the demonstration of "family values" modeled by imperial families. See also Larson, "Paul's Masculinity"; Young, "Being a Man"; Glancy, "Protocols of Masculinity."

Hadrian.⁹⁸ This virtue encompassed a man's moral excellence, his proper role as head of the household, and religious observance.⁹⁹ The writers of 4 Maccabees and the Pastorals made use of this virtue and created a dialectic of resistance and accommodation to Roman propaganda and occupation.¹⁰⁰ In a later essay, D'Angelo explores Philo's response to Roman moral propaganda about piety. She shows how Philo showcases Jewish "sexual probity, marital chastity, and familial devotion" as superior to that of Romans. In this rhetorical presentation of Jewish fidelity, Jews show Romans how to act appropriately.¹⁰¹

With these two essays, D'Angelo is moving away from Gleason and issues of elite masculinity *per se*. However, in the process, D'Angelo moves in a direction that Gleason has suggested. In her response to the essays in *New Testament Masculinities*, Gleason calls for "cultural specificity."¹⁰² Gleason writes, "to the extent that readers of early Christian texts, whatever their ethnicity, were not members of the educated elite, we must ask of each text's probable audience: What were its specific gender-norms? Jewish views on male nudity and male-male sexual contact, to mention just two examples, were clearly at odds with the views of the Greco-Roman elite . . ."¹⁰³ D'Angelo addresses the integration of Hellenistic views with those of Jewish people in Egypt in the writings of Philo. She shows how Jewish people had to deal with idealized imperial men and the effects of such propaganda on conquered peoples. More work with Jewish values and masculinity needs to be done, but D'Angelo has begun to move in that direction with her treatment of family values.

The second author who relies on classical scholarship about elite men is Tat-siong Benny Liew. Among other sources, Liew uses Craig William's book *Roman Homosexuality* to illuminate ancient sexual behavior and its implications for masculinity in New Testament texts.¹⁰⁴ The article "Mistaken Identifies but Model Faith," coauthored by Theodore Jennings and Tat-Siong Benny Liew, is an example of scholarship that looks into ancient sexual behavior as explicated by classicists

---

98. D'Angelo, "Εὐσεβεία," 139.
99. Ibid., 141.
100. Ibid., 139–40.
101. D'Angelo, "Gender and Geopolitics," 63–88.
102. Gleason, "By Whose Standards," 327.
103. Ibid.
104. See also Liew, "Re-Mark-able Masculinities."

and uses that research to understand characters in a gospel narrative.[105] The article does not purport to contribute to a hermeneutic of masculinity or to study masculinity as a whole. In fact, the word "masculinity" appears seldom in the article. I discuss the article here because it shows how research into ancient sexual behavior as a means to convey power can become a building block for New Testament interpretation. In this article, Liew suggests that the relationship between the centurion and the youth in Matt 8:5–13 could have sexual overtones. They argue that, in light of the ancient sexual connotations of the Greek word παῖς, interpreters should substitute the phrase "boy-love" or "boy" for παῖς.[106] These English translations recognize the sexual connotations of the original Greek.

Liew refers to Craig Williams, whose book was featured above, to argue that "the Roman military supposedly embodies the ideal of Roman masculinity . . ."[107] In order to make this point, Jennings and Liew refer to a specific phrase in Williams' *Roman Homosexuality*. There Williams discusses "military discipline" as the "ultimate bulwark of Roman masculinity."[108] This comment by Williams seems to be somewhat of an aside, however, because at that juncture in his argument, Williams is making a larger point about the refusal to bestow honor on a youth who wore perfume, which was a sign of effeminacy. Liew relies on this sidepoint from Williams and goes on to quote Tacitus, who tells of the indiscriminate penetration of "handsome youth" by Roman soldiers as a part of a military victory in 69 CE.[109] Other evidence from Williams may corroborate Liew's point about penetration, since, according to

---

105. Jennings and Liew, "Mistaken Identities." Jennings and Liew are not the only scholars who pursue research about ancient sexual behavior as a heuristic tool for New Testament interpretation. In "Sex and the Single Apostle," Moore adopts theories from Williams. For example, Moore adopts the distinction between men and un-men, which can be found in Williams, *Roman Homosexuality*, 7; Walters, "'No More Than a Boy,'" 31; Walters, "Invading the Roman Body," 41. For these references see Moore, Sex and the Single Apostle," 135. In *God's Beauty Parlor*, 136, Moore defines men as "adult male citizens," and unmen as "sexually passive or 'effeminate' males, eunuchs, barbarians, and so on." For more on sexual behavior using the scholarship of Gleason, see Swancutt, "Disease of Effemination."

106. Jennings and Liew, "Mistaken Identities," 468.

107. Ibid., 476n23.

108. Williams, *Roman Homosexuality*, 130.

109. Jennings and Liew, "Mistaken Identities," 475.

Williams, anyone "might potentially be subordinated."[110] However, while the excerpt from Tacitus allows Jennings and Liew to make a salient point about power and domination demonstrated through rape, some evidence might prove contrary to that view.[111] Missing in this article is a distinction between military men, who demonstrated their manliness and earned honor through physical prowess, and elite men who primarily demonstrated their manliness and earned honor on the stage. Williams does not seem to discuss soldiers, but Jennings and Liew use Williams to interpret a New Testament text about a soldier. It is possible that the rules for masculinity and honor among soldiers might differ from those among elite Greek or Roman men who lived a life of leisure. Some similarities might exist, but nuance is necessary, particularly about military masculinity and the endemic values it might instill.

Colleen Conway and Behold the Man

One book deserves special mention. Colleen Conway's *Behold the Man: Jesus and Greco-Roman Masculinity* is one of the first, if not the first, book-length project on masculinity and New Testament interpretation. First, I will describe some general characteristics of the book. Conway states that her book "explores the relationship between gender ideologies of the first-century Roman imperial world and conceptions of Jesus as the Christ in the New Testament. In particular, the book examines how cultural ideas of masculinity informed the various representations of Jesus in the writings of the New Testament."[112] In order to reach these goals, Conway employs a literary method that is sensitive to characterization, rhetoric, and gender. She analyzes male characters as men, and Jesus in particular, as men whose portrayals are influenced by the historical background of the writings. Her sources are primary texts, including the *Res Gestae*, Seneca's letters, and the writings of other elite men. The publications of Gleason, especially *Making Men*, help Conway

---

110. Williams, *Roman Homosexuality*, 77.

111. Saddington responded to this article two years later in "Centurion in Matthew 8:5–13," also in *JBL*. He does not disprove the suggestion that the centurion and his boy were lovers, but he does suggest that Jennings and Liew do not prove their case with the primary sources that they included. Saddington argues that the centurion's behavior in Matthew 8 does not necessarily correspond with the behavior of legionnaires or soldiers in the city of Rome itself. Instead we should look toward behaviors of soldiers in Galilee or further to the East, where they are removed from elite Roman standards.

112. Conway, *Behold the Man*, 6.

interpret these primary sources and consider how the ideologies inherent in these remains may inform the portrayals of Jesus.[113] As Conway indicates above, the focus of her book is Jesus. As such, her book stays focused on the portrayals of Jesus in a wide variety of New Testament texts, including the Pauline letters, the four Gospels, and Revelation. Because Jesus figures prominently in many writings, the scope of her book is therefore broad.

Of particular interest for this study is Conway's treatment of Luke-Acts and the portrayal of Cornelius in Acts 10. In the chapter entitled "The Lukan Jesus and the Imperial Elite," Conway argues that the narrative world of Luke-Acts is "completely at home within the masculine power structures of the Roman Empire."[114] The heroes of Luke's story act in bold and powerful ways. Jesus and his disciples are "models of masculinity."[115] Luke presents himself as educated, and Paul presents himself as highly educated as well. Jesus brings salvation and peace, and as Conway points out, "Given the frequency with which we other powerful men were named as saviors and bearers of salvation, this statement stands out as a bold challenge to imperial authority."[116] These portrayals place the men of Luke-Acts on an elite stage and indicate that they can compete with elites for power and influence. About Acts 10, Conway briefly discusses Cornelius as a "pious and God-fearing man" who "has the endorsement of local leaders" and who "engages in a remarkable display of deference."[117] Cornelius is one of several Roman officials who "highlight the status and virtue that accompany true masculinity."[118]

This study has some aspects in common with *Behold the Man*. The methods with which we approach masculinity in New Testament texts are similar. Conway demonstrates how an awareness of characterization, rhetoric, and gender can help the reader discern the constructions of masculinity in a text. While Conway may not identify those three factors as lenses to be combined, she seems to operate on the assumption that the three can work together to reveal gender ideologies. Like this study,

---

113. Gleason's work appears in ibid., 19, in the chapter entitled "How to Be a Man in the Greco-Roman World," where Conway discusses physiognomy.

114. Ibid., 127.

115. Ibid., 129.

116. Ibid., 130.

117. Ibid., 133.

118. Ibid.

Conway's book assumes that constructions of masculinity are part of an author's rhetorical agenda(s). Not only is the author of a New Testament text attempting to persuade the audience that Jesus brings salvation, but the author is also attempting to show that Jesus is a real man. The sources that Conway uses are similar to sources used in this study. For example, I consult the writings of elite men. In the case of the *Res Gestae*, our sources are the same, rather than similar. As Conway points out, the portrayal of Jesus in Luke-Acts appears to be a challenge to imperial authority in some ways. Like Conway, I also suggest that portrayals of men in Luke-Acts, Cornelius in particular, present a challenge or critique to imperial authority.

This study also has some important differences from *Behold the Man*. The portrayal of Cornelius and the construction of masculinity in Acts 10 comes to the fore. The scope of this study is therefore more narrow. The sources consulted for this study include the writings of elite men, but I also attempt to incorporate material remains to a greater degree, such as inscriptions, images, and coinage. I will delve into the ramifications and rhetorical impact of the portrayal of Cornelius as a representative of the Roman Empire. Because Cornelius is a military man, I will present historical background with regard to the Roman military and compare and contrast the constructions of masculinity among military men, rather than elites. Moreover, I will show how Luke turns the power of imperial men upside down through the power of the Holy Spirit, and interact with Conway on these issues.

RESEARCH FROM THE FIELD OF NEW TESTAMENT: MASCULINITY AMONG NON-ELITES

In the previous section, I discussed how D'Angelo, Liew, and Conway have used interpreted specific New Testament texts. The two scholars featured in this section—Stephen Moore and Eric Thurman—integrate ethnicity, class, and power to describe alternative ways of being men under Roman domination. By "alternative," I refer to the demonstration of one's masculinity that differs from the elite, dominant concepts and standards of masculinity, and to the demonstration of masculinity among non-elites. Proposing what I will call "alternative masculinities" for colonized peoples, both Moore and Thurman write about masculinity for subjects of the empire during the first and second centuries CE, and both underscore issues of control over self and others. However, Moore and Thurman envision masculinity beyond the elite; in this way, their scholarship addresses the masculinity proposed by Luke in Acts 10.

First we explore some of the published works by Stephen Moore and his contributions to a hermeneutic of masculinity. In his introduction to *New Testament Masculinities*, Moore contributes to masculinity studies and New Testament interpretation by configuring it as an extension of feminist studies which should be guided by feminists.[119] Moore grounds masculinity studies and New Testament interpretation in a literary approach. He collects and reviews four of the works that used masculinity research, listing others in his footnotes. Only eleven published works appear to be in circulation at the time of his writing.[120] Moore directs budding practitioners of this hermeneutic to seek understanding of masculinity without erasing the work that feminists have done, and without giving the implication that feminist interpretation needs development in order to be whole.

One specific essay written by Moore informs the study of masculinity among people who were not elite, powerful, or in control of others. In his essay on 4 Maccabees, coauthored with biblical scholar Janice Capel Anderson, Moore addresses masculinity as it takes shape among Jewish subjects of the Roman Empire. Published before *New Testament Masculinities*, it is one of the first applications of masculinity studies as a potential method of interpretation. Moore's argument centers on the concept of self-control and the characters in 4 Maccabees who demonstrate it. In 4 Maccabees, Antiochus tortures a Jewish father, mother, and their seven sons, forcing the mother to watch their torture and hoping to elicit homage from all of them. For Moore and Anderson, this story "subverts and supports the ancient hegemonic construction of masculinity."[121] In this narrative, Gentiles are associated with passion

---

119. The movement toward masculinity studies in New Testament interpretation takes place largely among English-speaking academic circles. However, one German essay addresses masculinity in a similar fashion to Moore. In a festschrift to Schotroff, Leutzsch notes the increased exploration of constructions of masculinity in Greek and Roman antiquity. Leutzsch, "Konstrucktionen von Männlichkeit," 600.

120. Moore, "'O Man Where Art Thou,'" 4n5.

121. Moore and Anderson, "Taking It Like a Man," 251. Moore and Anderson are comfortable with the ambivalence of 4 Maccabees regarding their position with hegemonic masculinity. They also see ambivalence in Matthew's presentations of masculin-

and Jews with reason.¹²² The story's emphasis on reason and self-control (ἐγκράτεια) shows the influence of Stoicism. Consider this statement from 4 Maccabees 5:22–23, as Eleazar critiques Antiochus: "You scoff at our philosophy as though living by it were irrational, but it teaches us self-control, so that we master all pleasures and desires, and it also trains us in courage [ἀνδρεία], so that we endure any suffering willingly . . ." In the following chapter of the story, Antiochus tortures Eleazar; as Eleazar falls to the ground, "he kept his reason upright and unswerving."¹²³ After his death, his wife exemples ἀνδρεία (manly courage) by refusing to submit to Antiochus. She also manifests self-control (ἐγκράτεια) in contrast to the rage of Antiochus. This essay indicates that the spectrum of ancient masculinity, though infused with and dependent upon class, does not always adhere to class. Fourth Maccabees provides examples of young, physically weak, or otherwise oppressed people who embody masculine virtues better than their ruler.¹²⁴ Although control over others might not be available to Jewish subjects of the empire, self-control was a masculine virtue within the grasp of conquered men and women. Though they were subjects, both males and females, men and un-men, could look to narratives for models of masculinity that resisted elite domination and created opportunities for dignity.

Second, we explore some of the published works by Eric Thurman, who investigates masculinity among men who were not elite or powerful in Roman society. While Moore takes a literary approach to masculinity as it is constructed in texts, Thurman takes a postcolonial approach. Investigating primarily Mark's Gospel, he formulates an alternative to the hegemonic ideals of masculinity and opens up possibilities for New Testament interpreters. In his essay "Looking for a Few Good Men: Mark and Masculinity," Thurman discusses the gender instability in Mark's Gospel. For Thurman, such instability is reflective of colonized locations.¹²⁵ Like classicist Carlin Barton, Thurman traces the political shift from republic to autocracy, which "denuded" many elite men of

---

ity. Moore, "Matthew and Masculinity."

122. Moore and Anderson, "Taking It Like a Man," 257.

123. 4 Macc 6:7.

124. Moore and Anderson, "Taking It Like a Man," 253–54. For more on self-control and masculinity, see Ivarsson, "Vice Lists and Deviant Masculinity," 163–84; Smith, "'Full of Spirit and Wisdom.'"

125. Thurman, "Looking for a Few Good Men."

their own authority and caused a crisis of masculinity among them.[126] Thurman proposes that suffering is a feminine trait; Mark's disciples, like Jesus himself, takes up a "feminized" position of "servile suffering in explicit resistance to Roman colonial models of domination."[127] Like Moore and Anderson's treatment of 4 Maccabees, Thurman sees an ambivalence in Mark that cannot be characterized as simple rejection or inversion of hegemonic masculinity. Instead, Thurman describes Jesus as a hybrid figure who resists through mimicry, defined as "the process of (imperfect) imitation of the colonizer by the colonized."[128] Mark's Jesus mimics hegemonic masculinity and yet presents an alternative way of being a man. This Jesus suffers, a trait reminiscent of "Greco-Roman philosophical discourses."[129] With this essay, Thurman offers interpreters a form of masculinity suited to the majority of first century Jewish subjects, who were likely familiar with suffering.

In a later essay, Thurman also argues for the presence of an alternative masculinity in Mark's Gospel. In this essay he compares Mark with a fictional narrative, relatively from the same time period. Thurman lays Mark's Gospel along Xenophon's *An Ephesian Tale*, dated to the second century CE.[130] He compares issues of masculinity and empire in both texts. He recognizes a paradox within hegemonic masculinity itself, ala Barton, but notes the expanse and change of masculinity in Greek novels as well. Novels written in Greek by Greeks were at least in part an attempt to reconfigure masculinity and establish Greek identity under Roman domination. Xenophon and similar novels use "tropes of eroticized resistance, especially virginity," to establish that identity.[131] Early Christian discourse, including Mark's Gospel, formulates resistance in a different way. "Christian narratives appear to construct an alternative male subject willing to represent itself, passionately and paradoxically, as 'suffering' and 'feminized' in its aggressive defiance of the dominant social order."[132] Suffering was simultaneously feminine and aggressive.

---

126. Ibid., 140, 143; Barton, "All Things," 90, 92.
127. Thurman, "Looking for a Few Good Men," 144.
128. Ibid., 139. Definition dependent on Homi Bhabha.
129. Ibid., 143.
130. Thurman, "Novel Men."
131. Ibid., 189.
132. Ibid., 192.

Both Greek novels and Mark's Gospel "valorize male suffering,"[133] and portray a male hero who prays and wavers slightly in time of crisis.[134] Both texts stop short of a fully organized attack on hegemonic masculinity yet both texts avoid complete assimilation to the dominant order. Both texts engage hegemonic masculinity but propose different ways of being masculine. Despite the lack of political power for many people during the Roman era, subjects of the empire could nonetheless take control of their own gender standards, embracing suffering and fashioning it into a masculine virtue.

These essays by Thurman are examples of how "malleable manliness" can be discerned in narrative contexts.[135] Though ambivalent in their presentation, male characters in narratives resist without totally surrendering their masculinity. Colonized people like Greeks and Jews were forced to create the means by which they would critique their oppressors. Through rhetorical discourse about masculinity, they fashioned a method of liberation. They created new options for the demonstration of masculine virtue and made courage available to un-men. No longer were power and control limited to Roman authority figures. Even though some literary texts signal the possibility that some elite Roman men failed to achieve masculinity, other texts show that the people under them established their own standards and found ways to be masculine in adverse circumstances.

OTHER ALTERNATIVES: MILITARY MASCULINITY AND MASCULINITY IN ACTS 10

The explication and review of classical scholarship allows New Testament interpreters to assess their texts in light of the dominant masculine ideals of the day. The works of Gleason, Williams, and Barton form a basis for New Testament interpretation but their scholarship also reveals clear limits. While elite Greek and Roman masculinity and honor was focused on self-control and the control of others, it was nonetheless *elite*. Elite writers were preoccupied with themselves; their critiques center on other elite men and share common concerns that might not extend past

---

133. Ibid.
134. Ibid., 202–3.
135. Ibid., 208.

their own upper-class circles. However, because masculinity was publicly performed and acted out in the home and in the forum, lower-class people were likely exposed to and influenced by these demonstrations. Colonized men, slaves, freed dependents, women, and children had to submit to the authority of these elite men; for elite men, such obedience reflected positively on themselves. Conversely, if subordinates did not obey, the masculinity of the elite man was likely at stake. Despite such pressure to submit, some texts indicate that colonized peoples found ways to resist, and in the process, they established alternative understandings of masculinity and honor.

While current classical scholarship on masculinity has its limits, so does current scholarship on masculinity and interpretation of New Testament texts. As was demonstrated in chapter 1, most interpreters of the New Testament have not addressed the characterization of Cornelius with regard to gender. Scholars have begun to formulate alternative masculinities, however, and more work needs to be done in that area. More primary sources on military masculinity and other alternatives need to be brought into the conversation so that our understanding of manliness can have greater depth.

The figure of Cornelius poses an interesting challenge to interpreters who use masculinity studies as a tool to discern the rhetorical impact of narratives. The narrator of Acts describes Cornelius as Roman, yet he is not clearly characterized as elite. Instead, he is a professional soldier, perhaps with his own standards and means of demonstrating masculinity. The narrator does not provide details about his eyes, voice, garments, or sexual behavior, all of which may have been important to elite men. He is a Gentile, yet he affiliates himself with Judaism and the religion of a colonized people. He prays regularly to the God of Israel and falls to the feet of a Jewish fisherman. He gives alms generously, yet he does not demand recognition for that generosity, as did other benefactors in that era.[136] Cornelius straddles empire and subject, polytheism and Judaism.

The presence of alternative masculinities in discourses of subject peoples of that time period, as described by Moore and Thurman, leads one to ask about other narratives that may propose alternatives. Male characters in New Testament texts hover along the edges and fringes of elite manhood, beckoning interpreters and spotlighting the need for a flexible understanding of masculinity in the first and second centuries

---

136. See Danker, *Benefactor*, for evidence and inscriptions about benefactors.

CE. In the chapters that follow, I will argue that the narrator of Acts characterizes Cornelius so that the audience will envision an alternative masculinity. The narrator creates an alternative gender vision by describing a Roman centurion as nonviolent, faithful, and generous. The lack of definitive markers of elite Roman masculinity in Acts 10 may indicate a rejection of the elite preoccupation with one's "gender temperature" as well as a proposal of masculinity that could be demonstrated through non-violence, prayer, and generosity.[137] Through his countercultural relinquishment of control, rejection of violence, and obedience to the Holy Spirit, Cornelius demonstrates a masculinity that critiqued the empire and highlighted different ways of being both honorable and Roman.

The map of masculinity drawn in this chapter shows that a change of elevation takes place in Acts 10. The mighty are brought down from their thrones and the lowly are lifted up.[138] With leading men like Peter and Cornelius in Acts, the emerging church charted a path that strayed from leisured Greeks and Romans and proposed exemplars of its own sort.

---

137. Gleason proposes the possibility of taking a man's "gender temperature," using the physiognomical guidelines of Polemo and others. Gleason, "Semiotics of Gender," 392.

138. See Luke 1:52.

3

Cornelius and the Virtue of Piety

INTRODUCTION

WHEN AN INTERPRETER LOOKS for constructs of masculinity in an ancient source, one often finds social dynamics that we do not typically associate with masculinity. The understandings of manliness in ancient remains are often intertwined with religious and political concepts, which are then conveyed in a rhetorical manner. Because of this tapestry of gender, religion, politics, and rhetoric, constructs of masculinity are often difficult to isolate, identify, and define. In her book *Behold the Man*, Colleen Conway describes this reality: "this study is founded on the conviction that gender categories are deeply embedded and entangled in the symbolic systems of any culture. It also assumes that such symbolic systems are open to analysis, critique, and deconstruction."[1] This chapter builds on Conway's convictions stated above. Although portrayals of masculinity in antiquity can be saturated with meaning, interpreters can begin to examine the complicated symbolic tapestries in literary and material remains. This kind of analysis illuminates not only the religious and political systems of ancient societies but also their understandings of the roles of men, whose stories we encounter through texts, inscriptions, and images.

---

1. Conway, *Behold the Man*, 9.

One way to examine ancient constructs of masculinity is to study virtues. A modern interpreter can learn about exemplars of masculinity, or "good men," through the study of ancient virtues. These virtues include wisdom, courage, temperance, justice, and piety.[2] Of particular import for this chapter will be the virtue of piety. I am interested in the language about and representations of piety in antiquity, especially in the first and second centuries CE. Piety can be studied through word fields, as well as through practical aspects of an ancient man's life, including how he observed time, what and with whom he ate, how he spent his money, and how he recognized death (both his own and that of others). The following study of word fields and behaviors associated with piety is not an exhaustive one. The sources that refer to piety, be they literary or material, are numerous, and the men whom these sources describe are equally as numerous.

What is most relevant for this chapter is that in Acts 10 Cornelius is portrayed as a pious man. Cornelius has aspects of piety that belong to a variety of men, both Gentile and Jew. Using common language that was likely familiar to his audience, Luke characterizes Cornelius as a man whose piety is similar to Roman emperors such as Augustus, Nero, and Trajan. The piety of Cornelius also connects him to Roman military officers who showed respect and reverence toward their commanding officers and toward one another. Yet Luke does not endorse wholesale the ways in which men displayed their piety and their virtues in general. Luke's man Cornelius does not behave in every way as other model men of his day. Luke uses language that evokes and yet subverts elite Greco-Roman, military, and Jewish understandings of piety among men. Luke refashions piety so that the God of Israel, not the Roman emperor, is the true sovereign. Through the characterization of Cornelius, Luke provides guidance to the followers of Jesus and presents them with an alternative to Roman virtues and Roman dominance.

This chapter will explore how the characterization of Cornelius in Acts 10 intersects and interacts with the language and images related to the piety of elite Greco-Roman, military, and Jewish men.[3] Each relevant

2. Noreña, "Communication," 152; Feldman, *Jew and Gentile*, 201.

3. I do not want to convey that elite Greco-Roman, military, and Jewish men were distinct historical categories. For example, Josephus was a Jewish general, a Roman citizen, and a client who was employed to tell the story of the war between the Romans and the Judeans. These realities cannot be easily compartmentalized. Nor do I want to convey that the sources that inform this study are easily compartmentalized. For

word or phrase discussed here has its own semantic range, although the definitions of the words can overlap. Essential to this philological exploration will be the work of Fred Danker.[4] In addition to the overlapping definitions of words, each image mentioned in this chapter can also convey multiple layers of meaning. Yet these dense layers of meaning and the frequency of the words in extrabiblical remains do not occlude the character of Cornelius. Instead, Luke uses common words, phrases, and concepts about piety that his audience would likely encounter and understand. Luke employs and repeats these words, phrases, and concepts as narrative tools in order to persuade the audience to envision a world in which the mighty are brought down from their thrones (Luke 1:52) and the men who serve Yahweh are lifted up.

Finally, this chapter will explore how the characterization of Cornelius reinforces two themes: 1) continuity with Judaism, and 2) inclusivity in the Way. Although Cornelius is a Gentile God-fearer, the same words that Luke uses to describe the piety of Cornelius in Acts 10 are also used by Philo in his description of Moses. Cornelius is a hybrid man, committed to the God of Israel but described in such a way that audiences from diverse backgrounds would recognize in him multiple expressions of piety. The combination of these two themes—continuity and diversity—creates a man for all seasons, but not a man for all gods.

CORNELIUS AND THE PIETY OF ELITE GRECO-ROMAN MEN

The words and phrases Luke uses to describe the piety of Cornelius in Acts 10 are also found in extrabiblical descriptions of the piety of elite Greco-Roman men. These elites include emperors and client kings. Outside of Luke-Acts, these words and phrases evoke polytheistic Roman rulers. However, Luke uses them to propose not the sovereignty of the emperor, nor of Greco-Roman gods and goddesses, but the sovereignty of the

---

example, nearly all, if not all, extant sources are elite in the sense that they were recorded on materials that survived. Elite Greco-Roman men sometimes trumpeted their military experience or expertise. Colonization forced Judeans to adapt and perhaps to change their understanding of what a good Jewish man does. Yet some distinction is possible, and attempts at nuance will be made throughout the study.

4. While several of Danker's works may be useful in this sort of inquiry, his book *Benefactor* is most helpful. *Benefactor* also helps the interpreter consider a variety of inscriptions, a medium that is sometimes neglected among New Testament scholars.

God of Israel. In this section I will briefly discuss the definition of virtue and its etymological relationship to the Latin word *vir*. I will then focus on the Greek words εὐσεβεία, δικαιοσύνη, ἐλεημοσύνας πολλὰς τῷ λαῷ, and μιμνήσκω, all of which appear outside and inside of Acts 10. I will show how each word appears outside the New Testament, and how Luke turns each word toward the God of Israel.

Although the English word "virtue" may not indicate its gendered original, the ancient concept of virtue was intertwined with masculinity. The concept of virtue appears in many ancient, extrabiblical contexts, notably in Plato's *Republic*, and Aristotle's *Nicomachean Ethics*. Aristotle defines virtue as a "settled disposition of the mind determining the choice of actions and emotions, consisting essentially in the observance of the mean relative to us, this being determined by principle, that is, as the prudent man would determine it."[5] In this definition, virtue is linked to the choices of a man. The English word "virtue" is also linked to masculinity by its etymological relationship to the Latin word *vir*, often translated by the English word "man." Another translation for *vir* could be the phrase "manly man." Conway notes this connection between manhood and virtue when she states that "to become a *vir* in the Greco-Roman world, one was required to demonstrate manliness through the practice of particular virtues."[6] The historian Karl Galinsky makes a similar point in his book about the reign of the emperor Augustus: "One of the principal connotations of *virtus* . . . was manly valor on the battlefield," as well as "a result of moral effort."[7] Virtue and masculinity are therefore intertwined. This connection should not be overlooked by interpreters who study ancient masculinity. As Carlos Noreña notes, *virtus*, defined as "manly courage displayed in any public action," can be found on approximately 13 percent of denarii coins found and dated from the reign of Vespasian (69 CE) to the reign of Septimius Severus (235 CE).[8] Given the gendered nature of the words *virtus*, masculinity was advertised on coins for nearly one hundred and fifty years.

Not every male could be a *vir* or demonstrate *virtus*. These words imply high status and occasionally a leadership position. Richard Alston

5. Aristotle *Eth. nic.* 2:15 (Rackham, LCL).
6. Conway, *Behold the Man*, 22.
7. Galinsky, *Augustan Culture*, 84.
8. Noreña studied a sample of 148, 421 coins from the time period noted. *Virtus* was featured on 13 percent of them. Noreña, "Communication," 149.

has noted that most *viri* were elite Greco-Roman men, although some military men could be considered *viri* in certain locales.[9] Conway states that a good king demonstrated his virtues. "Closely integrated to the idea of the good king," writes Conway, "and central to Greco-Roman masculine ideology, are the achievement and display of virtues . . ."[10] In addition, the virtues of the Roman emperor were communicated in a variety of ways, including triumphal processions, public buildings, distributions of grain and coin, sacrifices, and portraits on coins.[11] Elite men, kings, and emperors showed themselves to be *viri* through these media. From this perspective, piety is linked to power.

In Acts 10, Luke makes his own statements about piety, masculinity, and power. Luke directs his audience away from Roman sovereignty and toward the ultimate authority in the narrative, which belongs to the God of Israel. Luke accomplishes this mission by means of the repetition of key words and phrases related to piety. First I will provide the historical background and usage of the Greek word εὐσεβεία in extrabiblical sources, and then demonstrate how Luke redefines the word with reference to Cornelius in Acts 10:2.

Εὐσεβεία

The Greek word εὐσεβεία has a similar meaning to the Latin word *pietas*. Because of this shared semantic range, one can study the appearances of both words in order to learn about the men who exemplify this virtue. D'Angelo connects these two with this statement: "εὐσεβεία appears to carry the implications of *pietas*, the Roman and imperial virtue that best approximates 'family values' combined with religious observance."[12] D'Angelo goes on to state that in the Greek version of the *Res Gestae*, Augustus' monumental inscription, the Latin word *pietas* is

---

9. Soldiers were not always able to control the boundaries of their bodies, which was an essential component in elite masculinity. Occasionally soldiers may have to endure physical punishment, despite their Roman citizenship. However, Alston states, "In some parts and among soldiers themselves, the soldiers' control over violence and their relatively high status as representatives of the empire qualified them as *viri*." Alston, "Arms and the Man," 220.

10. Conway, *Behold the Man*, 178.

11. Noreña, "Communication," 146.

12. D'Angelo connects these concepts in the texts of 4 Maccabees and the pastoral epistles in the New Testament. D'Angelo, "Εὐσεβεία," 141.

translated with εὐσέβεια.¹³ The two words are therefore interchangeable in this context. The definitions of the words are similar as well. Green and Scheid define *pietas* as "the typical Roman attitude of dutiful respect towards gods, fatherland, and parents and other kinsmen . . . and worship of the gods."¹⁴ Likewise, Bauer, Danker, Arndt, and Gingrich define εὐσέβεια in this way: "to be profoundly reverent or respectful, devout, godly, pious, [and] reverent."¹⁵ While the following extrabiblical sources revolve around the Greek term, the definition of the Latin term can help us understand the full meaning of the concept.

Piety can be attributed to many different elite Greco-Roman men, but material remains often attribute εὐσέβεια to Roman rulers, including Augustus, Nero, and Herod. In the *Res Gestae*, Augustus states that he built temples to Mars, Jupiter, Apollo, the divine Julius, Minerva, Juno, the Lares, and the Grove of the Caesars.¹⁶ Augustus restored the Capitol, which was associated with Jupiter, and eighty-two temples that were sacred to deities.¹⁷ According to Mary Beard, "each new emperor took the office of *pontifex maximus*," defined as "the headship of the whole of state religion."¹⁸ In addition to the chief religious post of the empire, Augustus held the priestly post of *augur* and participated in priestly colleges.¹⁹ Archaeologists have excavated statues of Augustus in which his head is covered with a veil, which signified his role as priest and his emphasis on piety. In an inscription found near the city of Acraephiae in Greece, the emperor Nero is also called "pious" (εὐσεβείας).²⁰ Herod is named a pious friend of Caesar in a Judean inscription from the first century CE.²¹ These inscriptions do not indicate that all people who read the

13. Ibid., 143.

14. *OCD*, 1182.

15. BDAG, 413.

16. This chapter uses the translation and citation system of the *Res Gestae Divi Augusti* (Shipley, LCL). About the temples built by Augustus, see *Res gest. divi Aug.* 3:19.

17. *Res gest. divi Aug.* 3.19–21; Danker, *Benefactor*, 270.

18. Beard et al., *Religions of Rome*, 204–5.

19. *Res gest. divi Aug.* 1:7.

20. The inscription is dated to approximately 67 CE. See inscription 814, *SIG* 2:506.

21. Inscription 427, *OGIS* suppl. 1:638. Herod demonstrated his own piety toward Augustus and the gods in Caesarea Maritima. Josephus describes this building project in *War* 1:414. Herod had a large temple built in Caesarea, and placed in it two colossal statues of Augustus and the goddess Roma. Barbara Burrell states that these statues portray Augustus as the god Zeus Olympios and Roma as the goddess Hera of Argos.

inscriptions considered Augustus, Nero, and Herod to be pious. Instead, these remains indicate that those who authored the inscriptions wanted the recipients to be named as such. In any case, the word εὐσεβεία appears to represent a desirable virtue among elite Greco-Roman rulers.

In addition to inscriptions, the exemplary piety of emperors could also be communicated through coins and images. According to Joan Taylor, a coin was issued in 16 BCE that showed emblems of the priestly offices of Augustus.[22] Carlos Noreña states that *pietas* was featured on 20 percent of denarii dated from Augustus to Septimius Severus.[23] Many of these coins featured not only the word *pietas* but also the image of an emperor on the other side of the coin. The Ara Pacis altar of Augustus, located in Rome and dedicated in 9 BCE, shows Augustus wearing a veil as a symbol of the priestly office, and standing with other priests as he makes a sacrifice for peace.[24] Trajan's arch at Beneventum, dated to the second century CE, shows Trajan standing next to the god Jupiter, as Trajan forms a treaty between Rome and barbarians.[25] The proximity of the emperor to the gods and the exemplary piety shown in these remains encourages viewers to consider the emperor the most pious man in the empire.

In addition to emperors and rulers, the word εὐσεβεία can also be used in inscriptions that feature other elite Greco-Roman men. According to Clayton Lehmann, the purpose of dedicatory inscriptions was to fulfill the obligation of *pietas*.[26] In this case, one man could have an inscription made to honor another man. Yet men could also commission inscriptions to honor themselves. The *Res Gestae* is an inscription of this type. Danker provides two more examples of this type. In the first example, Antiochus I of Kommagene had a large shrine and mausoleum built at his gravesite, and the inscription placed there reads: "I considered piety not only the most secure possession but also the most pleasurable enjoyment for human beings, and the same judgment held

---

Burrell, "Palace to Praetorium," 259.

22. "A coin was issued in 16 BCE showing emblems of the priestly offices to celebrate Augustus' becoming *pontifex* in 48 BCE, *augur* in 41-40 BCE, *quindecemir sacris faciundis* in c. 37 BCE, and *septemvir epulonum* in 16 BCE." Taylor, "Pontius Pilate," 562.

23. Noreña, "Communication," 155–56.

24. Brent, *Imperial* Cult, 35.

25. Beard et al., *Religions of Rome*, 2:27.

26. Lehmann, "City and the Text," 388.

to be the cause of my prosperous power and of its most blessed use...."[27] Antiochus continues, again referring to his own piety, "When I took over the ancestral reign, as expression of my pious thoughts I declared the kingdom that was subject to my thrones to be the common abode of all the Gods..."[28] In the second example, Attalos dedicates an inscription to the goddess Aphrodite but in doing so, he announces his own piety. This inscription reads, "I have in every respect demonstrated my piety, as well as goodwill to my home town, both in my liturgies and in all other services rendered blamelessly by me..."[29]

With these extrabiblical appearances in mind, we can consider Luke's use of εὐσέβεια in Acts 10:2. Luke describes Cornelius as εὐσεβής almost immediately; the only phrase that precedes it is a reference to Cornelius' military cohort. Luke introduces Cornelius in this way: "In Caesarea there was a man named Cornelius, a centurion of the Italian Cohort, as it was called. He was a devout man..." (10:2). It is likely that Luke relies on the frequent extrabiblical usage of the word εὐσεβής, often translated as "devout" in English, in order to use language that his audience would understand. Although the word can be found frequently outside of the New Testament, Luke limits the meaning of the word in his story and maintains that piety should be defined as reverence toward the God of Israel. Werner Foerster states that εὐσέβεια "mostly stands for the worship of the gods" as well as "the broader sense of respect for the orders of life," but for Luke, the word refers to the proper respect shown to Yahweh.[30] According to Danker, two passages in Acts "illustrate aspects of shift in registration of the *euseb-* family from a non-Jewish or non-Christian milieu to Jewish Christian circles."[31] One of these passages includes a description of Cornelius. In this passage, Luke combines the adjective εὐσεβής with the phrase φοβούμενος τὸν θεόν ("one who feared God"). The combination indicates to the audience that piety toward Greco-Roman gods or to the emperor is not meant

---

27. Danker dates this inscription to the middle of the first century BCE. See inscription 41 in Danker, *Benefactor*, 238.

28. Ibid.

29. Danker does not specify a date or location for this inscription. See inscription 10 in ibid., 73.

30. Foerster, "σεβάομαι," 177.

31. Danker, *Benefactor*, 343. The second passage is Acts 17:22–23. See below for a discussion of this passage.

here. Luke provides the object of the worship—τὸν θεὸν (God) —to distinguish Cornelius from men who demonstrate their piety toward Roman authorities. Likewise, one of Cornelius' soldiers is also εὐσεβῆ (10:7). Luke repeats this word soon after its reference to Cornelius. The repetition of the word, despite the absence of the phrase φοβούμενος τὸν θεὸν, reinforces the piety exemplified by Cornelius.

Elsewhere in Acts, the word εὐσέβεια allows Luke to shape a common imperial virtue into a virtue suited only to those who serve the God of Israel. This configuration of piety contrasts with extrabiblical references to the virtue. In Acts 3:12, Peter rejects any personal power or piety (εὐσεβείᾳ) which may explain the healing of a lame man. Peter states, "You Israelites, why do you wonder at this, or why do you stare at us, as though by our own power or piety we had made him walk?" Peter attributes healing power to the God of his ancestors. "And by faith in his name," Peter continues, "his name itself has made this man strong, whom you see and know; and the faith that is through Jesus has given him this perfect health in the presence of all of you" (3:16). Despite the Israelites' familiarity with the God of their ancestors, Luke gives the audience the impression that the Israelites may have interpreted it as the work of Peter and John. Here opposition from some Jewish groups begins to develop, and Luke clarifies the issue about which they may disagree. The God of Israel is at work, not human beings. This clarification about the true source of power also challenges elite Greco-Roman understandings of piety. In contrast to Antiochus I and Attalos, who announced their own εὐσέβεια through inscriptions, Peter refuses to take credit for the healing and associates the name of Jesus with the miracle. In this story, in contrast to some Jewish and Gentile understandings, Peter and John demonstrate a piety that does not draw attention to itself.

The word εὐσέβεια also appears in Acts 17:23. Danker points out a similar redirection of the meaning of the word here, where Paul informs the Athenians, who had been "extremely religious" toward an unknown God, that they have been worshiping the God of Israel.[32] Danker writes, "Luke carefully introduces the term *deisidaimonesteros* in his appraisal of public piety at Athens and preserves the *euseb-* form for Paul's favorable verdict concerning the provision Athenians had made for recognition of the 'Unknown God.' This deity is, of course, the God of Israel . . ."[33] In

---

32. Acts 17:22.

33. Danker, *Benefactor*, 344.

this appearance of the word, the Athenians practice piety but they do not know to whom their piety is directed. This is not a virtue for Luke. It is possible that Luke is critiquing the Athenians, whom Luke describes as interested in whatever was "newer" (καινότερον, 17:21). Through Paul's corrective response, Luke indicates that people should know whom they worship, and that, despite their ignorance, the God of Israel has been active all along.

Like Cornelius, Peter, John, and Paul know and fear the God of Israel. Unlike many of the elite Greco-Roman men mentioned in association with the word εὐσεβεία, the protagonists in Acts demonstrate piety toward the God of Israel. These positive examples of piety in Acts stand in contrast to Herod in Acts 12. Angry with the people of Tyre and Sidon, Herod received a visit from the people, who "depended on the king's country for food" (12:20).[34] Herod put on his royal robes, took a seat on a platform, and delivered a speech to them. The people shouted "The voice of a god, and not of a mortal!" (12:21–22). In contrast to Peter in Acts 3:12, Herod accepted the acclamations and did not give glory to God. Because he allowed the people to think he was a god, "the Lord struck him down and he was eaten by worms and died" (12:23).[35] Herod's death appears to be a direct result of his unwillingness to show reverence toward God.[36] Luke's graphic description of how he died raises the stakes regarding piety in the narrative. The way that Herod died tells Luke's audience that the lack of piety is an internal sickness with serious consequences.

---

34. Penner and Vander Stichele note that Herod's anger may render him effeminate. "Consumed by their passions," some portrayals of men may indicate "an implicit effeminization" through the lack of self-control. Penner and Vander Stichele, "Gendering Violence," 200.

35. For a parallel version of this event, see Josephus, *Ant.* 19:343–50 (Feldman, LCL).

36. It is not uncommon for emperors to be called "Son of God," or for rulers to be considered divine. Emperors were sometimes considered divine after their deaths. Yet for Luke, Herod's acceptance of these claims is wrong. According to Klauck, allowing the people to think he was a god broke the first commandment: "I am the Lord, your God. You shall have no other gods before me" (Exod 20:2). Klauck, *Magic and Paganism*, 39–44.

Δικαιοσύνη

The use of the word δικαιοσύνη (righteousness or uprightness) is the second way in which Luke highlights the piety of Cornelius and directs reverence toward the God of Israel, rather than toward Roman emperors. In Acts 10:22, the emissaries of Cornelius describe him as "an upright and God-fearing man, who is well spoken of by the whole Jewish nation . . ." Like εὐσέβεια, δικαιοσύνη can be found in reference to elite Greco-Roman men and emperors. Analogous to the Latin word *iustitia*, the word δικαιοσύνη refers to the "upright" nature of one's behavior and to the ability to discern and do justice. Danker translates this word as "uprightness" with regard to one's relationships with people.[37] "Two principle features of Greco-Roman character," Danker writes, are "piety toward God and uprightness in association with fellow beings."[38] The word appears in honorific inscriptions as a virtue praised by both Greeks and Romans, as well as in Luke-Acts, where it is often translated as "upright" or "righteous."[39] Δικαιοσύνη could be correlated with behaviors such as treating other people with fairness, respect, and dignity, acting with integrity and honesty, and otherwise demonstrating one's right relationship with God among other people.

Δικαιοσύνη, or the analogous Latin concept of *iustitia*, appears in extrabiblical references as a virtue of the emperor Augustus and a characteristic of war. Augustus dispensed justice through published edicts and imperial tribunals.[40] According to Noreña, Augustus emphasized and wished to revive the ancestral virtues of *clementia, iustitia, pietas*, and *virtus*.[41] In Rome, around 27 BCE, the Roman senate "set up a golden shield in the new senate house, named *Cura Iulia* after Julius Caesar."[42] The shield was inscribed with the four virtues that Noreña specifies.

---

37. Danker, *Benefactor*, 343.

38. Ibid., 489.

39. Ibid., 345.

40. Noreña mentions these activities as a factor in the relatively small representation of the virtue of *iustitia* on coins from Augustus to Septimius Severus. *Iustitia* appears on only 2 percent of denarii found and dated to that time period. Noreña suggests that coins that celebrated that virtue were not necessary, given Augustus' other activities related to justice. Noreña, "Communication," 157.

41. Ibid., 152.

42. Galinsky, *Augustan Culture*, 80. A marble copy of the shield can be seen in ibid., 87, figure 37.

According to Galinsky, the words *iustitia* and *pietas* on the shield "refer to the fact that the war against Cleopatra—and Octavian was careful to present it largely as such and not as a civil war against Antony—was a pious and just war."[43] If this shield gives us any indication, during the reign of Augustus, *iustitia* and *pietas* carried the connotations of both virtue and violent conflict. In this context, waging war can be a sign of justice and piety.[44]

Justice and piety also refer to an elite Greco-Roman man named Menas in an honorific inscription dated to the second century BCE. In a testimony to the trustworthy nature and credentials of Menas, people from the town of Sestos, located in the Chersonese, describe Menas as "pious and honest." [45] The word δίκαιος here translates to the English word "honest." These qualities allow Menas to supervise the city treasury. In this context, δικαιοσύνη means that Menas will be fair and just with people, and that he can be trusted with an important responsibility.

In Luke's story, δικαιοσύνη does not refer to the virtue of the emperor, or to the waging of war, or to the city treasury. In Acts 10:22 the emissaries of Cornelius call Cornelius δίκαιος. The emissaries arrive at Peter's home and say that Peter should come with them to the home of Cornelius. Luke builds the character of Cornelius by having other characters describe him as upright, just, and honest. The word conveys that Cornelius' emissaries are not trying to trick Peter. Given the power imbalance between a Roman centurion and a Judean subject, the audience may have imagined Peter to be suspicious about the summons. If the centurion was trying to intimidate or harm Peter, Peter may have been in danger. Yet the word δίκαιος indicates that Cornelius is sincere in his attempt to do what the angel had commanded, that is, to bring Peter to his home. In this way, the word use has more in common with the honorific inscription about Menas. However, Luke adds to his story the God of Israel. While Cornelius is honest, he is merely following the orders of the angel of God. He has a responsibility not to his city, but to God.

Elsewhere in Luke-Acts, the word δικαιοσύνη often refers to Jesus and to the teachings of Jesus. This correlation between Jesus and

---

43. Ibid., 80.

44. Augustus waged war against the Parthians during his reign, as he indicates in *Res gest. divi Aug.* 29:2. See also Galinsky, *Augustan Culture*, 155–56.

45. Inscription 17 in Danker, *Benefactor*, 94.

Cornelius also builds the character of Cornelius and places Cornelius in good company. In the infancy narrative of Luke's Gospel, Jesus is surrounded by righteous (δίκαιοι) people, including Zechariah, Elizabeth and Simeon.[46] All these characters give glory to God. Later in Luke, Jesus accuses the Pharisees of not knowing what righteousness is.[47] The Pharisees choose the best seats at meals, trust in themselves, and pretend to be righteous.[48] At the crucifixion, a Gentile centurion recognizes that Jesus is righteous.[49] In Acts, the designation of Jesus as righteous continues to appear. Peter and Ananias refer to Jesus as "the Righteous One."[50] The righteousness of Cornelius distances him from the Pharisees and connects him to the characters who know what genuine righteousness looks like.

Ἐλεημοσύνας πολλὰς τῷ λαῷ

One of the ways that elite Greco-Roman men demonstrated their piety was through financial donations to various causes. One's reverence toward deities and other authorities could be made public by donations and commemorated through inscriptions that recorded the purpose of those donations.[51] The word fields associated with this sort of piety revolve around the theme of generosity. While these word fields do not appear in the characterization of Cornelius, Cornelius is a man who gives alms generously (ποιῶν ἐλεημοσύνας πολλὰς τῷ λαῷ). By having him give alms generously, Luke challenges the prevalent dynamics of reciprocity and recognition for one's financial donations. This challenge from Luke critiques the dynamic of benefaction and rejects the ways that benefactors "lord it over" subordinates (Luke 22:24–27). In Acts 10 and elsewhere in Luke-Acts, the positive examples of generosity give

---

46. Luke 1:6; 1:17; 2:25.
47. Luke 5:32; 12:57; 14:14; 15:7; 18:9; 20:20.
48. Luke 14:14; 18:9; 20:20.
49. Luke 23:47.
50. Luke 3:14; 7:52; 22:14.

51. Danker identifies these word fields as the ευεργ- family, σωτήρ and its cognates, and words related to εὐποιεῖν. In Acts 10:38, Luke likely uses the word εὐεργετῶν to "parody and prod" Greco-Roman systems of benefaction. In this reference, Jesus is the true benefactor, who "went about doing good and healing all those who were oppressed by the devil." I owe this insight to Dr. Ray Pickett.

"without expectation of return" (Luke 6:35) and do not insist on recognition for it. The one who serves is the greatest (Luke 22:27).

Outside of the New Testament, donations of money toward city projects or public buildings can often be found in relationship to the prevalent social dynamic of patronage. Generosity with money, or benefaction, was a public means of demonstrating one's connection with a patron or client as well as one's piety toward Roman gods, goddesses, or the emperor. In the patronage system, generosity was recognized publicly and the recipient was expected to return the favor in some way. According to Richard Saller, patronage entailed a "reciprocal exchange of goods and services."[52] Goodman describes this dynamic, when he states that for most Romans, "the primary purpose of generosity was reciprocity. To the rich and moderately well-off, the very poor were thus invisible. Charity, in the sense of giving to the needy as a virtue for its own sake, was not a concept that Romans understood."[53] While some Romans may have understood the concept of charity, reciprocity most likely prevailed as the framework in which one spent money on others' behalf. Roman Garrison argues that the classical Greeks did not have a concept that meant "alms" or giving to the poor.[54] Along with the expectation of honor in return for generosity, "benefactors were often commended for their outstanding moral character traits."[55] Giving generously was paired with recognition. One man could recognize another man for giving generously, or a man could even recognize his own generosity.

Elite Greco-Roman men were sometimes described as generous, including the emperors Augustus and Trajan, the Roman client king Herod, and Dio Chrysostom. These men gave money toward the renovation of public spaces and other demonstrations of religious and political loyalty to the emperor. In the *Res Gestae*, Augustus states that he repaired the *Capitolium* and the Theater of Pompey in Rome "at enormous expense, and without having my name inscribed."[56] It is ironic that Augustus later drew attention to the expense, and included it in his list of deeds in order to be recognized for generosity. Philo states that Augustus gave corn and

---

52. Saller, *Personal Patronage*, 1.
53. Goodman, *Rome and Jerusalem*, 235.
54. Garrison, *Redemptive Almsgiving*, 38–39.
55. Joubert, "One Form of Social Exchange," 18.
56. *Res gest. divi Aug.* 4:20 (Shipley, LCL).

money to the people in Rome through the monthly dole, while never putting "the Jews at a disadvantage."[57] Pliny highlights the generosity of the emperor Trajan with the Latin word *liberalitas*, "which appears no less than a dozen times in the address."[58] An early second-century inscription outside the *Circus Maximus* in Rome recognizes Trajan for his generous donation of additional seats to the arena.[59] Likewise, an inscription in the Markets of Trajan in Rome identifies Trajan as "most generous."[60] According to Noreña, the trend relating generosity to the emperor "became quite explicit during the reign of Trajan."[61]

The Roman client king Herod also donated his money toward public building projects that demonstrated his piety, here defined as political and religious loyalty to the emperor. Herod renovated the temple in Jerusalem, perhaps "with an eye to winning eternal fame as a builder for himself and perhaps to enlisting divine support for his reign by an expensive dedication."[62] Josephus does not look kindly on this display of generosity, and considers Herod's expenditures as a sign of being consumed by his desire for honors. "For Herod loved honours, and being powerfully dominated by this passion, he was led to display generosity wherever there was reason to hope for future remembrance or present reputation..."[63] The dynamic of reciprocity comes to the fore in these assessments of generosity. The giving of large amounts of money does not necessarily garner the kind of reputation and recognition one desires, but in these examples it nonetheless results in some kind of recognition.

The elite Greco-Roman writer Dio Chrysostom, writing during the late first and early second centuries CE, also represents himself as someone who gives generously but who does not receive the kind of recognition he expects. Keeping a promise that was "by no means easy to make good and involving no small outlay of money,"[64] he attempted to renovate an old building but was met with resistance from the city's

---

57. Philo, *Embassy* 157 (Colson, LCL).
58. Noreña, "Communication," 161.
59. Ibid., 162.
60. The Latin term here is *liberalissimus*. Noreña, "Communication," 162.
61. Noreña states that the virtue of generosity (*liberalitas*) appears on approximately 12 percent of coinage found and dated from Augustus to Septimius Severus. Ibid., 156.
62. Smallwood, *Jews under Roman Rule*, 92.
63. Josephus, *Ant.* 16:153–5 (Marcus, LCL).
64. Dio Chrysostom, *Conc. Apam.* 3 (Crosby, LCL).

residents. "But there was a lot of talk," Dio states, "and very unpleasant talk too, to the effect that I am dismantling the city; that I have laid it waste, virtually banishing the inhabitants; that everything has been destroyed, obliterated..."[65] Dio touts his own generosity by saying that he comes from a long line of generous men,[66] and that he has spent more for public benefit than men with more financial resources.[67] Dio did not sell grain at a profit, although he could have.[68] He paid a high price for a piece of land and then placed colonnades and workshops on it, for the benefit of the people.[69] Yet the people do not appear to be grateful. These orations indicate that Dio expected a different kind of response to his generosity. These orations also indicate that reciprocity is operating *inter alia*. Dio characterizes himself as the exemplar of generosity, but his donations do not result in reward.[70]

The Generosity of Cornelius

With these extrabiblical references about elite Greco-Roman men in mind, we can now turn to the characterization of Cornelius in Acts 10. Cornelius is humble, respectful, and reverent toward God (εὐσεβής), honest and fair with other people (δίκαιος). Now we discuss his generous almsgiving toward needy people. In Acts 10:2, Luke describes Cornelius as a man who "makes many alms," or who gives alms generously. The word for alms is ἐλεημοσύνη.[71] Rudolf Bultmann defines this word as "benevolent activity," and always in reference to the poor.[72] The word is formed from the same stem as the Greek verb for mercy (ἐλεέω). Because of this etymological relationship, it is fair to assume

---

65. Ibid., 8.

66. Dio Chrysostom, *Tumult*. 3 (Crosby, LCL).

67. Ibid., 6.

68. Ibid., 8.

69. Ibid., 9.

70. Evidence from the period also provides examples of what not to do with one's money. These examples include the stories of men who spend too much or who spend it in the wrong places. In "Dinner with Trimalchio," (*Satyr.*), Petronius tells the story of the freedman Trimalchio, who lays out an extravagant dinner that appears gaudy and excessive. In the play entitled "Trinuumus," by Plautus, one character says, "You do a beggar a bad service by giving him food and drink; you lose what you give and prolong his life for more misery." Plautus, "Trinuumus, or Three Bob Day," 339 (Nixon, LCL).

71. For more appearances of this Greek word, see Tobit 4, 12, and 14.

72. Bultmann, "ἔλεος," in *TDNT*, 486.

that the deeds of Cornelius could be considered merciful. His actions are in accord with the teachings of Jesus in Luke: "Be merciful, just as your Father is merciful" (Luke 6:36). The modifying phrase τῷ λαῷ tells the audience that Cornelius' money goes toward the people. The noun λαός occurs multiple times in Acts as a reference toward the people of Israel.[73] According to Strathmann, Acts 10:2 is one of these occasions. Strathmann writes, "This technical usage may be fully seen when λαός means Israel with no elucidatory additions, so that the writer does not even consider the possibility of there being any other λαός."[74] By this definition, Cornelius is merciful toward the people of Israel.

The generous almsgiving of Cornelius appears again in 10:4; the angel of God says to Cornelius, "Your prayers and your alms [ἐλεημοσύναι] have ascended as a memorial before God." The same word is repeated to emphasize that alms is a commendable demonstration of piety toward God and to the people of Israel. According to Tannehill, repetition can educate the reader about what is most important.[75] The repetition of the word ἐλεημοσύναι, noted by a divine voice as well as that of the narrator, leads the audience to believe that Cornelius does the right thing with his money. David Rhoads points to this kind of repetition in his analysis of the Gospel of Mark. Rhoads writes, "The simplest form of repetition is that of certain key words and phrases. These verbal threads may occur within episodes."[76] This is the kind of repetition we see with ἐλεημοσύναι in Acts 10:2 and 10:4.

Elsewhere in Luke-Acts, the way that one spends his or her money can be a reflection of one's piety toward God, one's concord with the teachings of Jesus, and one's humility with other people. Prior to Acts 10, Luke sets up the expectation that alms go to the poor and to people who may not be able to reciprocate. In the Sermon on the Plain in Luke, Jesus states that one should lend one's money without expectation of return (6:36). This kind of giving distinguishes the followers of Jesus from creditors who demand interest. In Luke 22, the disciples argue about which disciple is the greatest. Jesus corrects their misguided notions about greatness, and states, "the kings of the Gentiles lord it over them; and those in authority over them are called benefactors. But not

73. Strathmann, "λαός," in *TDNT*, 52.
74. Ibid., 53.
75. Tannehill, *Narrative Unity of Luke-Acts*, 2:75.
76. Rhoads et al., *Mark as Story*, 47.

so with you; rather the greatest among you must become like the youngest, and the leader like one who serves" (22:25–27).[77] Jesus characterizes the benefaction of elite Greco-Roman men as something akin to tyranny and greed. But the followers of Jesus are not to crave greatness for their actions. While Cornelius does receive recognition for his generosity, his commendation comes from an angel, and from the people of the Jewish nation.[78] Luke sets Cornelius apart from other benefactors by describing Cornelius as a man who does not *seek* recognition for his donations. The exemplars of generosity in Luke-Acts serve the poor and do not "lord" their wealth or authority over others. The lame man in Acts 3 sat outside the Beautiful Gate, asking for alms.[79] Attributing the miracle to the God of Israel, Peter serves the lame man and does not seek recognition for it. In Acts 9, Tabitha makes clothing for poor widows.[80] Peter raises the widow from the dead, enabling her merciful works to continue. As with Acts 10:2 and 10:4, Luke calls the activity of Tabitha ἐλεημοσυνῶν.[81] Cornelius, Peter, and Tabitha all serve the poor and as such could be considered true benefactors in Luke's story.

Μνημονεύω and Μιμνήσκω

In Acts 10:4, the angel of God tells Cornelius that his prayer and alms have ascended as a memorial (μνημόσυνον) before God. The Greek words related to remembrance and memorials now come to the fore. Like the other key words above, μνημονεύω, μιμνήσκω, and their noun forms describe the piety of elite Greco-Roman men. However, in Acts, remembrance takes place in the presence of the God of Israel. God remembers and notices men as examples of piety. This is yet another way that Luke turns words that are commonly encountered in imperial contexts toward the sovereignty of Yahweh.

Immortality was a tantalizing prospect for many elite Greco-Roman men, who may have envisioned themselves as memorable. These men

---

77. This reference contrasts with the example of the rich ruler in Luke 18:18–22. Kyoung-Jin Kim describes this pericope: "The narrative of the Rich Ruler (18:18–22) introduces a man who does not give up his wealth for the sake of the poor, so that he turns out to decline to follow Jesus." Kim, *Stewardship and Almsgiving*, 195.

78. For more about the testimony of the entire Jewish nation (Acts 10:22), see below.

79. Acts 3:2.

80. For more on Tabitha, see Spencer, "Women of 'the Cloth,'" 134–54.

81. Acts 9:36–43.

had the means to afford the materials on which their names and deeds could be inscribed. Inscriptions, tombs, coins, and other monumental remains helped elite men preserve their virtues for future generations. One could commission inscriptions about oneself or one's family members, or to show gratitude to a patron, the emperor, or to deities.[82] The emperor Augustus established the *Res Gestae*, inscribed near the end of his life, as a record of his own deeds, and as a way of helping future emperors and Roman citizens remember his contributions to the empire. On the other hand, the people who were subject to Roman rule could have inscriptions made to honor their ruler. This is the case with the decree of the inhabitants of Busiris, Egypt, in honor of their prefect. The inscription, dated to the middle of the first century CE, reads, "Therefore it is appropriate that [the prefect's] god-like favors be inscribed in sacred letters for all time to remember."[83] Regardless of subject, inscriptions on stone give the impression of a lasting legacy that will not be forgotten.

Other kinds of material evidence also convey the desire to be remembered, and the desire to have one's virtues and victories commended by others. These remains relied on iconography and symbols as well as words. The symbols made their messages available to people who did not read. Coins were a way to commemorate an emperor's achievements through symbols and brief captions. According to R. Jackson Painter, the "Nike types" of coins "celebrated the victories of the emperors" from the time of Trajan.[84] Another way that emperors encouraged the Romans to remember was through monuments such as arches. The Arch of Titus in Rome commemorates the siege of the temple in Jerusalem in 70 CE. On that arch are Roman soldiers, carrying away the sacred symbols and holy things of Judaism. Martin Goodman states that the arch was "dedicated not by Titus but by Domitian."[85] Domitian emphasized the achievements of his predecessor Titus and wanted the people to remember the war. With Domitian on the throne, the victory over Judea would not easily slip from Roman memory. In addition to the emphasis on the war found on the arch, the emperor Domitian "was still in 85 issuing coins

---

82. According to Danker, gratitude needed to be demonstrated publicly. Ingratitude was a cardinal sin. Danker, *Benefactor*, 436.

83. Ibid., 226.

84. Painter, "Greco-Roman Religion," 111.

85. Goodman, *Rome and Jerusalem*, 467.

with the caption Judaea Capta."⁸⁶ These coins featured representations of humiliated Judean people. In the cases of these imperial remains, the memory of Roman victory cannot be separated from the memory of Judean humiliation.

While some elite Greco-Roman men and emperors used inscriptions, symbols, and coins as memorials, in Acts 10, prayer and almsgiving are memorials. The prayer and almsgiving in Acts 10:4 signify a piety that Luke wishes to commend and convey to his audience. The most credible voice in the narrative—a voice associated with the God of Israel—recognizes the piety of Cornelius and lifts up his example as the proper way to show reverence. A form of the Greek verb μνημονεύω appears again in Acts 10:31 (ἐμνήσθησαν). Luke repeats this verb and this event by having Cornelius tell his story to Peter. As we saw with the Greek words associated with generosity, Luke uses repetition as a narrative tool to persuade his audience to embrace Cornelius as a model of piety and as the kind of man whom others should imitate.

In Luke-Acts, remembrance is intertwined with the theme of mercy. We see this connection in the merciful deeds (ἐλεημοσύναι) of Cornelius, which are then remembered by God. In the Magnificat, Mary remembers the mercy of the Lord, who has helped his servant Israel. Soon thereafter, in Luke 1, Zechariah states that God has shown mercy and remembered the covenant with his ancestors. In Luke 16, Abraham says to the rich man, who had not shown mercy to Lazarus, that he had already received good things. In these references, mercy is an enduring form of piety and a promise from God.⁸⁷ In all of these references God is the one who remembers. God remembers people whom others may forget.

In this section I have shown that Luke uses language about the piety of Cornelius that intersects and interacts with extrabiblical

---

86. Ibid.

87. One can also discern a connection between memory and death in Luke-Acts. In Luke 22, Jesus offers the disciples bread and wine, and tells them eat and drink and remembrance of him. In Luke 23, the criminal hanging on the cross next to Jesus asks Jesus to remember him when he comes into his kingdom (23:42). The man at the empty tomb tells the women to remember what Jesus had told them, that he would die and rise again. "And they remembered..." (24:6–8). On the road to Emmaus, the risen Jesus interpreted the scriptures for two people, who then recall how their hearts burned within them while he spoke (24:31–32). While some men wanted to be remembered through the medium of stone, it seems that Luke wishes Jesus to be remembered through bread, wine, and flesh, all of which pass away.

language about the piety of elite Greco-Roman men, including Roman emperors. Key words and phrases here include εὐσεβεία, δικαιοσύνη, ἐλεημοσύνας πολλὰς τῷ λαῷ, and μιμνήσκω. With every word or phrase, Luke directs his audience away from piety shown by or toward Roman authorities. Luke characterizes the piety of Cornelius with the same words that are used to describe the piety of elite Greco-Roman men, yet there are two important differences. Although the terminology is the same, Cornelius is committed to the God of Israel, and most elite Greco-Roman men were not. Moreover, Cornelius does not seek honor as most elites do.

CORNELIUS AND THE PIETY OF MILITARY MEN

When Luke introduces his audience to Cornelius, he immediately informs the audience that Cornelius is a Roman centurion of the Italian Cohort. While it is not unusual to encounter in ancient sources Roman military officers who demonstrate their piety, it is somewhat unusual to hear about a centurion who is dedicated to the God of Israel. In this section I will provide a brief historical overview of extrabiblical sources that inform our understanding of piety among Roman military men. Most of the historical evidence indicates that military men were polytheistic. The available evidence does not allow connections to be made through specific words and phrases. However, it is possible to place the piety of Cornelius in the context of the Roman military piety in general. In Acts, Cornelius is a pious military man like other men outside the New Testament. Yet Luke's exemplar of piety appears to negotiate life in the military with a life that demonstrates commitment to Yahweh. Some complications are inherent in this vision, particularly regarding the issue of sovereignty. In addition to a review of available extrabiblical evidence, this section will place Cornelius in the context of Luke-Acts, which features other military men who show respect and reverence toward the God of Israel and the Jewish people.

Piety in the Roman Military: A Brief Overview

In the Roman military during the first few centuries CE, a soldier's life was highly structured and oriented toward the preservation of the hierarchy of authority. Respect for commanding officers, the emperor, and one's comrades enabled the hierarchy to function and the military in general to carry out its mission. Piety as a concept includes this kind of respect and reverence for those in authority. The Romans tolerated private religious beliefs and the private religious practices of soldiers in the army as long as it did not interfere with the soldier's duties.[88] Helgeland describes this tolerance by saying that both soldiers and civilians needed "to fulfill their religious obligations to the imperial cult," but as long as these obligations were carried out, "they seem to have been free to practice their own cults—as long as they did not upset the tranquility of society or promote what the Romans regarded as immoral."[89] The fulfillment of one's duty and the need for order prevailed, yet there was some room for variety in one's own religious affiliations.

It must be said, however, that the religious and political lives of soldiers, as with other inhabitants of the empire, were intertwined and almost impossible to separate. The combination of the religious and political systems would have made it difficult for a military man to separate his service to the state from his relationship to the emperor and the gods. Extrabiblical evidence about piety in the military reflects this reality. A soldier's observance of time (the calendar) and a soldier's oath are two examples. A military calendar from Dura Europos, written on a papyrus dated to the third century CE, describes the observations of imperial birthdays and anniversaries, the accessions of emperors, and circus games, as well as sacrifices offered to Jupiter, Minerva, Mars, and Juno.[90] About the oath, J. B. Campbell writes, "The military oath symbolized the bond between emperor and soldier and was sanctified by religious ties and the Roman military tradition."[91] According to Campbell, "The nature of the obligations imposed by the oaths . . . was religious, in that the takers of the oath would invoke the vengeance of Jupiter on themselves in the event of perjury."[92] Given this evidence, a soldier's piety included

---

88. Helgeland, "Roman Army Religion," 1496.

89. ibid. Helgeland continues, "While we know of many Christians in the army, from at least the time of Marcus Aurelius, the army never searched them out until the time of Diocletian's preparations for the great persecution in the year 303." Helgeland, "Roman Army Religion," 1496.

90. Beard et al., *Religions of Rome*, 2:71–74. For more on the implications of the military calendar, see Cotter, "Cornelius," 291.

91. Campbell, *Emperor*, 7.

92. Ibid., 29.

reverence showed toward religious and political authorities, and this reverence had perhaps daily repercussions.

Pious Military Men: Some Extrabiblical Examples

Like elite Greco-Roman men, military men occasionally established inscriptions to demonstrate their piety toward the gods. Two of these gods were Jupiter Dolichenus and Turmasgada. Mary Beard describes Jupiter Dolichenus as "a god whose name proclaimed his origin in the small town of Doliche in northern Syria. About seventeen of his sanctuaries have been found . . . and over 550 inscriptions, plaques, and statues relating to the cult have survived."[93] An inscription to Jupiter Dolichenus has been excavated in Caesarea Maritima. A man named Viktor, likely associated with the military, "fulfilled a vow to Jupiter Dolichenus" and established what may be a small altar to commemorate the fulfillment of the vow.[94] Although the original vow is still obscure, Viktor had its fulfillment inscribed as a sign of his piety. In another inscription dated to the first or second centuries CE and excavated in Caesarea Maritima, a centurion of the *Legio XII Fulminata* had his name inscribed on a funerary altar or a votive altar to the god Turmasgada.[95] On the altar are symbols of military victory, the goddess Tyche, and symbols associated with Caesarea.[96] Justin Howell comments that the symbol of the eagle, also found on the altar, may resemble an image of the emperor as he is being crowned by a Victory.[97] Given the mixture of religious, political, and imperial images on these remains, the piety of military men appears to combine all of these features. Even the emperor Trajan can be seen demonstrating his piety at the beginning of a military campaign. Le Bohec states that "on Trajan's column we can see that the Emperor started every military campaign with the *suovetaurilia*, the sacrifice of a pig, a ram, and a bull, accompanied by military music . . ."[98]

---

93. Beard et al., *Religions of Rome*, 2:295.

94. Lehmann and Holum date this inscription between the late-first and third century CE. See inscription 124 in Lehmann and Holum, *Greek and Latin* Inscriptions, 18, 121–22.

95. Inscription 119 in Lehmann and Holum, *Greek and Latin Inscriptions*, 118–19.

96. Ibid.

97. Howell, "Imperial Authority," 34–35.

98. LeBohec, *The Imperial Roman Army*, 238.

During his military service, a soldier would have been surrounded by authorities to whom he was subject. These authorities include the emperor. Soldiers were often accompanied by military standards and images of the emperor, which commanded respect and reverence.[99] Dated most likely to the first or second centuries CE, an inscription by a senior centurion (a *primus pilus*) named Tiberius gives honor to the emperor Tiberius.[100] Justin Howell cites a relevant inscription about a centurion. In this inscription—a funerary stele in Rome—a centurion, with an eagle on each side, pours out a libation onto the altar.[101] This cultic ritual moment most likely indicates that the centurion is performing a duty associated with his piety toward the emperor as well as to the Roman gods.[102] Livy writes in his *Histories* that Roman commanders gave appropriate sacrifices before battle: "the Roman consuls before leading their troops into battle offered sacrifices."[103] In these references it is sometimes challenging to distinguish the recipient of these sacrifices. This dynamic further illustrates the intricate nature of piety among military men and the combination of religious and political reverence shown by them.

The establishment of inscriptions and sacrifices required money. Military men could use their financial resources, gathered from their army salaries, to demonstrate their piety toward one another, the emperor, and deities. In order to determine how much money centurions had at their disposal for such demonstrations, a brief introduction to the salaries earned by soldiers, and specifically centurions, would be helpful. According to Le Bohec, centurions made approximately 3750 denarii per year, from the reign of Augustus to the reign of Domitian, after which the pay increased to 5000 denarii per year.[104] While this salary may pale

---

99. Howell, "Imperial Authority," 34.

100. Lehmann and Holum state that this inscription is "said to be from Caesarea." About the inscription's date, they suggest that "the letters most resemble those of alphabets in the first and second centuries." See inscription 145 in Lehmann and Holum, *Greek and Latin Inscriptions*, 131–32.

101. Howell, "Imperial Authority," 34–35. This inscription dates to the third century CE.

102. Ibid.

103. These consuls were Decius and Manlius, and they were preparing for battle near the foot of Mount Vesuvius. Livy, *Hist.* 8:14 (Foster, LCL).

104. Le Bohec, *Imperial Roman Army*, 212, table 39. Webster asserts a somewhat different pay scale for centurions. He states that centurions received 1500 denarii a year

in comparison with the salary of a tribune, a centurion, like other soldiers, received regular and steady pay.[105] In addition to a steady salary, a soldier would have received upon discharge a bonus of anywhere from 3000 denarii during the time of Augustus to 8250 denarii in 212 CE.[106] A *primus pilus* centurion, the highest-ranked centurion in the cohort, could receive enough money upon discharge to acquire equestrian status, that is, 400,000 sestercii (the equivalent of 100,000 denarii).[107] These numbers indicate that military men had at their disposal the funds to commemorate their own piety or to show their piety toward others in a public, lasting way.[108]

How military men spent their money can be interpreted as an extension of their piety. For example, piety can be shown in the case of a fellow soldier's death. Wendy Cotter asserts that "groups of soldiers arranged for their own funeral rites and expenses, and stipulated that plaques be raised in their name."[109] The burial association fees were dedicated from the soldier's pay.[110] The erection of monuments was a pious duty and a sign of respect for one's comrades.[111] Soldiers could

---

or more. Webster, *Roman Imperial Army*, 259.

105. The regular nature of army salaries distinguished soldiers from day laborers and peasants, who may not find work every day. Some centurions may have received additional income from bribes. Centurions were responsible for granting furloughs to soldiers under them. Soldiers may have to bribe their centurion in order to take a leave of absence. In order to study furloughs, Speidel uses evidence from papyri and ostraca. Speidel, "Furlough in the Roman Army," 333, 340.

106. Le Bohec, *Imperial Roman Army*, 213.

107. Webster, *Roman Imperial Army*, 260. According to Jones, a denarius was equal to 16 asses (another unit of Roman money). A sestercius was equal to 4 asses. From this comparison, the value of a sestercius is one-fourth of the value of a denarius. Jones, *Dictionary of Ancient Roman Coins*, 86.

108. Not all expenditures by military men reflected their piety. Goodman tells of a centurion who loaned money to a Judean named Judah, with interest (*Rome and Jerusalem*, 77). Note the contrast between this evidence from Goodman and Luke 6:34–35, where Jesus says, "If you lend to those from whom you hope to receive, what credit is that you? Even sinners lend to sinners, to receive as much again. But love your enemies, do good, and lend, expecting nothing in return." Note also the contrast between the centurions who make money off of Judeans and Luke 3:12–13, where John the Baptist tells soldiers not to extort money from anyone and to be satisfied with their wages.

109. Cotter, "Cornelius," 290.

110. Webster, *Roman Imperial Army*, 272.

111. Ibid.

set up tombs for their comrades as well, or "a centurion could use his salary to have a mausoleum built over his body."[112] In dangerous situations such as battle, soldiers could be assured that their comrades, if not themselves, would provide at the time of their death the recognition that they deserved. In light of this kind of expenditure, one can see the multifaceted nature of military piety. In this context, duty, respect, and reverence should be extended not only to one's superiors but also to fellow soldiers.

Military Piety and Judaism

As the above examples show, most of the extrabiblical evidence about military piety is related to polytheism. Scholars have very little historical evidence about Roman soldiers who affiliate themselves with the God of Israel, and the evidence that does exist does not indicate a genuine interest on the soldiers' part to show piety toward God.[113] Josephus tells the story of the Roman commander Metilius, who offered to convert to Judaism when his garrison was under Judean siege. Josephus writes, "thus, brutally butchered, perished all save Metilius, he alone saved his life by entreaties and promises to turn Jew [ἰουδαΐσειν] and even to be circumcised."[114] In this case, the conversion of Metilius to Judaism happens under duress. About this story Shaye Cohen comments, "Metilius seems to mean that he will defect from the Romans, join the Jews, and have himself circumcised as proof of his new loyalty. The God of the Judeans has no part in Metilius' calculations."[115] According to Cohen, the Tosefta tells of Roman soldiers who convert to Judaism on the fourteenth of Nisan in order to participate in the paschal feast at Passover.[116] Jacob Neusner's English translation of this Tosefta passage states that there were "soldiers and guards in Jerusalem who immersed and ate their

---

112. Le Bohec, *Imperial Roman Army*, 251.

113. This lack of evidence indicates that Cornelius is an unusual centurion, and that Luke-Acts proposes its own understanding of the Roman military and piety toward Yahweh.

114. Josephus, *War* 2:450–54 (Thackeray, LCL). Cohen indicates that the Greek verb ἰουδαΐζειν has three meanings: "to give political support to the Judeans," "to adopt any of the distinctive customs and manners of the Judeans," and "to speak the language of the Judeans." Cohen, *Beginnings of Jewishness*, 65.

115. Cohen, *Beginnings of Jewishness*, 155.

116. Tosefta *Pisha* 7.14.182L (Neusner, *Tosefta*, 151). See also Cohen, *Beginnings of Jewishness*, 65.

Passover-offerings in the evening [of the day on which they converted and were circumcised]."[117] In this case as well, conversion to Judaism appears to be for reasons other than one's piety toward the God of Israel.

In light of the lack of extrabiblical references to Roman soldiers who adhere to Judaism in some way, one could ask what difficulties might result if a Roman soldier did indeed adopt Jewish practices. E. Mary Smallwood states, "military service at the behest of gentile rulers was always bound to cause difficulties for the Jews of the Diaspora because of their dietary laws, which made their inclusion in gentile units impractical, and their inability to carry out any duties on the Sabbath."[118] The Jewish practices associated with piety toward the God of Israel—dietary laws and Sabbath observance—complicated the completion of military duties. By describing the participation of observant Jews in the military as "impractical," Smallwood seems to suggest that it would be difficult for a soldier to find kosher food every day. Sabbath observance, which differed from the military calendar and the overall understanding of time among Gentiles, would mean that Jewish soldiers could not do their duty one day a week.

In addition to Torah observance, a Jewish soldier would likely encounter conflicts associated with sovereignty. The oaths taken by all soldiers, the military calendar, the standards, images, and rituals, all presume Roman sovereignty. These observances reflect a commitment to the emperor and the gods as the true sources of authority and the supreme religious and political powers. Jewish piety, however, envisions Yahweh as the true source of authority. Based on that core belief, a person who adopts Jewish practices will likely avoid activities that will conflict with that commitment. Perhaps because of these complications, according to some primary sources, Jews were exempt from military service. Privileges were granted to Jews under Julius Caesar; one of these privileges was that troops were not to be raised in territories of the Jews.[119] Josephus tells us about an edict issued by the consul Lucius Lentulus, in which Jews who were also Roman citizens in Ephesus were exempt from military service "in consideration of their religious scruples."[120] Similar

---

117. Tosefta *Pisha* 7.14.182L.
118. Smallwood, *Jews under Roman Rule*, 127.
119. Josephus, *Ant.* 14:204 (Marcus, LCL).
120. Ibid., 14:228.

exemptions were granted in Delos.[121] While all the primary sources do not agree,[122] Smallwood writes about another exemption of Jews from military service in Asia, which was granted in 49 CE.[123]

In these ancient references, piety toward the God of Israel appears to be an insurmountable obstacle to military service. The exemptions resolved these complications by allowing Jews not to participate in the military. While Jews exempted from military service, they were also protected from harassment. When soldiers in the Roman military treated Jews poorly, Roman rulers occasionally punished those soldiers. Cohen states that "the emperor Augustus decreed that anyone caught stealing 'the sacred books' of the Jews was to be punished severely; in the first century C.E. a Roman soldier in Judea desecrated a Torah scroll, and the only way the Romans could quiet the subsequent disorder that erupted was to behead the offender."[124] Not only were Jews exempted from military service; Roman military men were not to harass and molest Jews and their sacred objects.[125]

Military Piety and Cornelius the God-Fearer

With this evidence in mind, we can turn to the characterization of the centurion Cornelius in Acts, and how Luke portrays the piety of Cornelius and other military men in his story. The issue of God-fearers now comes to the fore. In Acts 10, Cornelius is a Gentile God-fearer. Despite his affiliation with the military, Cornelius fears, respects, and shows reverence to the God of Israel. As a God-fearer, he would not have had to cope with the conflicts associated with Torah observance and military life. He did not have to observe the same dietary restrictions as circumcised Jews or proselytes did. Other Jewish practices, such as the observance of Sabbath, do not appear to be issues of debate in Acts. Luke does not mention the Jewish practice of Sabbath observance with

121. Ibid., 14:232.

122. In his story of the emperor Tiberius, Suetonius writes, "Those of the Jews who were of military age, he assigned to provinces of less healthy climate, ostensibly to serve in the army; the others of that same race or of similar beliefs he banished from the city; on pain of slavery for life if they did not obey." Suetonius, *Tib.* 36 (Rolfe, LCL).

123. Smallwood, *Jews under Roman Rule*, 127.

124. Cohen, *From the Maccabees*, 181. For more on the desecration of the Torah by the Roman soldier, see Josephus, *Ant.* 16:6.2; 20:5.4; *War* 2:12.2.

125. Clearly these policies had more effect before the Roman-Jewish war in 66–70 CE.

regard to Cornelius. Nor does Luke mention Sabbath observance with regard to other Gentiles in Acts.[126] Perhaps it is simply understood that Gentiles do not have to observe the Sabbath. The category of God-fearer allows Cornelius and other Gentiles to practice their piety and still work and live under Roman rule.

A brief orientation to God-fearers and the scholarly debate about them will be helpful here. God-fearers are Gentiles who are in some way affiliated with the God of Israel. Their adoption of Jewish practices such as prayer or almsgiving showed some allegiance to God, but male God-fearers were probably not circumcised. Certain primary sources point to their existence and involvement in Jewish synagogues or communities. Book 20 of Josephus' *Antiquities* describes Helena of Adiabene and her son Izates, who demonstrate some level of commitment to the Jewish God.[127] Two inscriptions point to the involvement of Gentiles in Jewish communities: a Bosporan manumission letter freeing a slave who is to honor God, and an inscribed stele in Aphrodisias that differentiates God-fearers from proselytes.[128] These primary sources use language related to the Greek verb σεβόμαι, as does Josephus in the instances noted above.

Scholars have debated whether the available primary sources point to a widespread phenomenon of Gentile adherence or to local, sporadic Gentile involvement in Jewish communities and synagogues. A. T. Kraabel suggests that the available primary sources do not prove the existence of God-fearers, at least to the number that most scholars assume.[129] From this perspective, the God-fearers are a Lukan innovation. Thomas Finn suggests that although a technical vocabulary for God-fearers had not yet been developed by the time of Luke's writing, some God-fearers did exist, and refers to Juvenal, Josephus, and Philo for support of this view.[130] While the sources do not allow us

---

126. When Luke mentions the Sabbath in Acts, he uses it with regard to the activities of Jews or Paul (Acts 1:12; 13:14, 27, 42, 44; 15:21; 16:13; 17:2; 18:4).

127. Josephus, *Ant.* 20:32–48. The phrase σεβόμενοι τὸν θεὸν also appears in *Ant.* 14:110.

128. The manumission letter is dated to the first century CE, and the Aphrodisias inscription is dated to the third century CE. For discussion of both these sources, see Levinskaya, "Inscription from Aphrodisias."

129. Kraabel, "Disappearance of the 'God-Fearers,'" 113–26.

130. Finn, "God-Fearers Reconsidered." For another perspective see Wilcox, "'God-Fearers' in Acts."

to posit large numbers of God-fearers or an organized terminology that referred to them, recent scholarship appears to suggest that some Gentiles did adopt some Jewish practices and become affiliated with Judaism in various ways.

Shaye Cohen has attempted to categorize the ways in which Gentiles related to Judaism, three of which are relevant to Cornelius.[131] In his article "Crossing the Boundary and Becoming a Jew," Cohen delineates seven different ways in which Gentiles could relate to Jews:[132] 1) "admiring some aspect of Judaism"[133]; 2) "acknowledging the power of the God of the Jews"[134]; 3) "benefiting the Jews or being conspicuously friendly to Jews"[135]; 4) "practicing some or many of the rituals of the Jews"[136]; 5) "venerating the God of the Jews or ignoring the pagan gods"[137]; 6) "Joining the Jewish community"[138]; and 7) "converting to Judaism and 'becoming a Jew.'"[139] In Acts 10, Luke presents Cornelius as a Gentile who benefits the Jews financially through almsgiving and who adopts some Jewish practices such as prayer. Luke gives no indication that Cornelius has renounced the pagan gods, although the προσκυνεῖν gesture before Peter may appear to be a physical gesture of veneration toward the God who sent Peter. The fourth category about the adoption of Jewish practices fits the portrait of Cornelius best. Piety and righteousness for Cornelius take shape in the concrete practices of prayer and almsgiving.

By reshaping piety toward the God of Israel into ethical practices such as humility, respect, honesty, and generous almsgiving, all of which can be exemplified by Gentiles and military men such as Cornelius, Luke makes an overall point about how one can live under the empire and still claim that the God of Israel is the one true sovereign. Wendy

---

131. Other God-fearers and those who revere God in Acts include Lydia (16:14), and Titius Justus (18:7). Cornelius is the only character who is called a God-fearer twice (10:2, 22).

132. Cohen, "Crossing the Boundary."

133. Ibid., 15.

134. Ibid.

135. Ibid., 17.

136. Ibid., 20.

137. Ibid., 21.

138. Ibid., 24.

139. Ibid., 27.

Cotter states that Luke's audience may have expected a different sort of piety from a centurion: "in the imagination of anyone listening to a story about a centurion, the centurion would have always have had a Roman face."[140] While Cornelius is a Roman military officer and a representative of the empire, he demonstrates his piety toward Yahweh in ways that Luke considers important. Prior to Acts 10, Luke gives very little indication that Cornelius has had difficulty negotiating his military obligations to the state and his pious practices toward the God of the Judeans. This is because Luke's primary traits of piety do not revolve around circumcision, food laws, and Sabbath observance. The category of God-fearers eases the tensions between piety toward the God of Israel and the demands of military life. The category of God-fearers also makes piety toward the God of Israel accessible to more people.

In addition to the reshaping of Jewish piety and the fundamental changes regarding Torah observance, Luke is also making a point about the proper object of piety. About this claim, Gary Gilbert states, "by contesting Rome's claims, transposing Roman expressions of authority to Jesus and the early church, and offering alternative models of world rule, Luke-Acts creates a counter-discourse that responds to and resists Roman imperial authority and in so doing, seeks to constitute an understanding of being a Christian in the Roman world."[141] Luke avoids any confusion about the true source of power in the narrative by juxtaposing a representative of the empire with the Holy Spirit. In Acts, God (θεός) refers to the God of Israel. Luke clearly characterizes Cornelius as a God-fearer twice (φοβούμενος τὸν θεόν, 10:2, 22). Cornelius prays to God constantly (δεόμενος τοῦ θεοῦ διὰ παντός) in 10:2, and divine recognition of his prayer occurs twice (10:4, 31). In these references, Luke supplies the object of the piety of Cornelius and repeats it for emphasis.[142] The God of Israel, rather than Roman authorities, deserves reverence, and Cornelius recognizes this reality through his pious practices.

It is important to note that Cornelius, as a representative of the empire, is an unlikely proponent of piety toward the God of Israel. Justin Howell has argued that Luke may be using irony in Acts 10 to critique centurions who participate in the imperial cult. Howell argues

---

140. Cotter, "Cornelius," 283.

141. Gilbert, "Luke-Acts and Negotiation," 87.

142. For more on the possibility that Cornelius is merely adding another god to his polytheistic pantheon, see the following section.

that "the target of Luke's critique is . . . centurions exercising authority and benefaction in the emperor's behalf."[143] This kind of benefaction and exercise of authority for the emperor was one aspect of the imperial cult.[144] Howell also suggests that Luke is using irony as a way "to mock or critique an opponent."[145] This irony appears "in his characterization of centurions."[146] For a definition of irony, Howell refers to the writings of Aristotle and Quintilian, and indicates that irony contains "a contemptuous element"[147] that gives a positive impression when the author intends to convey a negative impression.[148]

While Luke may indeed be critiquing centurions who participate in the imperial cult, I wish to clarify the identity of the opponent in Acts 10. I suggest that the opponents in Acts 10 are Roman sovereignty and Roman dominance. Cornelius the character is not the target of Luke's critique. On the basis of narrative analysis, I assert that Luke does not critique Cornelius specifically. The functions of Acts 10 in the narrative are to convey the positive nature of the integration of the Gentiles and the submission of a Roman representative to the power of the God of Israel. Luke needs the conversion of Cornelius to be a positive development in order for the overall narrative to work. If Luke crafted his narrative so that the audience would envision Cornelius as a character who appears positive but who is actually negative, the rhetorical impact of the integration of the Gentiles falters. Luke conveys the sincerity of Cornelius and his participation in the Way by several means. Already noted above are the repeated emphases on the piety of Cornelius toward the God of Israel, as opposed to other gods. In addition, the encounter between Peter and Cornelius is led by the Spirit; both Peter and Cornelius find one another through divine visions. Early in the narrative, the Hebrew Bible prophecy of Joel foreshadows the integration of the Gentiles, and Peter announces this prophecy in a speech that follows the appearance of the Holy Spirit at Pentecost (Acts 2). The Holy Spirit appears again at Cornelius' house, in an event that mirrors the first Pentecost (10:44–46). Peter conveys to the Jewish authorities at Jerusalem in Acts 11 and 15

143. Howell, "Imperial Authority," 26.
144. Ibid.
145. Ibid., 41.
146. Ibid., 40.
147. Ibid., 42.
148. Ibid.

that this development was inspired by the Holy Spirit, and it is a result of God's initiative. In light of these narrative elements, I suggest that it is possible to critique the empire by presenting a representative of the empire whose piety is directed toward the God of Israel.

Early in the narrative, Luke also characterizes other military men in a positive way. These positive characterizations may contrast with the audience's expectations, but these military men appear to be genuinely interested in demonstrating their piety toward the God of Israel. While these other military men may not be called "God-fearers" in the story, they nonetheless contribute to a pattern of respectful military men who wish to live in a pious way. Luke proposes a kind of piety that they as Gentiles and military men can fulfill. In Luke 3:14, soldiers come to John the Baptist and ask, "And we, what should we do?" John replies, "Do not extort money from anyone by threats or false accusation, and be satisfied with your wages." This reply implies that it was possible to complete one's military duties and be pious toward the God of Israel. In Luke 7:1–10, a centurion shows reverence toward Jesus, recognize his power. Jewish elders say that the centurion "is worthy of having you do this for him, for he loves our people, and it is he who built our synagogue for us." The positive recommendation by Jewish characters in the narrative carries additional rhetorical impact. According to Shaye Cohen, "when a Jew describes a Gentile as 'pious' or 'reverent' without further qualification, the reference is probably not to the Gentile's selfless dedication to Isis or Heracles. The Jew is probably calling the Gentile an 'adherent.'"[149] While the words for piety and reverence do not appear explicitly in Luke 7, the phrase "he loves our people" may communicate something similar. These two examples of pious military men—the soldiers in Luke 3 and the centurion in Luke 7—imply that Cornelius is not alone in his sincere interest in demonstrating piety toward the God of Israel. While most of the extrabiblical evidence about piety among military men reflects reverence shown toward Roman deities and the emperor, in Luke-Acts there is no other sort of piety among military men than the piety shown toward the God of the Judeans.

---

149. Cohen, "Respect for Judaism," 419.

CORNELIUS AND THE PIETY OF JEWISH MEN

While Cornelius is a Gentile God-fearer, Luke crafts his characterization so that Cornelius emerges as a model of piety toward the God of Israel and a model man for the Way. Luke shows his audience a Gentile man whose traits evoke virtuous Jewish men, as well as the virtues of elite Greco-Roman and military men. Goodman provides a relevant caveat: "The relationship between Rome and Jerusalem was complicated by the fact that a Roman could be Jewish and a Jew could be Roman."[150] Although Jewish identity under Roman occupation was complicated, this section will attempt to show that the characterization of Cornelius intersects and interacts with extrabiblical and biblical descriptions of Jewish men, notably Moses and Jesus. The links to Moses help persuade the audience that the movement's continuity with Judaism will not be lost. The links to Jesus help persuade that audience that Cornelius, despite his ethnicity, is truly righteous. This paves the way for other Gentile men to be considered pious, righteous, and similar to Moses.

In order for Jewish audiences to consider Cornelius an exemplar of piety and virtue, Luke needs to remove some obstacles in the story.[151] These obstacles include purity, circumcision and dietary laws, in addition to a soldier's participation in the imperial cult.[152] The narrator establishes standards of judgment that persuade the audience to consider the removal of those obstacles to be positive changes.[153] These standards of judgment are strengthened by the involvement of God and of Hebrew Scripture. The integration of Gentiles comes from Hebrew Scripture prophecy (Acts 2 and 15). Both Peter and Cornelius receive vi-

---

150. Goodman, *Rome and Jerusalem*, 163.

151. Adherence to the God of Israel likely entailed some resistance from elite Greco-Roman men as well. Both Jews and Gentiles knew that Jews thought the God of Israel was the Lord of the universe (Cohen, *From the Maccabees*, 60–61). Romans knew that Jews refused to worship any other god apart from the God in Jerusalem (Goodman, *Rome and Jerusalem*, 392). For some elites, the problems associated with adherence to Yahweh were related to the abandonment of the state gods. Dio Cassius states that the title "Jew" applies to anyone who "affects their customs." Cassius, *Rom. hist.* 37:17 (Cary, LCL). He describes Domitian's actions against elite people who adopted Jewish practices; Domitian slew or exiled elites who "drifted into Jewish ways" and were therefore guilty of atheism. *Rom. hist.* 67:14. Tacitus states that adopting Jewish practices such as circumcision is despising the gods (Tacitus, *Histories* 5:5).

152. I owe this insight to David Rhoads.

153. For more on standards of judgment, see Rhoads et al., *Mark as Story*, 44–45.

sions from God directing to them one another in Acts 10. Peter's vision addresses issues of purity and the removal of food laws. Peter becomes hungry, a sheet containing unclean animals is lowered from heaven, and a voice says, "Get up, Peter, kill and eat" (10:13). Peter is reluctant to do so, saying, "By no means, Lord; for I have never eaten anything that is profane or unclean." Yet the voice asserts that God is indeed directing this fundamental change. Beverly Roberts Gaventa notes that "Peter's vision is repeated three times" and "the Jerusalem inquiry replays the entire episode yet again. This feature suggests, not the heavy hand of an intrusive editor of earlier sources, but Luke's insistence that his audience pay particular attention to this story."[154] About circumcision, Peter states in his speech at the home of Cornelius that "God shows no partiality, but in every nation anyone who fears him and does what is right is acceptable to him" (10:34–35). While meeting with the Jewish authorities in Jerusalem, Peter identifies himself as the apostle to the Gentiles and reports to them that the integration of the uncircumcised was the result of God's work (15:7).[155] The Jewish authorities relent and agree, through their representative James, that "we should not trouble those Gentiles who are turning to God" (15:19). James states, "therefore I have reached the decision that we should not trouble those Gentiles who are turning to God, but we should write to them to abstain only from things polluted by idols and from fornication and from whatever has been strangled and from blood. For in every city, for generations past, Moses has had those proclaim him, for he has been read aloud every Sabbath in the synagogues" (15:19-21). The remaining purity-related stipulations named here do not include circumcision or Sabbath observance, yet these Jewish authorities consider the remaining stipulations to be in line with the teachings of Moses. Thus a fundamental change in purity has been brought about by God, and the movement is still in line with its Jewish roots.

Luke also removes barriers related to purity by involving the Holy (i.e., pure) Spirit in the baptism of Cornelius. Baptism was a Jewish rite of purification that used water as a cleansing agent. In Acts 10, Cornelius is baptized and purified with water. Peter says, "Can anyone withhold the water for baptizing these people who have received the Holy Spirit just as we have?" (10:47). The arrival of the Holy Spirit is another sign

---

154. Gaventa, *Acts of the Apostles*, 163.

155. This conflicts with Paul's self-identification as apostle to the Gentiles in Gal 2:7.

that Cornelius is indeed acceptable, pure, and virtuous. Peter refers to this purification as "cleansing their hearts by faith" (15:9).[156] Because of this cleansing, God makes no distinction between the people of Israel and Gentiles (11:12; 15:9). In this way, purification, baptism, and the Holy Spirit are woven together. The Holy Spirit's activity resulted in a unified people, among whom there are no differences based on ethnic lineage or pious practices. As long as Gentiles, including Cornelius, fulfill the stipulations made by James in Jerusalem, all of them belong to the people of God. With regard to Cornelius, this means that he and other Gentiles, despite their Gentile ethnicity and observance of only some Jewish practices, can be model men for Luke's audience.

Another obstacle to envisioning Cornelius as a model man may be related to participation in the imperial cult. Howell suggests that there is evidence for centurions' participation in rituals and priesthoods associated with the imperial cult. As evidence, Howell cites a chief centurion in Campania had a poem inscribed on a temple to Augustus' grandsons.[157] This poem calls Caesar a god, and it states that, after his reign, Augustus will return to his throne in heaven where he will rule the world. Such language could be attributed to the God of Israel as well. Further evidence can be found in an image carved of stone, in Rome, that shows a centurion standing in a shrine and pouring a libation onto an altar.[158] From Howell's perspective, this ancient evidence makes it reasonable to assume that centurions were involved in the imperial cult.

If this is the case, the audience of Luke's story may have associated centurions with the imperial cult. Jewish audiences in particular may have seen involvement in imperial rituals as an obstacle, and it is likely that they would have considered such activity to be idolatry. Luke's story as a whole emphasizes practical piety and specific activities that indicate one's loyalty or adherence to the God of Israel. Concrete acts of faithfulness, such as being satisfied with one's wages (Luke 3:14) and giving alms (Acts 10:2, 4), show one's fidelity to the God of Israel. However, practices that attribute supreme authority to the emperor, such as sacrifices, present a problem for those who envision the God of Israel as the supreme

---

156. All foods are made clean in Acts 10 as well.

157. For the original Latin, see inscription 137 in *ILS* 1:36. For comment, see Howell, *Imperial Authority*, 33.

158. Noted above, this stele dates to the third century CE. For comment see Howell, "Imperial Authority," 34–35.

authority. Sacrifices, prayers, and language like the poem noted above belonged to idolatry and could not be easily reconciled with the worship of the God of Israel.

Luke does not appear to resolve this issue entirely. Within the storyworld and from the viewpoint of the characters, participation in the imperial cult does not take center stage. The issue of "cleansing," however, does arise, and this action may refer to idolatry. The divine voice tells Peter, "What God has cleansed, you must not call common or unclean," (ἐκαθάρισεν, Acts 10:15). Peter later states that God has demonstrated to him that no human being is to be called unclean (ἀ κάθαρτον λέγειν ἄνθρωπον, 10:28). The verb καθαρίζω appears again in 15:9, where Peter states that the hearts of the Gentiles have been cleansed (καθαρίσας τὰς καρδίας). The cleansing of the Gentiles takes place at God's initiative and has lasting impact for Gentile men such as Cornelius. Perhaps Cornelius has been cleansed of idolatry, and his participation in the imperial cult is no longer an obstacle for him, for the other characters, and for the historical audiences as well. His piety is exemplary despite his imperial responsibilities as a centurion.

While the God of Israel is the supreme authority in Luke's story, Luke's stance on whether or not Cornelius participated in the imperial cult is ambiguous. The necessities of military life and conflicting sovereignties inherent in Judaism and the imperial cult complicate this question. A centurion (Cornelius, in this case) may have not had a choice about his responsibilities toward the cult. It is possible that Luke deliberately leaves the question open. It may be helpful here to pose two opposing options. First, Cornelius could have maintained allegiance to the God of Israel, adopted Jewish ways, and continued to participate in the imperial cult. Second, the conflicts involved in Judaism and the imperial cult were insurmountable, and Cornelius was not able to fulfill his military duties.

First, if Luke is proposing that Cornelius could be committed to the God of Israel, demonstrate his affiliation with Judaism, and carry out his responsibilities associated with the imperial cult, Luke is showing that although the sovereignties collide, God is able to overcome any conflict. In Luke, John the Baptist provides a straightforward answer to soldiers who ask what they should do in order to "bear fruits worthy of repentance" (3:8). John tells the soldiers not to extort money from anyone and to be satisfied with their wages (3:14). John's answer implies that it is indeed possible for soldiers to bear fruits worthy of repentance and to participate in the kingdom of God. In Acts 10 and 15, Judaism itself adapts and evolves so that circumcision and food laws are no longer required. These developments show that fundamental change is part of the story. Change has been predicted in Hebrew Bible prophecy. The Spirit is poured out on all flesh (Acts 2:17) and the fallen house of David will be rebuilt so that all people will seek the Lord, and even all the Gentiles over whom God's name has been called (15:16–17). Cornelius' involvement in the imperial cult, then, is yet another obstacle that has been removed and another sign that affiliation with the God of Israel can take a variety of forms.

However, if Luke is proposing that the imperial cult is to be set aside, and that Cornelius is to be "cleansed" by no longer participating in it, Luke story takes on additional religious and political significance regarding issues of sovereignty. Affiliation with Judaism and adopting Jewish practices means giving up rituals and responsibilities associated with the imperial cult. One cannot be loyal to the emperor and to the God of Israel. The supreme authority of the God of Israel should not be challenged by other lords or gods. The God of Israel is "lord of all" (Acts 10:38). The good news of God is the news of Jesus, who died and rose again. Jesus, not the emperor, was the one who was appointed as judge over the living and the dead (10:42). In this scenario, Cornelius recognizes the ultimate sovereign by affiliating himself with Judaism, rather than with the imperial cult.

While these issues are not easily resolved, Cornelius emerges as a righteous and God-fearing man whose commitment to the God of Israel is secure. Luke does resolve any tension that may exist, both for the characters and for his audience, about who the God of Israel is. God works through men like Peter, who obeys the command to preach about Jesus. God also works through men like Cornelius, who acknowledges the power of God and demonstrates their faith through prayer and almsgiving.

THE LANGUAGE OF JEWISH PIETY: MOSES AND CORNELIUS

In addition to the removal of barriers regarding circumcision, food laws, Sabbath observance, purity, and idolatry, Luke uses specific words and phrases that link the Gentile Cornelius to Moses the Jewish patriarch. While the Way is ethnically diverse and fundamental changes regarding purity have taken place, the leaders of the Way maintain a connection to Judaism through Moses. In contemporary extrabiblical sources, Moses is described with words and phrases that intersect with the words and phrases in the characterization of Cornelius. These specific words and phrases are sometimes the same words that describe pious elite Greco-Roman men: εὐσέβεια, δικαιοσύνη, and other words relating to almsgiving, prayer, and testimony. Yet unlike most of the extrabiblical sources about elite Greco-Roman men, these Jewish men recognize the God of Israel as sovereign. Through the characterization of Cornelius, Luke suggests that the men of the Way have not lost their way, and that they will usher in an era that is both old and new.

First we turn to the Greek word εὐσέβεια. In the writings of Josephus and Philo, εὐσέβεια is associated with piety toward the God of Israel and the exemplary piety and masculinity of Moses. In *Against Apion*, Josephus defends Judaism and argues, "I would therefore boldly maintain that we have introduced to the rest of the world a very large number of very beautiful ideas. What greater beauty than piety?"[159] Josephus goes on to that that even Jewish women and children recognize that εὐσεβεῖν "must be the motive of all our occupations in life."[160] Moses was "the great lawgiver under whom they were trained in piety [εὐσέβειαν] and the exercise of the other virtues . . ."[161] The characterization of Moses in Philo's works includes piety as well. Feldman argues that for Philo, "it was through piety that [Moses] gained the offices of king, legislator, prophet, and high priest."[162] Conway suggests that masculinity and piety were linked in the characterization of Moses in the writings of Philo. Philo introduces Moses as the "greatest and most perfect of men"[163] Conway writes that in the writings of Philo, "a more pious soul indicates a more masculine status, or vice versa. Becoming more pious

---

159. Josephus, *Ag. Ap.* 2:293 (Thackeray, LCL).

160. Ibid., 2:181.

161. Josephus, *Ant.* 1:6 (Thackeray, LCL).

162. Feldman, *Philo's Portrayal of Moses*, 258. I acknowledge here an apologetic aspect to the writings of Philo. Philo may be writing to Greco-Roman audiences, saying that the qualities that they admire (εὐσέβεια, δικαιοσύνη, etc.) come from Judaism. I also acknowledge the Hellenistic influence on the writing of Philo.

163. Conway, "Gender and Divine Relativity," 485.

and becoming more masculine are one and the same . . ."[164] These extra-biblical references indicate not only that piety was a virtue worth having, but also that Moses exemplified it. Luke describes Cornelius as εὐσεβὴς in Acts 10:2. Cornelius has the kind of piety that Moses had, and they could both be described as *pious* and as *men*. Cornelius is a good man whose belief in the God of Israel meets the criteria for piety. In the words of Conway, "Thus, faith in Christ concerns two quintessentially masculine virtues combined with the messianic expectations of Judaism. Belief in Jesus is what enables one to be a true man."[165]

Second, we turn to the Greek word δικαιουσύνη. In Acts 10:22, Cornelius is characterized as δίκαιος. Josephus' writings characterize the Jewish patriarchs Moses and David as δίκαιος as well. In Josephus' works, δικαιουσύνη is a sign of a good, just leader. In the *Antiquities*, Moses "used to decide the disputes of those who sought his aid, and all came to him, thinking that only so would they obtain justice [δικαίου] . . ."[166] The outcome of Moses' decisions was justice [δικαιουσύνη] rather than πλεονεξίαν.[167] About the qualities of a good leader, Josephus writes that when men "attain to power and sovereignty" their characters may change, resulting in "audacity, recklessness," and "contempt for things human and divine."[168] Instead of these vices, leaders need piety (εὐσεβείας) and righteousness (δικαιοσύνη). Cornelius has both of these qualities. Through this language about piety and virtue in general, Luke is presenting a model man who maintains a connection to great Jewish leaders like Moses but whose ethnicity takes the Way into a more inclusive identity.

Third, we turn to the words and concepts related to almsgiving and generosity. In Acts 10, Luke describes Cornelius as a man who gives alms generously (ποιῶν ἐλεημοσύνας πολλὰς τῷ λαῷ, 10:2). His expenditures of money reflect his piety toward Yahweh and generosity toward the Jewish people.[169] We see similar generosity in the portrayals

---

164. Ibid., 479. Conway directs her readers to Philo, *QE* 1:7.

165. Conway, *Behold the Man*, 134. Conway makes this suggestion with regard to Acts 24:25, where self-control comes into play as a masculine trait. However, Conway's assessment also applies to Acts 10.

166. Josephus, *Ant.* 2:66 (Thackeray, LCL).

167. Ibid., 2:67.

168. Ibid., 6:263–65.

169. Although similar to the generosity of Moses, the generosity of Cornelius con-

of Moses in the writings of Philo and Paul in Acts. In a study of the characterization of Moses in the writings of Philo, Feldman states that in Philo, Moses "did not treasure up gold or silver, did not levy tributes, did not possess houses or chattels or livestock or a staff or slaves or any other accoutrements of luxurious living."[170] Moses "was not extravagant in dress or in food and did not display his grandeur . . . he was liberal in his expenditures on behalf of his people (*Mos* 1.153)."[171] Moses is one of those true men (ἀληθειῶν ἄνδρες) who are "superior to the temptations of money . . ."[172] Instead, good, pious men such as Moses give their money away as a sign of self-control, rejection of greed, and generosity toward the Jewish people.

Money gathered from the community supported the poor and the temple in Jerusalem.[173] Before the Roman-Jewish war in 66–70 CE, when the Jerusalem temple was destroyed, adult Jewish men were expected to give alms to the temple. These alms were voluntary contributions that supported the "maintenance of the regular communal sacrifices in Jerusalem . . ."[174] Paul refers to giving alms in his speeches in Acts 24. In

---

trasts with other characters in Luke-Acts. Metzger identifies these contrasting characters as people who "overspend on themselves" (Metzger, *Consumption and Wealth*, 137). In Luke-Acts, overspending on oneself is sometimes associated with death. These characters include the man who builds big barns in Luke 12, whom God identifies as a fool. This is the opposite of Acts 10, when Cornelius' giving draws positive recognition from God. The man dies that very night. In Luke 16, the rich man who wore purple clothes ignored the needs of Lazarus and later went to hell. In Acts 5, Ananias and Sapphira attempt to keep money for themselves, and they are both struck dead immediately. Unlike these characters, Cornelius does not store up for himself treasure on this earth (Luke 12:21).

170. Feldman, *Philo's Portrayal of Moses*, 58. Feldman refers here to Philo, *Moses* 1:151.

171. Ibid., 58–59.

172. Philo, *Dreams* 124 (Colson, LCL).

173. Goodman writes that "the impoverished Jew looked not to an individual patron but to the charity of the community as a whole." Goodman, *Rome and Jerusalem*, 238.

174. Ibid., 454. Philo refers to this collection of money as first-fruits which are then sent to Jerusalem (Philo, *Embassy* 156–57). Tacitus refers to the collection of these monies from converts to Judaism in a less than positive way: "For the worst rascals among other peoples, renouncing their ancestral religions, always kept sending tribute and contributions to Jerusalem, thereby increasing the wealth of the Jews," (Tacitus, *Histories* 5:5, Jackson, LCL). After the temple was destroyed, the Romans continued to expect payment in the form of a "*fiscus Judaicus*." Although the Jerusalem temple to the God of Israel no longer existed, the funds went toward the renovation of the temple of

a speech that highlights his exemplary Jewish piety and behavior, Paul states, "Now after some years I came to bring alms to my nation and to offer sacrifices" (24:17). Like Cornelius, Paul gives alms (ἐλεημοσύνας ποιήων) to his nation. A Roman centurion who represents the empire now joins Moses and Paul in supporting a temple that, by the time Acts was written, had already been destroyed. These ethnic, political, and religious implications were likely not lost on Luke's audience, who would have experienced the Roman-Jewish war perhaps twenty to thirty years before. Cornelius is therefore a unique hybrid of Gentile and Jew, yet his adherence to the God of Israel is clear in the narrative.

Jewish Piety and Cornelius: Prayer and the Testimony of the Jewish Nation

In addition to specific words and phrases that link Cornelius to Moses and other Jewish leaders, Luke portrays Cornelius as pious toward the God of Isarel in two more ways. Cornelius prays constantly (δεόμενος τοῦ θεοῦ διὰ παντός) and the entire Jewish nation speaks well of him (μαρτυρούμενος τε ὑπὸ ὅλου τοῦ ἔθνους τῶν Ἰουδαίων). Cornelius prays to the God of Israel and the people of Israel give testimony about his piety (Acts 10:4, 22, 31).[175] These connections show that the Way in Acts is still connected to Judaism.

The first way that Luke connects Cornelius to Jewish piety is through prayer to the God of Israel. Historical evidence about specific prayers and the ways that Jewish men prayed in the first and second centuries CE is scarce. Before the Roman-Jewish war, prayers were offered by priests in the temple in Jerusalem as well as by the laity. After the Romans destroyed the temple, the rituals of sacrifice and priestly prayer came to a halt. Cohen writes that prayers for the laity may have been similar to the Psalms, but prayer in general did not have a fixed form.[176] Prayer may have included the study and recitation of Scripture, praise, penitential prayer, and the Shema.[177] Despite the uncertainties about first- and second-century Jewish prayer, Cohen suggests that the Psalms,

---

Jupiter. Primary sources on this tax include Suetonius, *Dom.* 12:2; Josephus, *War* 7:218. See also Smallwood, *Jews under Roman Rule*, 345; Goodman, *Judaism in the Roman World*, 25–26; Feldman and Reinhold, *Jewish Life*, 289.

175. This testimony speaks to the public nature of honor in antiquity.
176. Cohen, *From the Maccabees*, 65.
177. Ibid., 70.

hymns, and extant prayers "imply that recitation of prayers was a prominent feature of Jewish piety."[178] Cohen also points out that "prayer was accessible to all and a much more personal experience than sacrifice."[179]

Two additional ways that Luke connects Cornelius to Jewish piety is through prayer. Luke indicates that Cornelius' prayer is not merely a diplomatic gesture. Using syntax related to the passage of time, Luke characterizes Cornelius as a man who prays *all* the time, or perhaps, he prays regularly.[180] The verb δέομαι in Acts 10:4, as elsewhere in Acts, indicates supplication and humility in the presence of an authority figure.[181] Luke clearly states that authority belongs to τοῦ θεοῦ (10:4, 31). Cohen suggests that "Gentile dignitaries can otherwise acknowledge or worship the God of Israel without compromising their paganism in any way."[182] While this may be possible, Luke's precision prevents such an interpretation here. The persistence of Cornelius' prayer to God appears to be more than gesture of respect. Luke states twice that Cornelius prays to God, twice we read that Cornelius fears God, and twice we read that God has recognized the prayer of Cornelius. The Holy Spirit falls on Peter and the guests gathered in Cornelius' house, and Cornelius and his entire household is baptized (10:44–48). Because Cornelius is committed to the God of Israel, and because God has recognized the prayer of

---

178. Ibid., 65. During the rabbinic period, beginning with the second century CE and extending perhaps to the sixth century, "being a man means using that uniquely male trait, self-restraint, in the pursuit of the divine through Torah study" (Satlow, "'Try to Be a Man,'" 20). Boyarin also notes that the study of Torah was a masculine pursuit in the rabbinic era. He writes, "The study of Torah is the quintessential performance of rabbinic Jewish maleness." Boyarin, *Unheroic Conduct*, 143.

179. Cohen, *From the Maccabees*, 65.

180. One could ask why Cornelius prays all the time. Cohen states that "the nature of statutory prayer in second-temple times is unclear" (Cohen, *From the Maccabees*, 68–9). Yet, given the evidence from the rabbinic tradition, it is possible to speculate that prayer included petitions. These petitions could seek knowledge of God as well as repentance and forgiveness. Cornelius may pray constantly or regularly to seek forgiveness for something. As a centurion, he may have been expected to participate in the imperial cult, an obligation which may lead him to seek forgiveness. Luke, however, does not indicate specifically that Cornelius repents or seeks forgiveness. For more on what Jewish prayer may have been like in second-temple times, see Cohen, *From the Maccabees*, 69–70.

181. Acts 4:31; 8:22, 24, 34; 21:39; 26:3.

182. Cohen, "Respect for Judaism," 414–15.

Cornelius, the audience of Acts can envision Cornelius as an exemplar of piety.[183]

The second way that Luke connects Cornelius to Jewish piety is through the testimony of the entire Jewish nation (μαρτυρούμενος τε ὑπὸ ὅλου τοῦ ἔθνους τῶν Ἰουδαίων, Acts 10:22). Cornelius sends three men to Peter's house; they are to bring Peter to the home of Cornelius. The embrace of the Jewish nation, signified by positive testimony, may result from multiplicity of ways that Cornelius shows piety toward Yahweh. The positive testimony also plays an important role in the plot. The comments from the emissaries of Cornelius persuade Peter to come with them, enabling Peter and Cornelius to meet and setting up the gathering where the Holy Spirit will fall upon them all. The testimony has a rhetorical function as well. The positive testimony persuades the audience that even though Cornelius is a Gentile, and a Roman centurion, the entire Jewish nation speaks well of him. Luke reinforces the diversity in the Way by characterizing both Gentiles and Jews as people who receive good reports from the Jewish nation.[184] In addition to Cornelius, Ananias in Acts 22 is a "devout man according to the law and well spoken of by all the Jews living there . . ."[185] In Acts, both Gentiles and Jews are capable of exemplary piety toward Yahweh. Although this change may be problematic for some characters in the story, God initiates the change and brings it about through pious Gentile men like Cornelius.[186]

In this section I have shown that Cornelius the Gentile has the piety of a Jew.[187] Cornelius has features of the piety of Moses in extrabiblical references, showing that the Way has maintained continuity with Judaism. Yet some changes have taken place. Luke does not describe Cornelius as a circumcised man, nor does Luke describe Cornelius as a person who observes food laws. Both of these marks of Jewish piety

183. Goodman writes that the ideal man in early rabbinic texts is subservient to God and reliant on divine help. This is certainly what we see in the characterization of Cornelius. Goodman, *Rome and Jerusalem*, 292.

184. Strathmann writes that one facet of the definition of the verb μαρτυρέω is to receive a good report. Strathmann, "μάρτυς," in *TDNT*, 496.

185. Acts 22:12. The phrase "according to the law" likely indicates Jewish piety in the form of Torah observance.

186. The giving and receiving of testimony in Acts is limited to men.

187. It is important to note that Cornelius has the piety of a Jew as Luke envisions Judaism for a man, without circumcision and food laws.

are removed in Acts 10, and model men in the narrative no longer need to observe them. Not only has piety changed, but also the exemplars of piety are now different. Now a model man can be a Gentile, and this development opens a new door to Luke's audience. Prayer and almsgiving are what makes a man in Acts 10. Men of diverse ethnic backgrounds can pray and give alms like Cornelius. Men who pray and give alms can now participate fully in the Way and perhaps even lead the Way.

The Power of Cornelius: Challenging Roman Domination

The piety of Cornelius involves humility, reverence, obedience, integrity, prayer, and generous almsgiving toward needy people. Within this configuration of piety is Luke's vision of the right way for men to use their power. There are significant contrasts between Luke's vision of how men should use their power, and how elite Greco-Roman and other military men use their power. Cornelius does not assert that the Roman gods are superior to the God of Israel. Instead, Cornelius listens to the voice of God and does what the angel of God commands him to do. Cornelius does not use his military authority to harm Judeans. Instead he kneels before Peter and welcomes Peter into his home. Cornelius does not use his power to suppress the Way. Instead, he uses his power to serve and advance the mission of God. Cornelius does not use his money to establish a monument in his own honor, or to honor the Roman gods and goddesses, or to honor the emperor. Instead, Cornelius gives his money to the needy people of Israel. In these ways, Cornelius is an example of how men can use their power for the benefit of others, and for the benefit of the Way.

By describing Cornelius as a man who uses his power to support and lift up, Luke reveals the flaws of elites and military men who seek to lord their authority other people and who seek honor for themselves. Once again we return to Luke 22:24–30, where Luke critiques "the kings of the Gentiles, who lord it over them" (22:25). Luke states, "But it shall not be so with you; rather than greatest among you must become like the youngest, and the leader like one who serves" (22:26). In Cornelius we see a pious man who serves the God of Israel and who obeys those whom God sends. While Cornelius may have the authority of a Roman centurion, he does not seek to be called "great" in the story. Instead, his humility and reverence indicates that he does not seek power for himself. Power in Acts 10 belongs to the Holy Spirit, who orchestrates the encounter between Peter and Cornelius and who "fell upon all who heard the Word" (10:44).

CONCLUSION

As the introduction to this chapter indicated, when one looks for masculinity, one often finds social and literary dynamics such as religion, politics, and rhetoric. There were a variety of different constructs of masculinity in the first and second centuries CE, and these constructs varied according to class, power, and convictions regarding sovereignty. It is striking to note that the characterization of Cornelius intersects and interacts with the portrayals of exemplary men from elite Greco-Roman, military, and Jewish circles. This intersection, and in some cases overlap, of characterization can be seen when one studies the virtue of piety among these groups. Accounts of pious men in extrabiblical and biblical sources give the interpreter a glimpse of "the good man." In Acts 10, Luke presents in Cornelius a good man whose pious practices can be recognized and imitated by a wide variety of people. Yet Luke uses the narrative tools of repetition and precision in order to convey that the true source of power is the God of Israel. Luke challenges the sovereignty of the emperor and of Roman dominance in general by being precise about the piety of his model men, including Cornelius. Wherever men come from, they need to lift up the God of the Judeans as sovereign and live their lives in accordance with that conviction.

4

Cornelius the Centurion

Masculinity and Empire

INTRODUCTION

> I wanted to hold the corpses of the Dacians; I did hold some.
> I wanted to sit on a seat of peace; I sat on one.
> I wanted to march in magnificent triumphal processions; I did just that.
> I wanted all the financial advantages of being a *primus pilus*; I had them.
> I wanted to see the Nymphs naked; I saw them.

THIS INSCRIPTION WAS FOUND on the tombstone of an anonymous *primus pilus* centurion, or the highest-ranking centurion in a cohort. Dated to the first half of the second century CE, it was excavated in a Flavian bath complex near Khenchela, in modern Algeria.[1] The inscription gives us a glimpse of the man's goals and perhaps a glimpse of military life in general. His goals included killing the enemy, relishing the peace that comes after victory, glorying in his victory, making money, and appreciating the beauty of the female body. The man's affiliation with the military gave him access to power, which may have been one of the reasons why men joined the Roman military.

In Acts 10 we encounter a centurion whose characterization seems to differ from that of the centurion described above. Although men are

---

1. The original Latin inscription can be found in *Bulletin Archéologique*, 94, inscription 2. I am grateful to Barry Hopkins at Jesuit-Krauss Memorial Library for his assistance with this inscription. See also Le Bohec, *Imperial Roman Army*, 235, 289.

frequently portrayed in ancient texts and inscriptions as elite repositories of power, some texts and inscriptions lift up male characters whose characterizations are more complex. Some of these more complex characterizations include military figures, whose relationship with power merits additional attention. These more complex characterizations embrace some aspects of masculinity and eschew other aspects of masculinity. The audience of a text can then ask, "What kind of man is this?" as well as "What kind of a military man is this?"

This chapter will explore the figure of Cornelius as one of Luke's model men. I will first place Luke-Acts in its literary context. Like other ancient texts, Luke's story presents the audience with examples to follow. Cornelius is an exemplary man whose features are worthy of recognition and imitation. Cornelius is also a Roman centurion, whom Luke presents with both realism and surprise. In this multi-faceted characterization, Luke engages but does not endorse Roman military masculinity. Some features of Cornelius are similar to portrayals of military men in texts and images in the first and second centuries CE (and beyond in some cases), yet other features of his characterization are dissimilar and subvert ancient expectations. I will argue that Luke uses the similarities to create verisimilitude and to root the character of Cornelius in common experiences of the audience.[2] I will then argue Luke uses the differences to highlight his rhetorical strategy with regard to masculinity, physical force, and empire. Luke leverages the memory of the war between the Romans and the Judeans, using those events as a contrasting background. Through contrast and geographical setting, Luke critiques

---

2. By "audience," I refer to the implied audience that can be inferred from the Luke-Acts narrative. From the two-volume set, we can infer that the audience was familiar with Judaism and Jewish Scriptures. We can determine this from the frequent references to Hebrew Bible prophecy and the employment of the term Messiah. This term appears as a positive description of Jesus, which leads the audience to consider the Way as a reformulation of Judaism. On this possibility see Brent, *Imperial Cult*, 74, 77, 148. Luke's theological vision of the Way as a reformulation of Judaism has also been discussed by Jacob Jervell, who argues that although the people of God are divided in Luke-Acts, "the history of the people of God, of the one and only Israel, continues among those obedient Jews who believe in Jesus." Jervell, *Luke and the People of God*, 15. Given the frequent references to Roman military figures in Luke-Acts, one can also infer that the audience is familiar with the Roman occupation of Judea. In addition to Roman occupation, the references to destruction in Luke indicate that the audience was likely familiar with the Roman-Jewish war (Luke 13:1–5; 17:22–37; 19:41–4).

Roman domination, proposes an alternative model of masculinity, and proclaims an alternative sovereign.

MODEL MEN

Many Greek and Roman texts, inscriptions, and images present male role models and exemplars for people to remember and imitate. These exemplary men most often emerge from elite settings and praise elite men such as emperors, senators, and other leaders. A prominent elite male role model during the early imperial period was Octavian, later known as the emperor Augustus.[3] The primary inscription associated with the reign of Augustus, the *Res Gestae*, reads, "I restored many traditions of our ancestors which were then falling into disuse, and I myself set precedents in many things for posterity to imitate."[4] As the one speaking in this inscription, Augustus describes his values and himself as models to be imitated by his descendants.[5] According to Colleen Conway, Augustus presents himself in the *Res Gestae* as the "ideal man—courageous, militarily successful, devoted to the gods, benevolent, just, beautiful, and so on."[6] The concept of Augustus as the ideal man and ruler was not limited to those who were able to read the *Res Gestae*. Scholar of the Augustan era, Karl Galinsky, describes the Augustan forum as a portrait gallery, where statues of exemplary men line the colonnade of the forum.[7] Galinsky states that these statues "were, as Augustus himself put it, to be viewed by the citizens as exemplars both for himself and for the *princepes* of future generations. Hence they were chosen to personify

---

3. The terminology of Colleen Conway, including the phrases "models of masculinity," "alternative masculinity," "model men," and "hegemonic masculinity" appear in this study, but these phrases can also be found in the writings of Stephen Moore and other interpreters who incorporate gender into their analyses.

4. *Res gest. divi Aug.* 8 (Shipley, LCL)

5. Ibid., 8:5. The Latin phrases for these concepts are "*exempla maiorum*" and "*imitanda posteris*." Cynthia Damon translates these phrases as "literally 'our ancestors' models,'" and "'to be imitated by our descendants,'" respectively. Damon, *Res Gestae Divi Augusti*, 22.

6. Conway, *Behold the Man*, 65. Conway also suggests that the emperor Augustus and later emperors were likely models "of all the best of Roman masculinity." Ibid., 23.

7. Galinsky, *Augustan Culture*, 204.

both civic and military virtues."[8] These *"summi viri,"*[9] as Paul Zanker calls the statues, were ancestors "prized for their value as *exempla*."[10] The marble statues were labeled with a brief title giving their name and honors awarded, as well as a longer description of their contributions to the empire.[11] Thus most residents of Rome could see great men and models of masculinity as their walked through the city. About this gallery, Suetonius writes, "next to the immortal gods he honored the memory of the leaders who had raised the estate of the Roman people from obscurity to greatness. Accordingly he restored the works of such men with their original inscriptions, and in the two colonnades of his forum dedicated statues of all of them in triumphal garb . . ."[12] In addition to public images, Paul Zanker suggests that some Romans set up portraits of Augustus and his family in the atriums of their homes, "a common practice"[13] that signaled "support for the new regime even at home."[14] Thus images of great men, especially Augustus, were widely distributed and visible in different venues. These artistic images display the dignity and power of specific men to literates as well as non-literates.

The presentation of exemplary men as role models also appears in other ancient texts; these models are occasionally military men. In *De Providentia*, Seneca describes good men who suffer and die "so that they might teach others to endure them; they were born to serve as a pattern."[15] While suffering makes the man for Seneca, Livy focuses on great men who are brave in battle: "What would you do then if your country called on you to die? Fifty thousand fellow Romans and allies lay slaughtered round you that very day. If so many brave examples could not move you, nothing ever will."[16] Dionysius of Halicarnassus finds exemplary men among Romans, as indicated by this statement: "Rome from the very beginning, immediately after its founding, pro-

---

8. Ibid.
9. Zanker, *Power of Images*, 211.
10. Ibid., 210.
11. Ibid., 211.
12. Suetonius, *Aug.* 31:5 (Rolfe, LCL).
13. Zanker, *Power of Images*, 265.
14. Ibid.
15. Seneca "De Providentia," 6:3, *Ep.* (Basore, LCL).
16. Livy quotes a military man named Titus Manlius Torquatus. Livy, *Hist.* 22:60 (Foster, LCL).

duced infinite examples of virtue in men whose superiors, whether for piety or for justice or for lifelong self-control or for warlike valor, no city, either Greek or barbarian, has ever produced."[17] In all of these texts, military men serve as patterns and exemplars for other men who wish to live a life of endurance, bravery, and virtue.

New Testament literature provides its audiences with model men as well. Luke presents a number of exemplary men in Luke-Acts, and Luke characterizes these men so that the audience will recognize his protagonists as male role models. By means of rhetorical characterization, Luke urges his audience to embrace his virtuous protagonists as models of masculinity, including Peter, Paul, Stephen, Philip, and Cornelius. These men bravely go where the Holy Spirit directs, endure suffering and imprisonment, and boldly carry their message to the ends of the earth. In these ways, Luke's male models conform to what some ancient audiences might have expected. However, Luke's "*summi viri*" are not always elite, nor do they all seek honor or possess wealth. Some of Luke's model men come from the lower classes in Judea, including Peter. Other models of masculinity in Luke are military officers from the middle of the military hierarchy, such as Cornelius and other centurions in the narrative. While the social locations of Luke's model men may differ, they have something in common. They proclaim the God of Israel as the true sovereign. Through this proclamation, Luke challenges elite Greco-Roman ideals and images of model men. When Cornelius kneels before Peter, Luke fleshes out the important theme announced in the Magnificat: "to bring down the mighty from their thrones and to lift up the lowly" (Luke 1:52). Luke's "*summi viri*" embody the virtues that undergird Luke's narrative. One of the most important of these virtues is allegiance to Yahweh. The great men in Luke-Acts are driven not by the emperor but by the God of Israel, and they advance to the far corners of the empire under the direction of the Holy Spirit. One of Luke's models of masculinity, Cornelius, will now take precedence in our discussion.

---

17. Dionysius, *Ant. rom.* 1:5 (Cary, LCL).

CONFORMING TO EXPECTATIONS: CORNELIUS AS THE EXEMPLARY CENTURION

The characterization of Cornelius in Acts 10 likely conforms to some of the audience's expectations about Roman military masculinity. As military officers, centurions had a degree of authority over other soldiers, interaction with civilians, and in some cases, authority over civilians. Luke describes Cornelius as an officer with these characteristics. Luke uses these similarities to create a narrative world that evokes historical realia. Luke also uses these similarities to help the audience accept Cornelius as a realistic military officer and role model, thereby firming up the credibility of his characters and the narrative as a whole. In this section, I will first provide a brief historical introduction to the Roman army and its structure and an overview of Rome's relationship with Judea. I will then discuss two similarities between Roman military masculinity and the portrayal of Cornelius.

Introduction to the Roman Army and its Structure

The Roman army had a complex structure and a wide variety of offices, responsibilities, and functions. The emperors in the first and second centuries CE used the army to expand the empire and to suppress rebellious territories, concentrating most of the military forces along the frontiers. Augustus claims that he had approximately half a million Roman citizens in his army; all of these citizens "bound themselves" to him by military oath.[18] Although the number of people employed by the army fluctuated, "the professional army at the disposal of the Roman emperor in the second century contained some 450,000 troops."[19] Per the emperor's orders, the main function of the army was to prepare for and to fight in war, states Yann Le Bohec. A soldier's "main task . . . is to kill without being killed."[20] Soldiers also maintained law and order

---

18. *Res gest. divi Aug.* 3 (Shipley, LCL). Augustus goes on to say that he "settled in colonies or sent back to their own towns after their term of service something more than 300,000 . . ." (Shipley, LCL). Augustus refers only to Roman citizens here, which would exclude auxiliary cohorts and units scattered throughout the empire. These auxiliary units could contain as many soldiers as the legions, which consisted largely of Roman citizens.

19. Campbell, *Emperor*, 4.

20. Le Bohec, *Imperial Roman Army*, 14. Le Bohec's literary and material sources range from the first century BCE to the fourth century CE. While he is quite specific

within the empire. They guarded fortresses and prisons, went on patrol, eliminated banditry, caught runaway slaves, and "ensured the security of officials by means of ships and escorts."[21] These duties kept Roman subjects under control, particularly in troubled provinces such as Judea, and subdued rebellion. Their police work included guarding "convicts condemned to the mines" and guarding "the corpses of the executed."[22] In addition to fighting in war and maintaining order within the empire's borders, soldiers also carried official letters and took on civil engineering work such as building roads and aqueducts. Le Bohec suggests that some emperors viewed the army as "no more than a relatively well-qualified workforce that cost the state nothing."[23] Given this range of tasks and responsibilities, soldiers were indeed a workforce, one that could fight, guard, suppress, escort, and build.

The Roman army was structured into cohorts, legions, specialty units and auxiliary units. A plethora of officers led and maintained the army's forces. Recruitment for all soldiers, including centurions, involved "a physical examination in which the examiner checked the general good shape of the young man, his masculinity, his eyesight, and then measured him to make sure that he was not below the minimum height required (5 ft 5 inches for a legionary.)"[24] Centurions commanded one hundred men in either a legion or an auxiliary unit.[25] A cohort consisted of six centurions and all their soldiers.[26] Scholars disagree about the rank of centurion; yet most agree that centurions did not belong to an elite officer corps. One could become a centurion by

---

about dating and location on some occasions, he does not always provide specific information. I will refer to specific dates and locations whenever possible.

21. Ibid., 14–15.

22. Ibid.

23. Ibid.

24. Ibid., 72. It is not immediately clear what Le Bohec means by the term "masculinity." This could mean an overall manly physique, or Le Bohec could be using a euphemism for male genitalia.

25. Speidel states that a centurion was in command of eighty men, rather than a hundred. Speidel, "Furlough in the Roman Army," 332.

26. A legion consisted of ten cohorts. Speidel, "Centurion's Titles," *Roman Army Studies*, 2:21.

rising up through the ranks[27] or by external appointment.[28] Le Bohec describes centurions as the equivalent of non-commissioned officers in the modern military,[29] and as officers who were "closer to ordinary soldiers than to the aristocracy."[30] Ramsay MacMullen also comments on the rank of centurion in the following way: "When one meets a centurion, one meets the army; whereas a provincial governor may better represent the Italian aristocracy, the equestrian order, or the ambitions of a predominantly civil career."[31]

Although not all centurions were equal, most centurions had responsibilities related to maintaining discipline among the troops.[32] Discipline could include physical coercion. Every morning, every soldier in a century reported to the centurion for the "morning muster," and "roll call."[33] Centurions carried a baton, also known as a vine staff, with which they could beat errant Roman citizen soldiers.[34] Such a baton was a privilege peculiar to the office. Roman citizenship carried with it the legal privilege of bodily protection, but while in the military, citizen

---

27. Dobson, "Significance of the Centurion," 404. Dobson suggests that centurions during the Republic rose up through the ranks. Le Bohec seems to suggest that rising through the ranks could happen during the imperial period as well. "Promotion was determined by the initial appointment—the higher up the ladder one started, the higher one finished . . ." Le Bohec, *Imperial Roman Army*, 44. Because of this dynamic, the Roman army was not an equalizer; every soldier did not enter into the army at the same level.

28. Le Bohec, *Imperial Roman Army*, 255. On external appointment and initial rank, Le Bohec states, "if he was the son of a notable he could hope for a centurionship." Ibid.,, 72.

29. Ibid., 255.

30. Ibid., 74.

31. MacMullen, *Soldier and Civilian*, 64. In this volume, MacMullen studies primarily the empire during late antiquity, approximately 200–400 CE. In some instances, MacMullen does not specify geographical locations. Specific dates and locations will be noted if available.

32. There is rank within the rank of centurions. The centurion of the first cohort in a legion had more prestige and the title of *primi ordines*. Campbell, *Emperor*, 102. From the position of *primi ordines*, a centurion could be promoted to the highest-ranking centurionate post in the legion, the *primus pilus*. Le Bohec, *Imperial Roman Army* 25, 43. For more on the internal structure of the centurion's rank and titles associated with that structure, see Speidel, "The Centurion's Titles," cited above, and Watson, "Documentation in the Roman Army," 504.

33. Davies, "Daily Life of the Roman Soldier," 314–16. For Roman military routine in the mid first century CE, see Josephus, *War* 3:85–88.

34. Le Bohec, *Imperial Roman Army*, 61.

soldiers were nonetheless required to obey superior officers.[35] The centurion enforced military discipline by exercising the right to physically coerce soldiers into obedience. The Roman emperor Titus gave to centurions the authority "to restrain, by resort of clubs, any who disobeyed orders" in the Jerusalem temple.[36] According to Campbell, centurions were essential officers who "stood for loyalty and discipline," a discipline that entailed physical coercion.[37]

Rome and Judea: An Overview

As the dominant empire in the Mediterranean during the first four centuries of the Common Era, Rome established its power over a large number of territories and maintained that power by military occupation. Judea was one of several provinces in which the Romans asserted their rule; as a province, Judea was subject to the laws and taxes stipulated by the Roman emperor and senate. Before the Roman-Jewish war of 66–70 CE, the Romans ruled Judea through a procurator and with the sometimes-uneasy cooperation of Jewish high priests in Jerusalem.[38] The Jewish high priests in Jerusalem had their own jurisdiction and oversaw the enforcement of local laws. While Jewish leaders concerned themselves with local legal issues, the Romans were most concerned with keeping the overall peace and maintaining order.[39]

Some aspects of governing Judea proved difficult for the Romans. Judea was not on the frontier of the empire, and provinces on the frontier were more prone to barbarian invasion.[40] Yet Judea was populated

---

35. Acts 22:25–30; 23:27.

36. The centurion was Liberalius. Josephus, *War* 6:262 (Thackeray, LCL).

37. Campbell, *Emperor*, 107. Campbell states, "The value of the centurions in preserving the loyalty and discipline of the army should not be overestimated . . ." Ibid., 109.

38. The first procurator of Judea was appointed in 6 CE. Rhoads, *Israel in Revolution*, 47.

39. Gallio, the proconsul of Achaia, distinguishes between Jewish law and a crime according to the Roman law in Acts 18:12–17. Some Jews bring Paul to Gallio, and Gallio states, "If it were a matter of crime or serious villainy, I would be justified in accepting the complaint of you Jews, but since it is a matter of questions about words and names and your own law, see to it yourselves; I do not wish to be a judge of these matters." Acts 18:14–15.

40. Provinces on the frontier of the empire had more soldiers than provinces that were not on the frontier.

largely by Jews, whose sovereign was the God of Israel. The city of Jerusalem drew Jewish pilgrims and residents together for festivals such as Passover, when the population of Jerusalem swelled exponentially. Rome tolerated these large gatherings but insisted on military supervision for purposes of control. Soldiers watched over the events in the temple from the vantage point of the Antonia Fortress, above the temple courts. While the Jewish high priests were not required to sacrifice to the Roman emperor, they were required, however, to sacrifice to the God of Israel for the purpose of the emperor's well-being. This compromise indicated Roman toleration as long as certain conditions were met. Should these sacrifices for the emperor's well-being stop, or should the peace be disturbed by rebellion, Roman soldiers could step in and take over with physical force.

During the troubled decades before the war, the tensions between Judeans and Romans grew and multiplied, and the Romans used military force to assert their power in the region. According to David Rhoads, "although the official Roman policy of religious toleration toward Jews was one of noninterference, there was often a vast difference between the official policy and the actual irritations despite this policy."[41] When Pilate, who was procurator from 26–36 CE, took money from the temple treasury to build an aqueduct, some Jews protested when he came to Jerusalem. In response, Pilate's soldiers "attacked the unarmed Jews, killed some, dispersed others, and as a result, suppressed the Jewish protest against Pilate's action."[42] During the procuratorship of Cumanus (48–52 CE), a Roman soldier made an obscene gesture toward worshiping Jews, and protest erupted.[43] The uproar led to a stampede, and some Jews were trampled to death. Procurator of Judea from 64–66 CE, Florus' abuse of power offended many Jews, and his abuses exacerbated the ever-growing divide between Judeans and the Romans. Florus refused to respond to Jewish concerns when conflict arose in Caesarea Maritima. Goodman writes, "In Caesarea, the long-running dispute between local Jews and local gentiles came to a head when some gentile youths provoked Jewish riots by sacrificing a cockerel in the alleyway outside a synagogue."[44] Florus did not punish the youths, triggering an

---

41. Rhoads, *Israel in Revolution*, 70.
42. Ibid., 61; Josephus, *War* 2:175–7; *Ant.* 18:60–62.
43. Josephus, *War* 2:223–7; *Ant.* 20:105–12; Rhoads, *Israel in Revolution*, 70.
44. Goodman, *Rome and Jerusalem*, 422–23. Conflicts and protests were also taking

uprising of Jewish residents. To suppress the uprising, Roman troops stormed the city, killing and looting in the market.[45]

It was in this climate that some lower-level priests and Eleazar, the captain of the Jerusalem temple, "took an action which was tantamount to a declaration of war."[46] They suspended the sacrifices for the emperor's well-being, breaking the agreement they had made with Rome and declaring Judea as a nation "outside the empire."[47] Combined with the other revolutionary forces and conflicts already circulating through the Judean countryside, this declaration of war led to a full-scale armed rebellion against Rome. The rebellion, characterized by conflicts among different Judean groups as well as with the Romans, led to a massive and bloody Roman military siege under the command of Vespasian's son Titus in 70 CE. According to Goodman, "Vespasian's image urgently needed the gloss of foreign conquest—the surest foundation of authority for a Roman politician—for him to be portrayed in the capital as warrior hero and saviour of the state."[48] Titus, the son of the man who became emperor, had also established his image by leading the siege of Jerusalem, in which the temple, its holy places, and the city as a whole were destroyed.

After the war, Roman dominion was established once again, but it is likely that Judeans never forgot the loss of life and the destruction in Jerusalem. At the hands of Roman soldiers, the locus for God's activity was desecrated and the walls of its courts brought to the ground. Jewish residents in Jerusalem, who could see the ruins of the temple and of the city in general, were confronted daily with the reality of Roman rule. Even for Judeans who did not live in Jerusalem, the military force and domination of Rome were apparent. In postwar Judea, procurators ruled over the Judean people directly, using troops at their own discretion. To the Judeans, Roman soldiers most likely represented the power of the empire, which had not hesitated to assert its rule by means of force. Roman soldiers had penetrated Judean territory and maintained

---

place in Scythopolis and Damascus; see Josephus, *Life* 24–27; *War* 2:487–98.

45. Goodman, *Rome and Jerusalem*, 423.

46. Rhoads, *Israel in Revolution*, 98. Goodman suggests that the cessation was sacrifices was a declaration of war by "members of the ruling elite" instead of lower-level priests. Goodman, *Rome and Jerusalem*, 422.

47. Rhoads, *Israel in Revolution*, 99; Josephus, *War* 2:409–10.

48. Goodman, *Rome and Jerusalem*, 439.

its dominance through continued military occupation, and through reminders such as taxes, monuments to Roman victory, and visual reminders on coins that circulated throughout Judea.

Conforming to Expectations: The Military Realm

With these historical introductions in mind, we move toward Luke's rhetorical strategy with regard to military officers and masculinity among men in the emerging church. The first similarity between the portrayals of centurions outside Luke-Acts and those inside Luke-Acts revolves around the issue of control. Centurions were responsible for controlling other soldiers. Control over others is an important element in Roman masculinity as a whole and especially in Roman military masculinity. Good military men kept their inferiors in line. The portrayals of centurions outside Luke-Acts show this type of control in action. In this section, I will discuss the similarities between the ways that some ancient sources portray centurions, and the ways that Luke portrays them. I will argue that these similarities are part of Luke's strategy of verisimilitude and reliability in his narrative world.

Extrabiblical literary texts portray centurions in both positive and negative ways. The positive portrayals reveal centurions who act bravely and maintain control over themselves and their soldiers, while the negative portrayals show centurions who cannot control themselves or their soldiers. The authors of these texts characterize their centurions rhetorically, providing models of effective and ineffective leadership. Among the positive portrayals are two anecdotes in the writings of Josephus. Josephus tells of a centurion who overheard a plan of attack in Gamala, and together with his soldiers bravely slew the perpetrators before the plan could be carried out.[49] The leadership of the centurion prevented many deaths and showed that he and his army, not his adversaries, could gain the upper hand in a time of conflict. A different centurion in charge of Agrippa's soldiers also played a key role in the arrest of Agrippa. In this event, Josephus characterizes the centurion as an intelligent and brave leader who made the most of a dangerous situation. Independently infiltrating a group rejoicing at the death of Tiberius, the centurion heard that Tiberius was indeed alive, realized the grave penalties of their celebration, and quickly turned the tables on Agrippa.

---

49. Josephus, *War* 4:37.

He "pushed Agrippa off the couch and said, 'So you thought you would fool me with a false report of the emperor's death, and would not pay for it with your own head?'" The centurion's loyalty was to the emperor Tiberius, and he acted out of that loyalty despite the danger of being punished by Agrippa.[50] The centurion then enlisted his own soldiers to arrest and imprison Agrippa.[51]

The writer Valerius Maximus, who provided orators with material for speeches in the second century CE, presents a Roman centurion who showed great bravery and control, and yet who lacked control over his sexual urges. This portrayal contains both positive and negative aspects of Roman military masculinity, and presents an exemplary leader with a tragic flaw. The centurion, also named Cornelius, "had served as a soldier with great bravery and had four times received from his commanders the honour of the First Spear for his valour."[52] This centurion exhibited exemplary leadership skills, and his commanders recognized his ability to lead multiple times through the awarding of the title *primus pilus*. However, this influential centurion died in prison because he was accused of "having sexual intercourse with a freeborn youth."[53] The centurion appealed to tribunes for leniency, saying that he thought the youth was a prostitute. But the tribunes denied his appeal, and they imprisoned the centurion. Thus a capable and exemplary centurion effectively controlled his soldiers, but could not control his own body.

Negative portrayals of centurions and soldiers appear in Roman plays, where centurions seem out of control in many aspects. Some playwrights characterize military men in general as weak, incompetent, and emotional; these rhetorical examples of weakness encourage the audience to mock such behavior. In *Perikeiromene*, a play written by Menander, a "swaggering soldier" named Polemon mistakenly assumed that his wife was having an affair. He forced her to cut her hair,

---

50. It is not immediately clear from this anecdote if the centurion was intending to be loyal to the emperor from the beginning. At one point in the story, his loyalty appears to be to Agrippa. However, the centurion thought quickly and enlisted his own soldiers to prevent dishonor to the emperor.

51. The centurion, his soldiers, and other parties involved in this situation received conflicting reports about Tiberius. Eventually it becomes clear that Tiberius was in fact dead, and Agrippa was released from prison. For the entire anecdote, see Josephus, *Ant.* 18:225–37.

52. Valerius Maximus, *Mem.* 6:10 (Bailey, LCL).

53. Ibid,. 6:9.

and then he lay "upon the couch in tears."[54] "Oh, my darling, how powerfully you have conquered me!" he cried, as he realized that the suspicious man was his wife's brother, rather than her lover.[55] In the play, a woman conquered a soldier, and the soldier was woefully mistaken. These aspects of the story make for comedy in the Roman world, as the military warrior appears effeminized by his wife and by his own mistake. A similar literary dynamic takes place in the plays of Plautus, especially one entitled *The Braggart Warrior*.[56] The main character in this play brags about the people whom he has beaten in battle, but his servant, speaking in asides to the audience, states that the soldier is a "bragging, brazen . . . fellow, full of lies and lechery. He says that all the women insist on running after him. The fact is, wherever he starts to strut, he is the laughing stock of them all."[57] Instead of leading and controlling other soldiers, he states that he would rather hire mercenaries; "so that I can take a rest."[58] The slave manipulates the soldier with a scheme, which leads the soldier to say, "Am I to stand here . . . so handsome and heroic all for naught?"[59] The military character, who in some texts embodies bravery and effective leadership of other soldiers, here becomes the target of satire and comedy.[60]

Whether positive or negative, portrayals of centurions and soldiers in sources outside Luke-Acts are rhetorical fodder within their respective works. In some cases, the centurions maintain control over their soldiers, even in dangerous situations. In other cases, soldiers are not able to control their slaves, their wives, or even their own bodies, not to mention their soldiers. As these examples demonstrate, control is an important element of Roman military masculinity, and one that first- and second-century audiences would likely expect from literary works.

---

54. Menander, *Peri.* (Arnott, LCL). It is not clear from Menander's play if this soldier is a centurion specifically. However, the play is nevertheless instructive with regard to military masculinity and control in literary texts.

55. Ibid., Act 5 (Arnott, LCL).

56. The plays of Plautus are dated approximately to the beginning of the second century BCE. See Plautus, *Brag.*, (Nixon, LCL).

57. Plautus, *Brag.* Act 2:90, (Nixon, LCL). Despite the soldier's bad habits, the slave indicates that the soldier feeds him well, and "makes a good olive compote."

58. Ibid., Act 4:940.

59. Ibid., Act 4:1020.

60. Pierce, "Ideals of Masculinity."

Given the presence of centurions in literary texts, and their association with control over other soldiers, the audience of Luke-Acts was likely not surprised by the portrayals of centurions in control in Luke. Early in the narrative, Luke introduces his audience to a centurion who controls others. The centurion describes his authority over other soldiers: "I say to one, 'Go,' and he goes, and to another 'Come,' and he comes . . ." (Luke 7:8). This portrayal conforms to audience expectation in two ways: first, historically, centurions did have authority over other soldiers, even if they did not exercise it well in some literary portrayals, and second, the inferior soldiers were to follow orders. Luke makes centurions and soldiers part of the story of Jesus, and he characterizes them as men who effectively lead and control soldiers. Carrying out the directions of the angel of God in Acts 10, Cornelius is an exemplary leader who uses his military authority for the benefit of the mission of the God of Israel. The angel of God directs Cornelius to "send men to Joppa for a certain Simon who is named Peter" (Acts 10:5). The angel directs him to use his authority for the right purpose. "When the angel who spoke to [Cornelius] had left, he called two of his slaves and a devout soldier from the ranks who served him, and after telling them everything, he sent them to Joppa," writes Luke (10:7–8). The devout soldier was not only under the command of Cornelius; Luke describes the soldier as "τῶν προσκαρτερούντων," meaning, one who attached himself [to Cornelius] and who was faithful to him.[61] The verb προσκαρτερέω indicates a devoted willingness to serve whenever directed to do so. Cornelius does not take advantage of this authority over the soldier. Instead, he sends the soldier on a mission that will bring Peter back to his home, enabling the spread of Peter's message and the eventual baptism of Cornelius' household. The effective leadership and exemplary command of Cornelius facilitates the integration of Gentiles into the Way.

In addition to his command over other soldiers, Cornelius is also associated with the Italian Cohort. This "Italian Cohort" reference is another way in which Luke meets the audience's expectations, creating a realistic narrative world. About this cohort, military historian M. P. Speidel suggests that some passages in Acts are more historically

---

61. BDAG defines προσκαρέω as "to stick by or be close at hand, [to] attach oneself to, wait on, be faithful to someone, with dative of person and emphasis on continuity." BDAG, 881.

accurate "than has often been admitted."[62] He notes that a cohort, originally raised in Italy, could indeed have been present in Caesarea in the late first century CE.[63] Scholars have excavated a gravestone of a soldier from *cohors II Italica*. This gravestone likely originated in the 60s or 70s CE.[64] Its epitaph refers to the army of Syria, but Josephus and Tacitus state that "Judea was annexed to Syria after the death of Agrippa in AD 44."[65] Saddington also suggests that the Italian Cohort was not a literary invention. He proposes that the Italian Cohort "belonged to a superior category of auxiliary regiments . . . or citizen regiments; they were originally recruited from citizens and appear to have been especially prominent in areas where legions were not stationed."[66] The cohort reference places Cornelius in his military context and enhances the story's historical verisimilitude.

Other centurions in Luke-Acts also manifest control over other soldiers, and at least one of those centurions' characterizations seems historically plausible.[67] In addition to the example of the centurion in Luke 7, noted above, another example can be found in Acts 27. Here the centurion Julius is in charge of a ship full of prisoners, including Paul. Julius listens to the ship's owner and pilot, but makes decisions about where and when the ship will go, as well as how the prisoners should be treated (Acts 27:3, 11, 42-44). This type of leadership was not unusual for centurions, and it may indicate, as does Acts 27:42, that centurions led groups of other soldiers on ships as well.[68] Like the Italian Cohort, the Augustan Cohort has some degree of historical accuracy. Saddington has studied two inscriptions about the Augustan Cohort. The first inscription, found in Syria, mentions a prefect of the Augustan Cohort, who conducted a census.[69] The second inscription, found in

---

62. Speidel, "Roman Army in Judea," 224.

63. Ibid., 225-27. The gravestone was found in Austria, but it is possible that the soldier was buried in his home area, rather than where he was stationed.

64. Ibid., 226. On this gravestone, see also Saddington, "Military and Administrative Personnel," 2415.

65. Speidel, "Roman Army in Judea," 226.

66. Saddington, "Military and Administrative Personnel," 2415-16.

67. My primary goal is to show how Luke uses verisimilitude rather than to prove historical accuracy of the text.

68. See above for information on the escort duties of centurions and soldiers in the Roman army.

69. Saddington, "Military and Administrative Personnel," 2417.

Arabia, mentions a centurion of the Augustan cohort.[70] Saddington places both cohorts in Judea at some point after 40 CE.[71]

Luke portrays his centurions as men who have the authority to control soldiers, and these men use their authority wisely. The centurions in Luke represent the military power of the empire and yet they seem to act independently, often showing respect for Jesus and the followers of Jesus. Like other ancient texts, Luke characterizes these military men in rhetorical ways, urging the audience to choose the positive and reject the negative.[72] Inherent and implicit in these portrayals are constructs of gender and models of masculinity. Luke presents his exemplar, Cornelius, as a model man who knows when and how to use his authority. As a centurion, Cornelius is not a high-ranking officer. Nor does he command a large number of soldiers or wield a great deal of social influence. Luke challenges the elite ideals and virtues of men by characterizing Cornelius, a man who does not represent the aristocracy, as the embodiment of central virtues in the narrative. These central virtues include effective leadership of other men and the proper use of authority. Luke also presents these model centurions in historically realistic ways, making these characters more believable and reliable among his audiences.

Conforming to Expectations: The Civilian Realm

Members of the Roman army did not remain in camps or barracks during their entire time of service. As occupants and representatives of the empire throughout Roman territories, soldiers and centurions interacted with civilians and occasionally exercised control over them. Physical coercion may have been necessary when interacting with civilians. This section will explore how centurions interacted with civilians, as well as literary portrayals of that interaction outside and inside of Luke-Acts. I will discuss how Luke uses verisimilitude to meet audience expectation to create a plausible narrative, and to fashion a masculinity based on the correct use of military authority.

Le Bohec indicates that there were two legions stationed in Judea in the first and second centuries CE. One was the *Legio X Fretensis* in

---

70. Ibid., 2410.
71. Ibid., 2417.
72. Most if not all of Luke's centurions are positively portrayed.

Jerusalem from the time of Vespasian, and the other was the *Legio VI Ferrata* at Caparcotna in northern Judea from the time of Hadrian.[73] In Caesarea Maritima, ten inscriptions attest to the presence of the *Legio X Fretensis* in the late first century CE, most of which were found inscribed on an aqueduct.[74] These legions do not take into account auxiliary units that may have occupied Judea. According to R. Jackson Painter, during the Roman-Jewish war, "Judea was the scene of a large amalgamation of troops, consisting of the legions, Syrian auxiliary troops, and the local armies from Emesa, Commogene and Iturea."[75] Soldiers from the legions and, likely, soldiers from auxiliary units interacted with civilians in three ways: commerce, informal marriage, and sometimes sharing homes in cities.[76] According to Saddington, "army officers were more fully involved in 'civilian' life than modern experience would suggest."[77] He refers to a document "found on the skeleton of a Jewish woman named Babatha" in the early second century CE. The document "shows the centurion of an auxiliary regiment lending money to a Jew."[78] This reference shows at least some commercial interaction between military and civilian in Judea. Davies suggests that soldiers had to make trips to the mint or to granaries, which would likely have put them in contact with civilians as well.

MacMullen describes the connection of soldiers and civilians especially in cities: "Soldiers in cities daily rubbed shoulders with civilians, but even in their camps, the same was true."[79] In these cities were interactions from business and the formation of new social connections. According to MacMullen, businesses set up shop close to camp to attract customers from among the local soldiers, including wine shops,

---

73. Le Bohec, *Imperial Roman Army*, 172–73. Campbell also states that Judea "had a permanent legionary garrison." Campbell, *Emperor*, 4.

74. Lehmann and Holum, *Greek and Latin Inscriptions*, 71–77.

75. Painter, "Origins and Social Context," 213. Here Painter refers to Josephus, *War* 2:499, 544; 3:64–69.

76. It is likely that centurions and Judean subjects spoke different languages. Perhaps the military men spoke Latin or Greek, and the Judeans Aramaic or Hebrew. Or perhaps, they both spoke Greek. However, in Acts 10, no language barrier seems to exist. Peter and Cornelius understand one another without a translator.

77. Saddington, "Military and Administrative Personnel," 2415n15.

78. This document comes from the Babatha archive; see Lewis, *Documents*, 41.

79. MacMullen, *Soldier and Civilian*, 119.

taverns, and brothels.[80] Such interaction can be seen in an inscription from the first century CE. The inscription describes an order by Nero to line military roads in Thrace with taverns and rest houses.[81] Marriage, often informally arranged, was another way that soldiers and civilians interacted. During the first century CE, Roman soldiers were not to marry, by order of the emperor Augustus. However, the ban on marriage was not always enforced, and soldiers formed "common-law" marriages and long-standing relationships with women, which may have involved children.[82] Classicist David Potter states that the formation of relationships, informal families, and children were "inevitable," despite the ban.[83] Moreover, Potter writes that soldiers could be housed in civilian homes, "something the civilian communities dreaded."[84] Shared homes were divided by "an interior crosswall, suggesting at least a theory of separation, whatever the facts may have been."[85]

Scholars of Roman military history and some ancient texts show not only interaction between soldier and civilian, but also occasions when soldiers (including centurions) took control of civilian activities. Such was their duty as representatives of the power and superiority of the Roman military. Soldiers and centurions acted as a police force among civilians, maintaining law and order in cities, towns, and villages. Le Bohec indicates that the "troops stationed [in the province of Judea] had to watch the native inhabitants rather than the desert for the potential enemy."[86] He suggests that units commanded by a provincial governor

---

80. Ibid., 119–20.

81. *CIL* 3:14207; MacMullen, *Soldier and Civilian*, 119.

82. Campbell, *Emperor*, 302.

83. Potter, "Introduction," 12; Alston, "Arms and the Man," 217. Potter states that the emperor who lifted the ban, Septimius Severus (193–211 CE), was pressured to lift it, presumably by the military itself.

84. Potter, "Introduction," 13. Potter does not provide a specific location or date for this practice.

85. MacMullen envisions this sharing of homes as a necessity, and something that had to be done only if troops had to be stationed in a city where barracks were not available. According to MacMullen, most cities in the East had quarters for soldiers, reducing the need for civilian housing. Further interaction between soldier and civilian took place from the time of Septimius Severus, whose policies allowed for marriage and participation in clubs. MacMullen, *Soldier and Civilian*, 154.

86. Le Bohec, *Imperial Roman Army*, 172–73. These territories had few local police officers, relying instead of on Roman representatives to suppress bandits and to keep the territory from erupting into dangerous conflict.

"acted as a police force, particularly where there was no threat of an external attack."[87] Since Judea was not on the frontier, the possibility of attack was reduced, enabling the soldiers to turn their attention inward toward bandits and rebellion. In this situation, soldiers kept watch for conflict inside the province and suppressed resistance. Josephus states that Vespasian posted centurions in towns for that purpose.[88]

This evidence indicates that soldiers and civilians interacted in a number of ways. This interaction is not always portrayed as positive in ancient texts, however. Rhetorical characterization plays a role in these portrayals. In some texts, centurions appear to be effective leaders and masculine role models because of their ability to control civilians. Exemplary centurions in the writings of Suetonius include Cornelius, a centurion during the reign of Augustus. According to Suetonius, when the Senate was reluctant to give Augustus a consulship, Cornelius protested, "throwing back his cloak and showing the hilt of his sword."[89] He "did not hesitate to say in the House, 'This will make him consul, if you do not.'"[90] In other cases, the centurion appears gallant but falls short in his attempt to maintain law, order, and control over civilians. In the conflict at Jotapata between Romans and Judeans, a centurion was "killed by treachery," after the town fell into Roman hands. In this incident, a Judean fugitive extended his hand to the centurion and then fatally stabbed him with a spear beneath the groin."[91] In still other cases, centurions appear to be poor models of masculinity and control over civilians. Valerius Maximus provides us with a description of a greedy centurion who kidnapped a woman, held her for ransom, abused her, and was eventually killed for his misdeeds.[92] While this story is might not be historical, it does give a glimpse of relevant stories that circulated around the time when Acts was written.

Luke characterizes Cornelius and other centurions in his volumes as officers who share scenes with civilians, and who occasionally order

---

87. Ibid., 208. According to MacMullen, this was especially the case in Egypt. MacMullen, *Soldier and Civilian*, 60.

88. According to Josephus, Vespasian posted centurions in strategic locations in the east, in order to "allay anxiety in Italy." Josephus, *War* 4:440–2 (Thackeray, LCL).

89. Suetonius, *Aug.* 26:1 (Rolfe, LCL).

90. Ibid.

91. Josephus, *War* 3:329–35 (Thackeray, LCL).

92. Valerius Maximus, *Mem.* 6:ext.2.

civilians to carry out a specific task. These characterizations create a narrative world at least somewhat akin to audience expectation and lend a reliable tone to his narrative. The portrayal of the centurion in Luke 7 involves interaction with civilians. "He loves our people," state the Jewish elders, and "it is he who built our synagogue for us" (7:5). In Acts 10, Cornelius interacts with subjects of the empire, especially Judeans. He brings relatives and close friends to his home to greet and to listen to Peter (10:24). This gathering gives the impression that Cornelius has relatives and friends who are not necessarily employed by the military. Cornelius asked these relatives and friends to come to his home, and they agreed, with no protest noted in the story. Moreover, Cornelius orders two of his slaves to accompany the devout soldier on the mission to find and bring Peter back to his home (10:7–8). The centurion retains his power over some men in the story. They went to Joppa without comment and brought Peter back the next day. As we have seen above, centurions likely had slaves and servants, as does Cornelius. In this account, Cornelius acts as a man who is accustomed to giving orders, and his relatives, friends, slaves, and fellow soldier act as they are under his authority.

In addition to Luke's strategy of verisimilitude, one can also see Luke crafting the characterization of Cornelius so that he will be a positive example of how to interact with, and at times, control civilians. Luke embraces the use of military authority as long as it is used for the benefit of the Way. The angel of God directs Cornelius to use his authority to retrieve Peter; this divine directive endorses military authority in the service of the God of Israel. This directive also links the military and non-military in ways that lead toward constructive change. Peter, a key protagonist in the narrative, obeys Cornelius, which allows the audience to consider Cornelius as a suitable commander. Moreover, one can also see a similar pattern in the description of Julius in Acts 27. While at first Julius does not respond ideally to Paul,[93] he later allowed Paul to have his say, and kept all the men in the ship as Paul suggested (27:31–32). Julius commanded the soldiers not to kill all the prisoners (27:42–44), and Paul continued on his journey.[94] Luke uses repetition and positive

---

93. Acts 27:11: "But the centurion paid more attention to the pilot and to the owner of the ship than to what Paul said."

94. While on the ship, Paul announced, "For last night there stood by me an angel of the God to whom I belong and whom I worship, and he said, 'Do not be afraid, Paul;

portrayals of centurions to fashion a masculinity that takes control at key times, uses authority wisely, and is motivated by a goal of service toward the God of Israel.

We have explored the historical background of the Roman military, the responsibilities of centurions over other soldiers, and the ways in which centurions interacted with and sometimes controlled civilians. We have seen Luke characterizing Cornelius and other centurions in ways that are similar to what his audiences might have expected. These similarities shore up his narrative as a story that might really happen. The historical plausibility of the narrative also helps the audience accept and believe that Cornelius is a positive model of masculinity for men in the emerging church.

SUBVERTING EXPECTATIONS: CORNELIUS AS THE (UNUSUAL) EXEMPLARY CENTURION

While Luke makes use of verisimilitude in refashioning masculinity through the characterization of Cornelius, Luke also subverts audience expectation and characterizes Cornelius as a somewhat unusual centurion. These unexpected traits include the absence of physical coercion as a means of control over subjects of the empire and submission to the Holy Spirit.[95] Luke uses these surprising traits to reconfigure masculinity. This model man relinquishes control over the empire's subjects and does not act in the ways that centurions were reputed to act. Luke also uses the characterization of Cornelius, especially his submissive gesture before Peter, to critique Roman domination over Judeans and to propose the God of the Judeans as a sovereign more powerful than the emperor. This critique would have carried additional salience when compared to the experiences of the Judeans during the Roman-Jewish war. In addition, the geographical setting of Caesarea, a city oriented toward empire, adds a sharp edge to Luke's critique. This section will explore Luke's rhetorical strategy with regard to the surprising aspects of the characterization of

---

you must stand before the emperor, and indeed, God has granted safety to all those who are sailing with you,'" Acts 27:23–24.

95. In this study I assume that the Holy Spirit is interchangeable with the God of Israel.

Cornelius, beginning with submission to the God of Israel, known in Acts 10 as the Holy Spirit.

Subverting Expectations: Submission and Authority in Luke-Acts

While centurions were agents of the Roman government who had some degree of military authority, they were also subject to other military and political authorities. Like other officers in the army, centurions had to balance boldness and restraint, command and obedience. A good military officer gives orders and obeys orders, depending on his rank and his place in the hierarchy. Roman military masculinity prizes the ability to control others, but also integral to military masculinity and honor were the willingness to submit to one's commanding officer. Submission was a valuable trait that allowed the army to function effectively. "What is required of a soldier?" Le Bohec writes. "Firstly, to obey his superiors; secondly, to die in combat if the occasion demands."[96] Submission may entail bodily harm or death, but the true warrior and the real military man obeyed his superior officers, despite the danger.[97]

The writings of Tacitus present centurions as exemplars of submission as well as loyalty. The *Histories* tell of four centurions of the Twenty-Second Legion who valiantly attempted to protect the images of Galba during a mutiny.[98] Nonius Receptus, Donatus Valens, Romilius Marcellus, and Calpernius Repentinus "were swept away by the onrush of soldiers when they tried to protect Galba's images and were thrown into chains."[99] At a later point, the centurions were "ordered to be executed, for they had been pronounced guilty of loyalty—the worst of charges among rebels."[100] Tacitus also describes centurions as exemplars of submission and loyalty to the emperors, especially Sempronius Densus. Sempronius Densus "was a centurion of a praetorian cohort whom Galba had assigned to protect Piso; he drew his dagger, rushed to

---

96. Le Bohec, *Imperial Roman Army*, 105. Le Bohec goes on to say, "Obeying an order, even one that seemed absurd, and respecting one's superiors were part of the imperatives of the profession, and can be learned, just like the handling of arms or the building of defences." Ibid., 107

97. Barton states that the nature of Roman honor entails some lack of control. Barton, *Roman Honor*, 276.

98. Tacitus, *Histories* 1:56.

99. Ibid.

100. Ibid., 1:59.

meet the armed men, upbraided them for their crime, and drawing the attention of the assassins to himself by act and word, gave Piso a chance to escape . . ."[101] Tacitus found the epitome of submission and loyalty in the centurion Julius Agrestius. He "exhibited noble courage [*constantia*]" and proved his honor as a soldier.[102] Sent to discover the activities of Antonius and the legions held captive in Cremona, he returned to the emperor Vitellius with a report. Vitellius did not believe the report, and called the centurion's loyalty into question. Julius replied, "Since I must give you a convincing proof of my statements, and you can have no other advantage from my life or death, I will give you evidence that will make you believe."[103] The centurion then committed suicide. Tacitus comments on this incident by saying, "Some have reported that he was put to death by the orders of Vitellius, but all agree to his fidelity and courage."[104] The actions of Julius and other centurions in the writings of Tacitus put on display the connection among military masculinity ad submission, even to the point of death.

Some of Luke's military men submit to officers in the narrative, yet in Acts 10, Luke subverts ancient expectation by redrawing the lines of authority and sovereignty.[105] The differences between Cornelius and centurions in extrabiblical texts emerge when one considers just *whom* Cornelius obeys. Cornelius submits to the Holy Spirit and to Peter, and his obeisance is to the God of Israel. Luke characterizes his exemplary man as one who recognizes and obeys the God of Israel as the true sovereign. The audience may have expected Cornelius to follow the orders of a military officer, or to carry out a mission given to him by a tribune. Given the writings of Tacitus, one might expect Cornelius to preserve the images of the emperor, to profess loyalty to the emperor, or even to die to prove a point to the emperor. However, Cornelius does not have a commanding military officer in the narrative, nor does he serve the emperor. Luke challenges Roman military masculinity and the supreme

101. Ibid., 1:43.
102. Ibid., 1:54.
103. Ibid.
104. Ibid.
105. Political and religious realities were intertwined in the imperial period, and any separation of the two should be made with caution. I focus here on issues relating to military and political authority and power, knowing that they cannot easily be distinguished. For more on the religious aspects of the characterization of Cornelius, see chapter 3.

authority of the empire in three ways. First, he emphasizes the obedience of Cornelius to the angel. Second, Luke has Cornelius fall at the feet of Peter in a gesture that symbolized both political and religious submission. Third, through the response of Peter to this gesture, Luke redirects his audience toward the God of Israel.

The first way that Luke subverts audience expectation and refashions masculinity is through the interaction of Cornelius and the angel of God. Luke emphasizes the obedience of Cornelius to the angel three times. In a vision, he "clearly saw an angel of God coming in and saying to him, 'Cornelius'" (Acts 10:3). Terrified, Cornelius responds, "What is it, Lord? [κύριε]?" Luke indicates that Cornelius wasted no time in obeying the angel: "When the angel who spoke to him had left, he called two of his slaves" (10:7). The emissaries of Cornelius repeat the directions of the angel in order to explain their presence in Peter's house (10:22). Cornelius himself restates his immediate obedience in 10:30–33, saying, "Therefore I sent for you at once" (ἐξαυτῆς). The emphasis on obedience occurs in the voice of the narrator twice and once in the voice of Cornelius. Even Cornelius finds obedience a virtue. The repetition of this trait in Acts 10 draws attention not only to obedience as a positive characteristic but also to the source of authority in the narrative. Cornelius recognizes his commander in the angel of God and carries out the angel's orders immediately. Luke reorients his audience toward the authority of the God of the Judeans.

In addition to the interaction between Cornelius and the angel of God, Luke uses a symbolic gesture of submission to indicate the authority of the Holy Spirit and messengers sent by the Holy Spirit, and Cornelius' submission to God. When Peter enters the home of Cornelius, Cornelius falls to his feet and shows obeisance: "πεσὼν ἐπὶ τοὺς πόδας προσεκύνησεν" (10:25). While the verb προσκυνέω has a variety of meanings, Luke uses it here to indicate obeisance, reverence, and respect.[106] The writings of Josephus and other references in

---

106. The NRSV translates προσκυνέω as "worship" in Acts 10:25. This translation misleads the modern reader. Some appearances of the word in the writings of Josephus lend additional semantic range to the word in the first and second centuries CE and clarify its use in 10:25. In Josephus, the gesture appears between human beings and appears to be a sign of submission. When David and Jonathan say farewell, David "fell at Jonathan's feet and [showed obeisance], calling him the preserver of his life. But Jonathan raised him from the ground, and putting their arms about one another, they took a long and tearful farewell . . ." Josephus, *Ant.* 1:6.240 (Thackeray, LCL). For other

Luke-Acts provide instances of this type of obeisance. These instances illuminate the physical movement in the scene. Often in the *Antiquities*, προσκυνέω refers to a gesture that takes place between a person endowed with superior authority, such as a king or a prophet, and a subject. The definition of προσκυνέω in Acts 10 concurs with usage of the word elsewhere in Luke-Acts and in Josephus. In Luke 4, the devil shows Jesus "in an instant all the kingdoms of the world." The devil's promise of glory and authority comes with one condition: "if you . . . will show obeisance to me (προσκυνήσῃς, Luke 4:7). Such a gesture would indicate submission and obedience on Jesus' part. Jesus refuses to submit to that configuration of power. It is possible to translate the response of Jesus as "Submit to the Lord your God and serve only him" (4:8).

This encounter between the devil and Jesus provides additional insight into Acts 10:25 and a foundation for Luke's approach toward masculinity in Acts 10. As we have seen above, Cornelius knows when to take control, and in this instance, he relinquishes control as well. Men in the first and second century CE, especially military men, negotiated overt and covert hierarchies of authority. They demonstrated their ability to control others and the willingness to obey others. Here Cornelius relinquishes control by obeying the angel of God and by physically demonstrating his submission to Peter.

Peter's response to the προσκυνεῖν is the third way that Luke challenges Roman military masculinity and the centrality of control over other men. Instead of accepting Cornelius' gesture, Peter "made him get up, saying, 'Stand up; I am only a human being'" (ἄνθρωπός, Acts 10:26). Peter does not claim his authority or accept control over Cornelius. Peter does not endorse the submission of Cornelius. Peter does not claim political power, nor does he claim to be the superior officer of Cornelius. Instead of asking for submission, as the devil did in Luke 4:7, Peter rejects it.[107] In Acts 10:25, Luke reverses the scene in Luke 4:7, proposing a masculinity that does not seek recognition and superiority. Peter asserts his humanity, his lack of ties to the divine, and his equality with Cornelius. After the encounter, one can assume that

---

examples of the word in the writings of Josephus, as it occurs between human beings, see Josephus *Ant.*, 1:6.285, 334; 1.7.187, 211, 250, 268, 275, 330, 349.

107. Peter's rejection of the honor and authority inherent in προσκυνεῖν contrasts with Herod's acceptance of the claims that he was a god (Acts 12:22–23).

both Peter and Cornelius stand up, a physical recognition of equality before God.

While Cornelius is a model of masculinity for the audience of Luke-Acts, it is possible that Peter also functions as a model for Cornelius within the narrative. When Cornelius falls to the feet of Peter in 10:25, Peter indicates to Cornelius that honor should be directed toward God. Through Peter's admission of mortality and humble recognition of his own limitation, Cornelius learns how to be a man who honors God. God alone deserves allegiance. The parallel visions and obedient responses of Peter and Cornelius in Acts 10 link the two men together, yet Peter's response to the προσκυνεῖν distinguishes Peter as one who helps Cornelius understand the true nature of sovereignty. Peter insists that Cornelius is not to treat him as an emperor. Instead, sovereignty belongs to the God of Israel. Peter's response shows that he also embodies the virtues of humility and obeisance, both central to Luke's model men and to the story as a whole.

A number of dynamics in Acts 10:25–26 may have been surprising to ancient audiences. Cornelius' gesture toward Peter is unusual because Cornelius, a military officer, acknowledges a superior authority at work in an "unlettered" Judean (ἀγράμματοι, Acts 4:13). While some Roman military men show obeisance to the God of Israel in the writings of Josephus, Luke uses προσκυνεῖν to subvert Roman military authority and to present a man who understands the difference between the power of God and the power of Rome. This gesture coincides with Luke's theme of subversion in the Magnificat. Mary proclaims, "He has shown strength with his arm; he has scattered the proud in the thoughts of their hearts. He has brought down the powerful from their thrones, and lifted up the lowly" (Luke 1:51–52). The uneducated Peter represents the lowly. Michael Thomas comments on this theme, made clear in the προσκυνεῖν: "Roman centurions, even in their role as diplomats and peacekeepers, did not habitually fall in reverence at the feet of conquered peoples or their gods. This seemingly minor detail, which would have delighted Luke's Christian readers, functions as part of a clear message: eventually, Rome will submit to Christ."[108] In an histori-

---

108. Thomas, "World Turned Upside-Down," 459. Thomas argues that Acts 10 and other passages in Acts have elements of satire and carnival, "a popular festival form that draws on the power of art in order to undercut the politically and religiously powerful. Carnival, like previous ironic models, mocks the sacred and ridicules all that is

cal era dominated by elites who sought honor, and in a narrative world where the devil seeks honor, Luke redirects the audience toward the true nature of authority and honor. By means of a gesture of submission and its rejection by Peter, Luke critiques empire through a representative of empire, and proposes a masculinity that is based on obedience to the God of Israel alone.[109]

Luke's rhetorical strategy regarding masculinity and empire also makes itself known in the characterization of centurions elsewhere in Luke-Acts. Although the term προσκυνεῖν does not appear in Luke 7, the centurion seeks the power of Jesus, despite his own admission that military authority runs counter to that of Jesus.[110] In the barracks where Paul is kept in Acts 23, the centurion obeys Paul as if Paul were a commanding officer. When Paul asks the centurion to take "this young man to the tribune, for he has something to report to him," the centurion obeys. "So he took him," Luke writes, "brought him to the tribune, and said, 'The prisoner Paul called me and asked me to bring this young man to you'" (23:17–18). It was probably unusual for a centurion to obey a prisoner, but Luke shows it nonetheless. Julius the centurion, in Acts 27, also listens to Paul the prisoner; in response to Paul's admonition that all of the prisoners should stay on the ship, the centurion cuts loose a boat that could have been used to escape (27:31–32). None of these centurions indicate through dialogue or gesture that anything is unusual about seeking a Judean healer or obeying a prisoner. Instead, they simply recognize the authority in their midst and relinquish control over their actions. Conway suggests that in Acts, "belief in Jesus enables one to achieve true masculinity—to become a manly man."[111] However, more than belief is necessary. Manly men submit to the authority of the

---

unyieldingly authoritarian." Ibid., 454. For Luke, "upside-down" may be "right-side up."

109. Gilbert, "Roman Propaganda and Christian Identity," 255. Gilbert states, "the writer of Luke-Acts claims for Jesus and the church the same titles and achievements commonly associated with Rome: savior, bringer of peace, ascension into heaven, and ruler of the world. . . . Luke-Acts generates a vigorous critique of Rome and its claims to universal authority-indeed, a rival to Rome's claim to be ruler of the world." See also Gilbert, "Luke-Acts and Negotiation," 104.

110. Conway sees common ground between the centurion in Luke 7 and Jesus: "[The centurion] knows what it is like to speak and have his soldiers and slaves obey. Moreover, he recognizes in Jesus a similar power." Conway, Behold the Man, 133.

111. Ibid. It is not immediately clear what Conway means by "belief." It is possible that submission is a part of belief, in her argument.

God of Israel, obey messengers commissioned by God, and do what the messengers tell them to do.

The Holy Spirit Is in Control

Within the storyworld of Acts, Cornelius and other centurions submit to God, as does Peter when he insists, "Stand up; I am only a man." These men obey the God of Israel, known in Luke-Acts as the Holy Spirit. In Luke-Acts, the Holy Spirit is a creative power that equips people, including Jesus, to recognize and witness to the work of God. The Holy Spirit is the true authority, to which the protagonists submit. The Holy Spirit leads and directs the protagonists from the beginning of the narrative (Acts 1:8) to the end (28:25). In Acts 2, the prophecy of Joel indicates that the Spirit will be poured out on all flesh, and many of the events in the story signal that the prophecy has been fulfilled.[112] The Holy Spirit orchestrates the movement of the apostles through visions and dreams, and those visions and dreams guide the men to one another and toward people who have never heard of the Holy Spirit (8:14–17). As recipients of the Spirit's direction, the apostles and other characters are instruments and subordinates of the Holy Spirit. The characters are not physically coerced or forced to do what the Holy Spirit commands. Instead, they interact with and speak with the Holy Spirit, moving from one location to the other in response to the Spirit's guidance. Conway suggests that in Luke-Acts, "we enter a narrative world that is completely at home within the masculine power structures of the Roman Empire."[113] Conway is correct to suggest that the narrative world of Luke-Acts has within it a power structure that is based on authority and obedience.

However, the apostles are not in control. The apostles and Cornelius are not "fully capable of holding their own in the upper echelons of the masculine world of the Roman Empire."[114] The Holy Spirit fills them, directs them from within, and guides them from without with visions and other manifestations of the Spirit.[115] As a result, they are not "leading

---

112. Acts 2:17–21.

113. Conway, *Behold the Man*, 127.

114. Ibid.

115. Luke often uses the verb πίμπλημι to describe the way in which the Holy Spirit works. Using this verb specifically, in Luke, the Holy Spirit fills Jesus (1:15), Elizabeth (1:41) and Zechariah (1:67). In Acts, the Holy Spirit fills a diverse group in Jerusalem (2:4), Peter (4:8), John and friends (4:31), Paul (13:9). Other words describe the work of

men," as one might find in a novel or film. Nor are they "self-made men." Instead they rely on directions from the Holy Spirit.[116] When Cornelius and the people hear the words of Peter, the Holy Spirit falls on them, taking control of the proceedings: "ἐπέπεσεν τὸ πνεῦμα τὸ ἅγιον ἐπὶ πάντας τοὺς ἀκούοντας τὸν λόγον" (10:44). Peter likens this experience to Pentecost (2:1-4; 11:15), when the Holy Spirit took over the scene early in the story. As an agent of the Holy Spirit, Peter then commands them in the Spirit (προσέταξεν δὲ αὐτοὺς ἐν τῷ ὀνόματι) to be baptized (10:48). The Spirit's arrival has caused a reversal in power between Cornelius and Peter. While the Spirit is still in control, the Judean subject now commands the centurion and his household to be baptized, and they obey.

This Spirit's initiative and interaction with the characters in the story has rhetorical impact for the audience of Acts. Through the power of the Holy Spirit operating within key characters in Acts, Luke refashions masculinity for his audiences. Peter, Cornelius, and others emerge as models of submission to the God of Israel, and models of masculinity for the emerging church. Men can be empowered by the Spirit to lead lives of service and obedience. Their accomplishments are not their own, and they do not seek recognition for their deeds. Instead, they communicate with and respond to the Holy Spirit, the true source of power in the story. This rhetorical impact likely empowered audiences to serve one another and to listen for the voice of the Spirit. The baptism of Cornelius and Cornelius' household and close friends urges the audience to be baptized. Luke is showing his audiences that good men respond to the Holy Spirit and are baptized, for there is nothing to hinder them (10:47).

Subverting Expectations: Absence of Physical Force between Romans and Judeans

The second major difference between the expectations of Luke's audiences regarding Roman military masculinity and the characterization of Cornelius revolves around the issue of physical force or physical coercion.[117] Luke characterizes Cornelius as an officer who, despite his ability

---

the Holy Spirit in men in Acts: πλήθω and multiple forms of πληρόω.

116. The Holy Spirit directs the apostles in Acts 1:2; 8:39; 10:19; 11:12; 13:2, 4; 15:28; 16:6-7 (twice), 20:22-3. The Holy Spirit empowers and equips men to speak in Acts 7:55; 9:17; 10:38, 45; 20:28; 21:11; 28:25.

117. In this study, I use physical force or physical coercion interchangeably.

to use physical force on subjects of the empire, does not do so. Luke critiques the empire as a whole by describing the encounter between Cornelius and Peter as a series of events that are free of violent conquest. Physical force or coercion is not necessarily a foregone conclusion in every corner of the empire, and centurions were not necessarily brutal. However, it is reasonable to assume that when Acts was written, Roman-Judean tensions still circulated in Judea. In the Roman-Jewish war, Roman military men asserted their dominion through conquest and the use of force in Judea. Luke critiques this dominion through the presentation of an alternative model of military masculinity. It is also reasonable to assume that centurions had the training and authority to use force to subdue subjects of the empire who resisted Roman rule. Yet like other centurions in Acts, Cornelius does not act in the ways that the post-war Judean audience may have expected him to act. Cornelius does not force Peter into submission; nor does he seem to represent a threat to the Judean people. Instead, the opposite occurs. Cornelius does not use force. He is subject to the power of the Holy Spirit. To sharpen his critique of Roman dominion, Luke sets the encounter between Cornelius and Peter in Caesarea, a city saturated with empire. This section will explore how physical force plays a role in Roman military training, how it takes shape in literary portrayals and images of centurions outside the New Testament, and how it plays out (or not) in Luke-Acts.

Roman military masculinity valued physical combat and victory through the clash of bodies and weapons.[118] According to Richard Alston, the writings of Tacitus reveal military masculinity and its differences from elite Greco-Roman masculinity. While elite Greco-Roman men could control the boundaries of their own bodies, military men were subject to beatings in combat and from their own superiors.[119] Tacitus describes the mutinous soldiers of the imperial army, after the death of Augustus, as "men of low-status, trouble-makers, and rabble-rousers.

---

118. Elite Greco-Roman masculinity prized the ability of a man to control the boundaries of his own body, a dynamic not typically possible in the military realm. Walters writes, "Viewed from this perspective, the Roman soldier, symbol of all that is manly in Roman society, is dangerously like the slave, that ever-present, unmanly inferior and outsider." Walters, "Invading the Roman Body," 40.

119. "The status of being a respectable, freeborn Roman citizen was thus marked, at least in theory, on the corporeal level by bodily inviolability. Roman citizens, however low their social status, were not to be beaten, raped, or otherwise assaulted." Walters, "Invading the Roman Body," 38–39; Alston, "Arms and the Man," 218–19.

They were men who were subject to beatings and who were unfree."[120] The generals of these soldiers inspected the men and observed their scars. "Scars from battle were marks of honour in the Republican period, but these were scars from beatings administered by the centurions."[121] Distasteful to generals and elites, these soldiers were mutinous, undisciplined, and "enslaved to their officers and to their emotions."[122] The ability to control the boundaries of one's body and to protect it from harm thus distinguishes the elite from the non-elite, in this case, the elite from the soldier.[123]

Military training relied on physical coercion and created its own sort of masculine values and ideals. David Potter states that military service was "intended to enhance the aggressiveness" of young men.[124] "Pity was not a virtue; when the enemy turned in flight, it was time to strike him down."[125] According to Martin Goodman, "dehumanizing the enemy was the key to Roman military success . . ."[126] Organized training and military discipline "were calculated to transform a young man into precisely the kind of killer that the nature of combat demanded."[127] After the Romans defeated their enemies, the subjugation continued: "The Romans treated defeated enemies with a ruthlessness unusual in the ancient world . . . Roman soldiers expected to indulge in extreme violence in the sack of cities at the close of the siege. They treated a period of looting, rape and indiscriminate slaughter of civilians as a natural reward for soldiers as recompense for their efforts. It is unsurprising that many of their opponents preferred to make terms and surrender rather

---

120. Alston, "Arms and the Man," 216. Alston directs his readers to Tacitus, *Ann.* 1:16–49.

121. Ibid.

122. Ibid.

123. Fisher writes that even in elite circles, some forms of violence existed. Fisher defines this kind of violence as social insult or physical coercion. "The main settings for such insults and acts of violence are naturally the *gymnasia* and shared meals/drinking parties, and the main stimuli, the common factors of drink and sexual rivalries . . ." Fisher continues, "finally, it should be emphasized that casual violence against dependents and slaves, and the beating of children were all likely to have been common." Fisher, "Violence, Masculinity, and the Law," 75, 77.

124. Potter, "Introduction," 10.

125. Ibid.

126. Goodman, *Rome and Jerusalem*, 335.

127. Potter, "Introduction," 10.

than risk facing such savagery."[128] Outside of battle and organized campaigns, the emperor depended on the military to maintain law and order among themselves and throughout occupied territory; maintenance of the empire included the authority to use violent means, if necessary.[129] The emperor, and the empire as a whole, depended on men who could coerce subjects into submission.[130] Representatives of the empire such as soldiers and centurions could also abuse their power and coerce civilians into serving them or performing duties for them.[131]

Ancient literary remains show the relationship between military conquest and masculinity for both elites and non-elites. Roman military men and emperors displayed their manhood through subjection of other peoples to Roman rule. While the reign of Augustus could be characterized by *pax*, Augustan "peace" arrived after he expanded the empire and conquered numerous territories. *Pax* entailed domination.[132] In the *Res Gestae*, Augustus states, "The Parthians I compelled to restore to me the spoils and standards of three Roman armies . . ."[133] This compulsion likely involved military force, and Augustus takes credit for the accomplishments of his soldiers. Undoubtedly the threat of subjugation at the hands of the Roman military played a role as well. In the funeral procession of Augustus, "all the nations he had acquired, each represented by a likeness which bore some local characteristic, appeared

---

128. Goodman, *Rome and Jerusalem*, 338.

129. Campbell, *Emperor*, vii.

130. While a soldier's life could be characterized as masculine, it did have drawbacks. Two speakers in Plato's *Laws* discuss the children of Cyrus, who "spent all his life from boyhood in soldiering, and entrusted his children to the womenfolk to rear up . . ." Cyrus "overlooked the fact that his sons were trained by women and eunuchs and that the indulgences shown them as 'Heaven's darlings' had ruined their training." One speaker continues, "Such an upbringing can never produce either boy or man or greybeard of surpassing goodness." Plato, *Leg.* 3:694–96 (Bury, LCL).

131. Campbell suggests that Matt 5:41 is a reference to a soldier who could force a civilian to "go the second mile" and act as a guide for military men in the area. According to Campbell, "it is true that the soldiers who misbehaved in Egypt and Judaea were generally on service detached from their units, but this practice was widespread in the provinces in the empire. We hear more of military misconduct in Egypt precisely because there is more evidence from Egypt for life under Roman rule, and also evidence that relates to the common people." Campbell, *Emperor*, 250.

132. Galinsky, *Augustan Culture*, 132; Campbell, *Emperor*, 146.

133. *Res gest. divi Aug.* 5:29 (Shipley, LCL).

in the procession."¹³⁴ Augustus is a dominant man, and the procession gives the impression that his people remembered his as such. Vespasian celebrated his own dominance in an elaborate triumph over Judea, detailed by Josephus in this scene:

> The war was shown by numerous representations . . . affording a very vivid picture of its episodes. Here was to be seen a prosperous country devastated, there whole battalions of the enemy slaughtered; here a party in flight, there others led into captivity; walls of surpassing compass demolished by engines, strong fortresses overpowered, cities with well-manned defences completely mastered and an army pouring within the ramparts, an area all deluged with blood, the hands of those incapable of resistance raised in supplication . . .¹³⁵

The grandness of this triumph feeds into ideals of Roman dominance and the superiority of the Roman military. These military men rule, and they rule by means of force. Their celebrations include parades that show, scene by scene, violent takeovers and the subjugation of peoples.

Some ancient remains link centurions specifically to the authority to use physical force and to domination by means of force. Because of their batons, with which they maintained order among military ranks, centurions were peculiarly qualified to coerce men physically and to ensure domination. Alston comments on this connection: "Military service also gave soldiers increased power to inflict violence."¹³⁶ "The sticks were to chastise. They are as much a symbol of their superiority as the riding down of the barbarian."¹³⁷ Tacitus describes one centurion who was nicknamed "Fetch Another" because he frequently broke his stick on the back of another person. "Camp humorists had surnamed him 'Fetch-Another,' from his habit, as one cane broke over a private's back, of calling at the top of his voice for a second, and ultimately a third."¹³⁸ Gravestones sometimes depict centurions with their batons; one such gravestone was found near Prusa, in Bithynia.¹³⁹ Another gravestone,

---

134. Cassius, *Rom. hist.* 56:34 (Cary, LCL).

135. Josephus, *War* 7:142–44 (Thackeray, LCL); Suetonius, *Vesp.* 8:1.

136. Alston, "Arms and the Man," 218–19.

137. Ibid.

138. Tacitus, *Ann.* 1:23 (Jackson, LCL).

139. For a drawing of the gravestone, see Speidel, "Bithynian Gravestones," 183. The drawing is attributed to Lebas.

dated to the mid first century CE, features the centurion Marcus Favonius Facilis, stationed in Britain, baton in hand.[140] In some writings of Josephus, centurions are the aggressors. Centurions of Sossius climbed the walls of Jerusalem and "leapt into the city" during a siege.[141] Centurions and their dominance even become material for satirists; Juvenal's sixth satire states that if a soldier has a complaint, "he has appointed for him as judge a hob-nailed centurion with a row of jurors with brawny calves sitting before a big bench."[142]

One particular portrayal of a centurion in the *Jewish War* deserves special mention. This portrayal simultaneously highlights the brutality of centurions toward Judeans and exemplary Roman bravery in combat. The centurion Julianus, a man of "strength of body and intrepidity of soul," "single-handedly drove back the Jews...."[143] Josephus continues,

> the multitude fled in crowds before him, regarding such strength and courage as superhuman; while he, dashing this way and that through the midst of their scattering ranks, slew all whom he overtook, and no spectacle that met the eye of Caesar was more wonderful than that, nor more terrifying to his foes. Yet, after all, he too was to be dogged by Destiny, whom no mortal man may escape. For, wearing, like any other soldier, shoes thickly studded with sharp nails, while running across the pavement, he slipped and fell on his back, with a loud clash of armour, which made the fugitives turn.[144]

The Judean forces heard the clash of armor on the pavement, and "crowding round him struck at him at all sides with swords and spears."[145] Although he fought valiantly, he succumbed. "Caesar was deeply moved at the fall of so valiant a soldier."[146] Despite the ignominy of a death as-

---

140. Ferguson, *Backgrounds of Early Christianity*, 50. This gravestone can be seen in the Colchester and Essex Museum.

141. Josephus, *War* 1:149 (Thackeray, LCL); 1:351.

142. Juvenal, *Sat.* 16 (Ramsay, LCL).

143. Josephus, *War* 6:8 (Thackeray, LCL).

144. Ibid.

145. Ibid.

146. Ibid. In another instance, the centurion Priscus shot a Judean with an arrow, but in this instance, the Judean was gloating over the corpse of a Roman soldier. Josephus writes that the Judean was "trampling on the corpse, brandishing his bloody sword and with his left hand waving the buckler, he shouted lustily to the army, glorying over his prostrate foe and jeering at his Roman spectators, until, in the midst of his

sociated with one's own shoes, Josephus brings to light the Roman sense of military honor and presents an ideal Roman warrior in the centurion Julianus.[147]

In addition to literary portrayals, one might also consider visual images of military men. An essay by Davina Lopez is helpful at this point.[148] Lopez suggests that material remains and images of men during the first and second centuries CE can inform our interpretation of New Testament texts. Images reveal power relations and understandings of masculinity circulating during the time that the New Testament was written. Biblical scholars can study those images in order to compare and contrast constructs of gender in New Testament texts. Lopez draws attention to the work of gender historians and scholars of Roman art, who have concluded that images and depictions of men in antiquity say something about masculinity. "Images functioned as active participants in the political programs and agendas of their patrons, who used the representation of manliness as a vehicle for representing legitimacy of rule, authority, and military victory," writes Natalie Boymel Kampen.[149] Since images were a means of communication in the Roman world, Roman military masculinity was not solely a literary or textual phenomenon. Images of military men and their dominance over other nations made constructs of gender public and available to people who could not read.[150]

In her essay, Lopez discusses images on imperial coinage. These images of violence and domination communicate a military masculinity that asserts and maintains power over other nations. In general, coins are a means to disseminate information and images throughout the empire.[151] The Capta coin type features a representative of a subjugated

---

dancing and buffoonery, Priscus, a centurion, bent his bow and transfixed him with an arrow . . ." Josephus, *War* 6:175–76 (Thackeray, LCL). Josephus tells this story as if the Judean deserved death, and the centurion's actions seem justified in this rhetorical context.

147. For Barton, Roman honor involved desperation and adversity. Roman military masculinity thrived on the concept that desperate, risky situations made males into men. Barton, *Roman Honor*, 52–54.

148. Lopez, "Before Your Very Eyes"; Lopez, *Apostle to the Conquered*, 26–55.

149. Kampen, "What Is a Man?" 7; Kampen, "Gender Theory in Roman Art"; Osborne, "Sculpted Men of Athens."

150. Literacy was not widespread in the first and second centuries CE. It is possible that 85–90 percent of the people in the Roman Empire could not read.

151. Campbell, *Imperial Roman Army*, 121. Mattingly argues that the emperor played a central role in the development of and dissemination of his image. Mattingly,

people and a representative of the Roman military, often the emperor. The defeated person espouses a dejected physical posture, either seated and mourning, or bowing to the victorious warrior. The military man stands tall over the subject or stands behind the subject. This persistent symbolism appears in coinage from the reign of Augustus to the reign of Trajan. Coins minted during the Augustan era feature a military man standing over representatives of Parthia,[152] Domitian over Germanica,[153] and Trajan over Dacia.[154] Of the most relevance, however, are the Judea Capta coins.[155] On most of these coins, the reverse shows a female representative of Judea, depicted as a woman.[156] These coins appear most often during the reign of Vespasian,[157] but some appear during the reigns of Titus[158] and Domitian.[159] While coins were not the only way in which constructs of gender, Roman violence, and Roman dominance were circulated, they allow a glimpse into the masculine ideals of the empire and the experience of the nations subdued by it.[160]

The military men in these images are not all centurions, but the model Roman military man in these remains, both literary and material, seeks and maintains dominance over other nations. This dominance sometimes takes shape in celebration, as emperors parade their

Coins of the Roman Empire, 3:xlix, xlv. However, Galinsky argues that the emperor was not in control of his own image, and the depictions on coins were left up to the mint-maker. Galinsky, *Augustan Culture*, 30.

152. Mattingly, *Coins of the Roman Empire*, 1:ciii, 3.

153. Ibid., 2:xlv, 5.

154. Ibid., 3:lxix, 57.

155. The "Judea Capta" phrase refers to the legend on the reverse, in the exergue. According to Painter, the "Judea Capta" coins were "probably minted at Caesarea." She argues that these coins "were a visible means of showing imperial power and prestige in Palestine." Painter, "Greco-Roman Religion," 111n21.

156. Lopez, "Before Your Very Eyes," 121. Not all the Judean subjects appear as women on the Judea Capta coins. Other Judean subjects appear as men or children.

157. For examples of Judea Capta coins during the reign of Vespasian, see Mattingly, *Coins of the Roman Empire*, 2:xxxiii, xxxv, xlv. This volume provides pictures and descriptions of at least sixty-seven Judea Capta coins from the reign of Vespasian. On most of the examples, Judea is represented as a woman.

158. Ibid., 2:lxxvi.

159. Ibid., 2:xcii, 369.

160. One could also consider the cuirass of the statue of Augustus of Prima Porta. On this see Lopez, "Before Your Very Eyes," 123–33; Galinsky, *Augustan Culture*, 107. In addition to the material remains in Lopez's essay, see Lepper and Frere, *Trajan's Column*.

emblems through the streets, re-enacting their brutal victories. At other times, this dominance takes shape through suggestive, more indirect means, such as the centurion posing with his baton in his hand. At still other times, the dominance takes shape through the effeminization of Rome's enemies and subjects. Whatever the medium, Rome maintains a hegemony over subject peoples through forceful conquest. Rome asserts its power over Judea and other nations, and fashions its military men in a way that reflects that power.[161]

In contrast to these extrabiblical portrayals of Roman military men, Luke depicts Cornelius in a submissive posture to a Judean subject. This portrayal stands out as unusual for two reasons: first, centurions had the authority to use physical force if necessary, and second, many Roman literary portrayals and images idealize physical coercion at the hands of the military. In addition, it is possible that Roman military men could move beyond legal enforcement, abuse their power, and use undue violence. Even if physical coercion was not carried out, centurions and other military men represented the *threat* of force.[162] Given the memories of the war between the Romans and Judeans, which took place only one generation prior to the writing of Luke-Acts, the portrayal of a nonviolent and submissive centurion may have surprised Judean audiences. While the social location of Luke's audiences is not yet fully resolved among scholars, it is reasonable to infer from the narrative that Luke's audiences had some grasp of Roman occupation and the defeat at Roman hands, as well as the destruction it entailed. Luke uses these memories as a contrasting backdrop behind the interaction between Peter and Cornelius. Cornelius does not use physical force in the story, but Luke proposes that other characters do. In contrast to most extrabiblical sources, violent characters in Luke-Acts most often come from certain Jewish groups, Roman administrators, or client kings.

---

161. Goodman comments that the Roman attitude toward Judea was not always hostile, nor did Rome always seek to dominate Judea in a forceful way. "Roman comments about Jews were rarely hostile before the outbreak of war in 66. Far more common were amusement, indifference, acceptance, admiration, and emulation." Goodman observes that the most frequent views were "amusement at the celebration of the Sabbath, circumcised genitalia and strange food taboos . . ." Goodman, *Rome and Jerusalem*, 384.

162. About the threat of force, Goodman states, "Some emperors, including Augustus, came to the purple through military victories over their political opponents, but even those other emperors whose rule had started in more peaceful circumstances could still rely on the latent threat of force. Usually, the threat sufficed." Ibid., 371.

While the audience may have expected violence from Roman military men, Luke refashions military masculinity by characterizing Cornelius as a centurion who does not coerce Judean subjects physically and who treats these subjects as emissaries of God.[163] Luke disrupts the link between military men and the use of force, and he portrays Cornelius as a man who shows the utmost respect to Peter. In the words of Steve Walton, "Luke presents Roman officials and (especially) centurions positively, drawing attention to their godliness and justice."[164] Moreover, the events, dialogue, and interaction in Acts 10–11 are free of violence and Roman conquest, two themes that one often encounters in texts and images from the late first and early second centuries CE. As a military officer, and specifically as a centurion, Cornelius represented Roman law and order. His rank (and stick) equipped him to enforce that order. Instead, Cornelius submits to the Holy Spirit and gives up his power. As the προσκυνεῖν indicates, the source of power is the Holy Spirit, who directs the plot of Acts and the actions of the apostles. Luke presents a model man who relinquishes his authority to beat nations and subjects into submission. In the process, Luke reverses the hierarchy of authority and proposes a cosmic order based on the sovereignty of the God of Israel.

Luke's rhetorical strategy about centurions and physical force makes itself known in the descriptions of other centurions in Acts and the attribution of violent acts toward certain Jewish groups, a Roman administrator, and a client king. Luke directs his audience away from centurions as bastions of brutality and toward other sources of destructive power. While some military figures in Acts do use physical force, most centurions mitigate the coercion already being used against the protagonists, or they prevent bodily harm altogether.[165] Luke repeatedly portrays centurions as positive role models, emphasizing their respect for Jesus, Peter or Paul.[166] Physical coercion often comes instead from

---

163. As one who rejects violence, Cornelius stands in line with the teachings of Jesus in Luke-Acts. See Luke 6:27–31; 9:51–56.

164. Walton, "State They Were In," 22.

165. Relevant texts include Luke 8:29; 12:11; 22:52; 23:11; Acts 5:23, 40; 12:4; 21:33; 22:24, 27:42.

166. Luke 7:1–10; 23:47; Acts 10:25; 22:25–26; 23:17–18; 27:43. Some nuance should be noted here. The centurion at the foot of the cross of Jesus apparently proceeded with the crucifixion, despite his statement that Jesus was innocent (Luke 23). In addition, the centurion who stood near Paul in Acts may have allowed Paul to be

certain Jewish groups in the narrative.¹⁶⁷ Conway suggests that self-control was a manly trait, and that the presence of anger reveals the absence of self-control.¹⁶⁸ Given this framework, the anger, rage, and jealousy of some Jewish groups give the impression that these antagonists are not really men.¹⁶⁹ These negative examples of masculinity include Pilate¹⁷⁰ and Herod, who embraces violence as a means to control the movement in Acts, but who does not succeed in that quest.¹⁷¹ In contrast to these negative examples, Cornelius rejects violence and emerges as a positive role model for men in Luke's community.¹⁷²

Subverting Expectations: Geographical Setting and Critique of the Empire

The events in Acts 10 take place in Caesarea Maritima. By means of this geographical setting, Luke critiques the dominance of the empire and brings to light the superior power of the God of Israel. The city of Caesarea stood as a testament to Roman power and to Augustus,

---

flogged, had Paul not said that he was a Roman citizen (Acts 22).

167. Luke 22:54; Acts 2:22; 3:12; 4:1–3; 5:17–18; 5:30, 40; 6:12; 7:52, 58; 8:1–2; 13: 28; 14:19; 17:5; 18:12, 17; 21:27; 23:2, 10; 26:21. This pattern does not necessarily indicate an anti-Jewish perspective on Luke's part. Luke maintains his interest in Hebrew Bible prophecy (Acts 2:17–21; 15:16–18, among other examples) and his understanding of Jesus is based on the Hebrew concept of the Messiah (Acts 2:31; 3:18). The attribution of violence to some Jewish groups in Luke-Acts indicates intra-Jewish conflict between Luke's community and other Jews, who likely had competing visions of the people of Israel. As Penner and Vander Stichele indicate, violence "demarcates as righteous the insiders, who remain faithful in the face of threats to their lives, while depicting those outside of the community as lacking such virtue." Penner and Vander Stichele, "Gendering Violence," 195. Violence demarcates and denotes insiders and outsiders in Acts, but it can also indicate intra-Jewish conflict.

168. Conway, *Behold the Man*, 26–29.

169. Luke 4:28; Acts 23:10.

170. Luke 13:1–2; 23:24. The portrayals of Roman administrators and client kings in Luke-Acts are not consistent. The conflicting portrayals frustrate scholars who attempt to collate the representatives of the empire into neat categories. For a summary of views on Luke-Acts and empire, see Walton, "State They Were In."

171. Luke 3:20; 9:9; Acts 12:1–5, 19. In this way, Herod has something in common with demons, who also do violent acts but who are cast out. See Luke 4:35; 8:26–39; 9:37–43; Acts 5:16; 16:16–18; 19:11–12, 13–16.

172. About models of masculinity in Acts, Conway writes, "Luke's work is the most explicitly concerned with showing Jesus and the leading figures of the emerging Christian community as models of masculinity." Conway, *Behold the Man*, 129.

the first emperor. "King Herod the Great founded Caesarea Maritima between 22 and 10/9 BCE,"[173] and he established an elaborate harbor there.[174] The harbor, which extended out into the water, displayed the ability of Romans to control nature and to carve out of earth and water a symbol of Roman dominion. Herod also built an extravagant palace on the promontory overlooking the water. Excavators Ehud Netzer and others "have brought to light a palatial complex on two terraces, with porticoes, dining and reception suites, and a small Roman-style bath, well-integrated with the theater and the amphitheater."[175] According to Josephus, Agrippa promoted the connection between Caesarea and Rome with games and spectacles; he "celebrated spectacles in honour of Caesar, knowing that these had been instituted as a kind of festival on behalf of Caesar's well-being."[176] Murray states that Caesarea "became the administrative and military centre of the Roman government [in Judea], rivaling Jerusalem alone in influence over the country."[177] Vespasian made Caesarea a Roman colony, giving it the title *Colonia Prima Flavia Caesarensis*,[178] and the colony was "repopulated, in place of the former Jewish residents, with retired Roman soldiers."[179] For these reasons, residents of Caesarea would have been immersed in symbols, art, architecture, and festivals that celebrate the power of Rome, despite its distance from the city itself.[180]

Luke uses this geographical setting, known for its dominance and conflict with Judeans, to showcase an alternative authority and an alternative way of being a man. In some ancient writings, Caesarea was a pre-war hotspot for ethnic tension and a locale for Roman-Judean

---

173. Lehmann and Holum, *Greek and Latin Inscriptions*, 1.

174. Ibid.

175. Ibid., 12.

176. Josephus, *Ant.* 19:343 (Feldman, LCL). For more about Caesarea in the writings of Josephus, see *War* 1:408; *Ant.* 20:174. In *War* 7:37–39, Titus "celebrates his brother's birthday with great splendour" in Caesarea, "reserving in his honor for this festival much of the punishment of his Jewish captives. For the number of those destroyed in contests with wild beasts or with one another or in the flames exceeded two thousand five hundred." (Thackeray, LCL).

177. Murray, "Jews and Judaism," 131.

178. Painter, "Greco-Roman Religion," 111–12.

179. Goodman, *Rome and Jerusalem*, 460.

180. For more on the city and its connections with empire, see Raban and Holum, *Caesarea Maritima*.

conflict. About Caesarea before the war, Goodman states, "intercommunal violence in the city was temporarily crushed by the military force at the disposal of the governor Felix, and to resolve the issue embassies were sent from both sides to Nero in Rome, but when Nero favoured the argument of the gentile inhabitants, the Jews were not satisfied and Josephus reports the allegations of corruption."[181] Caesarea continued to be a place of political, religious, and ethnic tension during and after the war. According to Lee Johnson, ancient writings reveal that "Caesarea became the base of operations for the Roman military, first for Cestius, the governor of Syria . . . then for Vespasian . . . and finally for Titus."[182] In *Jewish War*, during the reign of the Roman administrator Florus, "within one hour more than twenty thousand were slaughtered, and Caesarea was completely emptied of Jews, for the fugitives were arrested by orders of Florus and conducted, in chains, to dockyards."[183] Yet in Acts 10, we find very few traces of Roman violence, minimal conflict between Romans and Judeans, and only mild tension between the authorities of Rome and the God of the Judeans. Instead, we see a Roman military man demonstrating his submission to an emissary of God, relinquishing his authority to control Judeans, and confessing with his body the power of the God of Israel. Cornelius' submission takes on additional significance and subverts the Roman power structure that would likely have been apparent to Luke's community. The city of Caesarea evokes a hierarchy of authority in which Rome is at the top, but Luke redraws those lines and places the God of the Judeans at the top.[184]

The positive characteristics of Cornelius stand out in comparison to the negative models of masculinity associated with Caesarea in Luke-Acts. In the narrative, Caesarea is the home of ineffectual Roman men who cannot control themselves or others. In Acts 24:24–27, the governor Felix exemplifies fear and weakness. Even though Paul discusses

---

181. Goodman, *Rome and Jerusalem*, 411.

182. Johnson, "Literary Guide," 42. Johnson here refers to Josephus, *War* 2:507–13; 3:409–13; 4.663; 5:140. Painter states that Vespasian and Titus "awaited the outcome of the civil war" in Caesarea, and that Titus was eventually declared emperor there. Painter, "Origins and Social Context of Mithraism," 215. Painter directs readers to Tacitus, *Histories* 2:79–80; 5:10.

183. Josephus, *War* 2:457 (Thackeray, LCL). Josephus may exaggerate here, but the numbers nonetheless indicate a bloody massacre.

184. For more on Caesarea as the setting for a critique of the empire and its representatives, see Howell, "Imperial Authority," 35–36.

"justice, self-control, and coming judgment," Felix "becomes frightened," and cannot control his emotions (24:25). Felix sends for Paul often, hoping for a bribe rather than Paul's thoughts on self-control (24:26). Some "Jews" control Felix rather than himself; he "wanted to grant the Jews a favor, Felix left Paul in prison" (24:27). Likewise, Festus wished "to do the Jews a favor" and asked Paul if he would like to be transferred to Jerusalem, where his opponents awaited him (25:9). Despite their affiliation with the empire, these men are controlled by the opponents of Paul. In Caesarea as well are the headquarters of Herod. After he ordered guards to be executed, he "went down to Caesarea and stayed there." These guards were unable to keep Peter in prison (12:19).[185] The geographical setting of Caesarea reveals Luke's strategy to critique the use of force through the absence of force, empire through a representative of empire, and negative exemplars of masculinity through positive exemplars of masculinity.

CONCLUSION

This chapter has discussed Luke's rhetorical strategy in Acts 10 and explored the characterization of Cornelius as Luke's model man. Cornelius has some features of centurions and Roman military masculinity that ancient audiences might have expected. These include the authority to control soldiers and civilians. Luke uses these similarities to ground his portrayal in verisimilitude and to encourage his audience to consider Cornelius a realistic male model. However, Cornelius also does some surprising things in Acts 10. He shows obedience toward the God of Israel, as opposed to a commanding military officer, and a makes a gesture of submission before a Judean. Cornelius' actions reveal Luke's rhetorical strategy with regard to masculinity, violence, and empire. Luke subverts ancient expectation in these ways, providing his community with a model of nonviolence and relinquishment before the God of Israel. Cornelius emerges as an exemplar of virtue and a different kind of man for the early church.

---

185. An exception should be noted. The evangelist Philip and his prophetic daughters live in Caesarea (Acts 21:8).

Conclusion

THESIS AND METHOD

THIS STUDY HAS ARGUED that Cornelius in Acts 10 is a model man for Luke's audience. While most scholars have focused on the role of Cornelius as a model Gentile, this study argues that he is also a model man. By means of the characterization of Cornelius, Luke lifts up a man whose key qualities are submission, piety, and generosity. The characterization of Cornelius has features that are both similar to and different from characterizations of men in contemporary extrabiblical evidence. Like some elite Greco-Roman and military men, Cornelius has the virtue of piety. His piety can be seen in the Greek words εὐσεβής, δίκαιος, and words relating to generosity. Unlike some other elite Greco-Roman and military men, Cornelius' piety is directed toward the God of Israel, a commitment that was likely complicated in light of his role as a centurion in the Roman military. The characterization of Cornelius also differs from some extrabiblical portrayals of centurions. Cornelius does not exercise his authority over Peter, a Judean subject. Luke portrays Cornelius' submission and giving up of control and authority through the gesture of προσυκνεῖν. In addition, Cornelius does not display the brutality toward Judean subjects that one might expect, given extrabiblical descriptions of centurions as well as the brutal subjugation of Judeans by the Romans described by Josephus in *Jewish War* and *Antiquities of the Jews*. Against the backdrop of the Roman-Jewish war, Cornelius' commitment, obeisance, and relinquishment of control appear all the more striking. The inclusion of Gentiles in general and Roman military men in particular reflects the diversity of the Way. Yet the characterization of Cornelius, which has some features in common with the characterization of Moses in the writings of Philo, also indicates that the Way has preserved continuity with Judaism.

Because this study analyzes features of a narrative such as characterization, rhetoric, gender, and standards of judgment, narrative criticism is a fitting method to use. A hermeneutic of masculinity can operate in conjunction with narrative criticism; in this study, the two have been fused in order to produce a reading that is attuned to narrative elements as well as constructs of masculinity in the narrative. A hermeneutic of masculinity is a way of reading ancient texts that critically assesses male characters, while keeping in mind ancient power imbalances between men and women, allowing for diversity among men, and recognizing rhetorical agendas. Feminist scholars have demonstrated how to think critically about portraits of female characters, and from feminists we have learned that there is no "unisex" approach to interpretation. Portraits of men in the New Testament can and should be critically explored using these feminist insights. However, analyzing portraits of men in the narrative is not "the flip side of the coin," as if men and women are granted equal time in the narrative or equal power in history. In order to preserve feminist work, interpreters of masculinity need to maintain the feminist assertions that New Testament texts emerge from patriarchal cultures and that our texts will reflect the cultures from which they arose.

WHAT KIND OF MAN IS THIS?

The argument in this book is based on the assumption that masculinity is a cultural construct that varies over time and space. Male is not neutral, and though we frequently encounter men in ancient sources, their masculinity (or lack thereof) can be further examined in light of ancient standards and values related to the behavior of men from that time and place. While available sources do not always allow us to pin down constructs of masculinity to a specific time and place, scholars can nonetheless set up historical parameters, and acknowledge the intricate and complicated nature of masculinity in the available sources. In some sources, and perhaps in all of them, politics, religion, and gender all come together in a single whole. Despite this complexity, scholars can

Conclusion

acknowledge that male characters are gendered. We can then ask: "What kind of man is this?"

First, Cornelius is a man who is a Gentile. To be specific, he is a Roman man. Although Luke does not explicitly call him a Gentile, the audience assumes that he is. Because of his role in the plot of Luke, as a Gentile convert, he represents the integration of the Gentiles into the Way. His conversion is foreshadowed by the baptism of the Ethiopian eunuch is Acts 8. The move toward Gentiles and the conversion of both Cornelius and the Ethiopian eunuch also represent the fulfillment of Hebrew Bible prophecy (Acts 2 and 15). The embrace of Gentiles as part of the movement in Acts is a result of God's initiative at Pentecost and at Cornelius' house in Acts 10. The events in Acts 10 lead toward the decisions made in Jerusalem regarding Gentiles who turn to God (15:19). The debate among Peter, the apostles, and the elders in Jerusalem results in stipulations that do not include some Jewish practices (15:19-21, 23-29). Even though Cornelius is a Roman God-fearer whose practices differ from circumcised Jews, Peter argues for his integration and for the embrace of Gentiles, for God "has made no distinction between them and us" (15:9).

Second, Cornelius is a man who is pious. He exemplifies the virtue of piety. Luke characterizes Cornelius as εὐσεβής, δίκαιος, and one who fears God. Cornelius prays constantly, gives alms generously, and is respected by the entire Jewish nation. Luke repeats these descriptions of Cornelius in the narrative by having Luke, Cornelius, and Peter tell the story of how they came together in Caesarea. Both Jewish and Gentile audiences likely recognized these varied traits as traits associated with piety. Yet Luke carefully asserts that Cornelius is committed to the God of Israel. In these ways, Luke shows his audience what a good man looks like.

Third, Cornelius is a man who is a Roman centurion. He represents the power of the empire to the other characters and likely to Luke's audience as well. He acts like a Roman centurion in some ways. He interacts with and controls other soldiers and civilians. Yet he acts like a Jew in other ways. He prays, gives alms, and submits to the will of the God of Israel. These two dynamics—a Roman centurion on one hand and a convert to Judaism on the other—do not easily mesh. Many Romans saw the emperor as sovereign, but for Jews, the God of Israel was sovereign. Luke does not indicate that any difficulties resulted from these competing sovereignties, however. In fact, Luke makes it appear entirely possible for a military man to live a life committed to Jesus and Yahweh (Luke 3 and 7). Because of this combination of unusual traits, Cornelius is a hybrid man, whose commitment to the God of Israel is clearly portrayed at the expense of any difficulties associated with the practical aspects of it.

Despite any inherent historical difficulties or unique situations in Luke's story, Luke is free to write his story and establish his own standards of judgment. Authors set their own standards for what is good and bad, what is manly and unmanly. For Luke, the ultimate authority is the God of Israel. Colleen Conway states that in Luke-Acts, "belief in Jesus enables one to achieve true masculinity—to become a manly man."[1] It is probable that Luke is making a statement not only about the masculinity of Cornelius but the masculinity of good men in general. According to Howell, "it is obvious that [Luke] himself holds the values (e.g., generosity and almsgiving) that he attributes to Cornelius."[2] Here we glimpse the implied author of the story and the values that he considers worthwhile.

By identifying the standards of judgment operant in Acts 10, and by identifying which standards exemplify manliness in the entire story, we see how Luke challenges some understandings of masculinity in his day. Conway argues that the "mainstay of manliness is self-control."[3] In a similar vein, Craig Williams associates masculinity with "control and dominion."[4] Yet in Acts, the Holy Spirit is in control from beginning to end. The male protagonists are not "leading men." Instead, they follow the directions of the Spirit. The Holy Spirit is the true source of power in the story, and the men who are positively characterized recognize the Spirit as the ultimate authority.

AVENUES TO EXPLORE: METHOD

While this study has addressed some issues regarding gender and the interpretation of male characters, specifically Cornelius, this study has also generated questions that it was not able to answer fully. In this section I will identify some avenues that could be pursued with further research.

1. Conway, *Behold the Man*, 133.
2. Howell, "Imperial Authority," 42.
3. Conway, *Behold the Man*, 69.
4. Williams, *Roman Homosexuality*, 141.

The first avenue that could be explored in light of this research has to do with word fields relating to masculinity. Word fields are collections of words with meanings that revolve around a topic in ancient literature. The development of word fields could help an exegete do word studies and to identify characters that stand out as exemplars or failures of masculinity. With the help of a concordance, scholars could use word fields to identify primary sources that may inform our exegesis. These words could be in Greek or Latin, depending on the primary source, although Greek words may be more helpful when searching through the Greek of New Testament texts.

Some possibilities with regard to word fields can be mentioned here. When ancient authors praised men, they employed language about the masculinity of their subjects. Some key words for manly men include ἀνδρεία and its verb form ἀνδρίζω.[5] The noun form, ἀνδρεία, is often translated as "courage" or "bravery." These translations obscure the gendered nature of the original. Ἀνδρεία also means "manliness" or more precisely, "manly courage." It may be worthwhile to use these gendered translations in an English version of a text, and to consider how they modify the meaning(s). Richard Alston also identifies the Latin terms *vir* and *libertas*. *Libertas* "was the defining characteristic of the Roman *vir*."[6] Since softness was sometimes associated with effeminacy, an exegete could search for the Greek or Latin words associated with "hard," or from a philosophical point of view, perhaps "reason."

AVENUES TO EXPLORE: SOURCES

The identification of word fields may not be enough to study constructs of masculinity in texts. A purely philological approach targets potential sources, but limits the scope of inquiry. Issues relating to masculinity may appear in texts that do not have the specific words that the exegete

---

5. A relevant question may be, "To what degree does Cornelius exemplify manly courage?" In order to answer that question, one may need to identify a risk that necessitates a manly and courageous response. Given the resistance to conversion to Judaism in some texts (Suetonius, Dio Cassius, and the general anti-Jewish bias of Tacitus), one could suggest that converting to Judaism constitutes a risk. Domitian ordered some elite converts to be exiled. One wonders if the conversion of people who were not elite would garner the same kind of attention.

6. Alston, "Arms and the Man," 208.

has identified in advance. Exegetes need to take into account other forms of characterization as well, including rhetorical overtones, sensitivity to roles that each character might play (in a narrative context) and to religious, political, and ethnic dynamics that may underlie praise or invective. Material remains, such as inscriptions, and images of men may also inform our understanding of masculinity. In this section I will discuss possibilities relating to philosophical sources as well as material remains.

One avenue that could be explored with regard to sources has to do with the virtues of ancient men. Often, the discussion of a man's virtues appears in texts that are influenced by Greco-Roman philosophy. Greco-Roman philosophers may also discuss virtues in the abstract, without reference to a specific man. These philosophical sources could help us explore how virtues can be used to characterize a man. These sources could also help us explore how virtues differ, based on the philosophical underpinnings of each source. For example, a good Stoic man may be different than a good Cynic man. It may also be useful to ask what virtues are shared among specific philosophical schools. Carlos Noreña identifies virtues emphasized during the reign of Augustus; these were the Latin *virtus, clementia, iustitia,* and *pietas*. These virtues differed somewhat from the four cardinal virtues in Greek philosophy, which were the Greek ἀνδρεία, σωφροσύνη, δικαιοσύνη, and σοφία.[7] An effort to be more specific about which virtues are relevant to New Testament study, as well as the influence of different philosophies, may help exegetes be more accurate with their assessments of good or ideal men.

This study has incorporated material remains as historical evidence, but further study could continue to incorporate monuments, inscriptions, and images in order to learn about ancient understandings of masculinity. Given the limited literacy of first-century people, images are an especially important source. Paul Zanker argues that images are a "visual language."[8] Images make statements about gender as well as about religion, politics, and power. According to Natalie Boymel Kampen, "images of manliness were produced most consistently and disseminated most widely through the public images of rulers and elite men. No matter how personally peculiar, decadent, or unpleasant they

---

7. Noreña, "Communication," 152.

8. Zanker goes on to state that "rarely has art been pressed into the service of political power so directly as in the age of Augustus." Zanker, *Power of* Images, v.

may have been, rulers and elite men were invariably shown as models of manly virtue and strength (of body or of character).... Images functioned as active participants in the political programs and agendas of their patrons, who used the representation of manliness as a vehicle for representing legitimacy of rule, authority, and military victory."[9] Public images of elite Greco-Roman and military men could help us understand the environment in which the Way developed. Two examples from the first and second centuries can serve as illustrations of this point. A coin with an image of Nero on one side has an image of the personified *Virtus* (manly valor on the battlefield) and his weapons on the other.[10] Not only does this image communicate the military accomplishments of the emperor Nero but also his paradigmatic masculinity. Another example comes from Trajan's column, dedicated in the early second century CE. On this column, one can see Roman soldiers brutally killing Dacians.[11] These images communicate Roman military might and the habits of Roman soldiers. The portrayal of Cornelius the Roman soldier in Acts differs considerably from this image, thus creating contrast and indicating diversity in the ways in which first- and second-century audiences understood and perceived military men.

Another helpful development with regard to ancient images and material remains would be the identification of criteria by which we analyze ancient images and art forms. Although Maud Gleason analyzes images and statues for what they say about gender, her criteria for discerning masculinity in images are not clearly delineated. In order to learn more about the many layers of communication found in images, New Testament scholars would do well to assert some general guidelines on how to analyze images as well as take more seriously their potential as historical sources.

AVENUES TO EXPLORE: CONTRASTS TO MASCULINITY

In order to study masculinity in antiquity, it may be helpful to explore portraits of characters that contrast with the traits and features associ-

---

9. Kampen, "What Is a Man?," 7. It should be noted that Kampen is working with the historical framework of late antiquity (third through the sixth centuries CE).
10. Smallwood, *Documents*, 33.
11. Lepper and Frere, *Trajan's Column*, 70–71, plates XVII–XX.

ated with masculinity. Studying male characters who appear effeminate, or perhaps studying female characters, could illuminate constructs of masculinity.

One way to study masculinity could be to develop word fields for the lack of masculinity. The lack of masculinity is one way that the ancients criticized one another. Effeminacy was a failure, scandal, or weakness that could be skewered or mocked when conflict arose. One's adversary may have a multitude of vices as well as effeminate behavior, all of which were subject to critique. When an ancient man critiqued another man, he may use words that indicate paradigms of effeminacy, such as the Latin words *cinaedus* and *androgynus*.[12] Some key words for effeminate men also include the Latin and Greek words for these adjectives: effeminate, womanly, softness, anger, rage, and loss of self-control. One could also consider the Latin words for "broken, emasculated, sinewless and degenerate,"[13] as well as the Latin words for softness and excess, and their Greek counterparts.[14]

Here it will be useful to identify some examples of critique that can be found in primary sources. When Josephus describes the Zealots in *Jewish War*, he accuses them of engaging effeminate behavior as well as indiscriminate violence: "With an unsatiable lust for loot, they ransacked the houses of the wealthy; the murder of men and the violation of women were their sport, they caroused on their spoils, with blood to wash them down, and from mere satiety unscrupulously indulged in effeminate practices, plaiting their hair and attiring themselves in women's apparel, drenching themselves with perfumes and painting their eyelids to enhance their beauty."[15] A relevant Greek phrase here is ἐνεθηλυπάθουν τῷ κόρῳ" ("indulged in effeminate practices"). In the *Sibylline Oracles*, the author denounces Rome as "effeminate and unjust" and "with you are found adulteries and illicit intercourse with boys..."[16] In Philo's story of Moses, Moses ridicules the sons of Jethro, who would

12. Gleason, "Semiotics of Gender," 391.

13. Richlin, "Gender and Rhetoric," 94.

14 14.. The particular word here is the Latin *mollitia*, which means "softness" and "excess, overemphasis on pleasure, heightened emotions, without self-discipline." Graver, "Manhandling of Maecenas," 611. Walters also refers to the Latin word *mollis* in his essay "'No More Than a Boy,'" 29.

15. Josephus, *War* 4:560–61 (Thackeray, LCL).

16. *Sib. Or.* 5:165–68 (Charlesworth, 1:396–97). For more on this oracle, see Goodman, *Rome and Jerusalem*, 486–88.

not allow girls to water their camels: "But Moses, who was not far off, seeing what had happened, quickly ran up and, standing nearby, said, 'Stop this injustice. You think you can take advantage of the loneliness of this place? Are you not ashamed to let your arms and elbows live an idle life? You are masses of long hair and lumps of flesh, not men. The girls are working like youths and shirk none of their duties, while you young men go daintily about like girls."[17] Through these references (vices, in these cases), modern readers encounter constructs of masculinity. Modern readers come to understand the traits associated with masculinity through a man's failure to demonstrate those traits. One also puts effeminacy in relation to other vices. Constructs of masculinity are therefore not isolated but placed in relationship with other vices. Despite the complicated nature of masculinity in antiquity, it may be helpful to gather the Greek words from these examples and other sources and search for these words in New Testament texts. Within a larger framework of inquiry, key terms and phrases can bring out important features of masculinity.

In some New Testament texts, the traits of male characters such as Jesus or Paul may be more closely associated with the traits of women. In her book *Our Mother Saint Paul*, Beverly Roberts Gaventa discusses "maternal imagery in the letters of Paul."[18] As Gaventa points out, Paul refers to himself as a nurse to the infant Thessalonians,[19] a woman in labor giving birth to the Galatians,[20] and as a mother providing milk to the Corinthians.[21] Paul describes both Jesus and himself as men who came from the wombs of their mothers.[22] From this interpretive perspective, Paul does not hesitate to embrace maternal and feminine imagery to describe himself and Jesus. If these traits, which were associated with women rather than men, made him effeminate in the eyes of his audiences, Paul does not seem to recognize it as a problem. Perhaps here we have another alternative form of masculinity. The followers of Jesus may have molded themselves and their faith in ways that contrasted with elite understandings of manliness.

17. Philo, *Moses* 1:54–55 (Colson, LCL).
18. Gaventa, *Our Mother*, 3.
19. 1 Thess 2:7; Gaventa, *Our Mother*, 17.
20. Gal 4:19; Gaventa, *Our Mother*, 29.
21. 1 Cor 3:1; Gaventa, *Our Mother*, 41.
22. Gal 1:15; 4:4; Gaventa, *Our Mother*, 51.

Marcus Borg has explored compassion as a trait of God and Jesus, and in antiquity, compassion may have been more closely associated with women as well. "For Jesus," Borg writes, "compassion was the central quality of God and the central moral quality of a life centered in God."[23] The Hebrew word for "compassionate" is closely related to the word for "womb."[24] Borg continues with this statement: "As a mother loves the children of her womb and feels for the children of her womb, so God loves us and feels for us, for all her children."[25] Not only are Jesus and God compassionate, but the followers of Jesus are also to be compassionate, which can be translated as "merciful."[26] Being compassionate to one another is a way of imitating God.[27] The followers of Jesus are to create a community in which compassion takes precedence. This embrace of language related to a woman's womb might not have been shared by elite men, whose writings sometimes indicate anxiety about effeminacy and traits associated with women.

While this study focuses on the portraits of men in antiquity, it is also possible that women can exemplify piety as well. It would be worthwhile to seek literature and images that portray women as pious, and to consider what traits might be associated with "the good woman." These depictions could be of elite Greco-Roman or Jewish women. One may ask here if those portraits of good women in antiquity indicate a man's idea of what a good woman should do or be. Given the androcentric nature of most literature from the first few centuries CE, this might always be the case. However, the question about pious women remains. The work of Ross Shepard Kraemer may be helpful with regard to virtuous Greco-Roman women, and the work of Tal Ilan might be helpful with regard to Jewish women.[28] In Luke's story, the characterization of Mary the mother Jesus might be fruitful. Mary's demure acceptance of the will of God is countered by her prophetic announcement in the Magnificat. In the portrait of Mary, Luke combines several aspects of piety: submis-

---

23. Borg, *Meeting Jesus*, 46.
24. Ibid., 48.
25. Ibid.
26. "Be merciful, just as your Father is merciful" (Luke 6:36, NRSV). Here mercy is associated with fathers, instead of mothers. Borg notes that compassion is associated with the womb for women, and the bowels for men. Borg, *Meeting Jesus*, 47.
27. Ibid., 46–47.
28. Kraemer and D'Angelo, *Women & Christian Origins*; Ilan, *Integrating Women*.

sion and bold prophetic critique. One could compare these aspects of piety, exemplified by a woman, to the aspects of piety exemplified by men in the narrative. Perhaps Luke is making a statement about pious qualities that should be shared by both men and women.

AVENUES TO EXPLORE: THE MASCULINITY OF CORNELIUS

Because of Luke's attention to detail in the characterization of Cornelius, one dissertation cannot fully explore the traits of Cornelius. We know a great deal about Cornelius, but there are also things that we do not know. Luke does not tell us all that we would like to know in order to determine what kind of man he is. He does not speak publicly, and according to Maud Gleason, public speaking is the hallmark of elite masculinity. This may indicate that Cornelius was not elite, and is therefore a representative of an alternative masculinity. Luke does not tell his audience what Cornelius looks like, which rules out physiognomy and the study of physical appearance. Luke does not tell us about Cornelius' sexual behavior, which may indicate whether or not he is manly (the penetrator) or unmanly (the penetrated). We do not know about his status before he joined the military, whether or not he was appointed directly to the post of centurion, or if he rose through the ranks to achieve the position. We do not know enough about military masculinity and its peculiar values to compare and contrast it with Cornelius' lack of brutality toward Judean subjects. For example, was Cornelius less of a man because he gave up his power and indicated his submission to a Judean subject? This study has suggested that he may have been perceived as an unusual centurion in this way, but more scholarship on the values held among military men needs to be done in order for us to be certain.

Another issue that could be considered regarding the portrait of Cornelius is the matter of self-control. Does Cornelius have self control? This is a complicated question to answer, especially among military men. In the military, one man is subject to the orders of another, and military men do not have control over the boundaries of their own bodies. Centurions carry batons to enforce physical discipline, even on Roman citizens, whose bodily boundaries are protected outside of the military. Yet self-control may enable soldiers to carry out their tasks and follow orders. Self-control in the military may help the hierarchy to function effectively. Even outside of the military ranks, self-control is a complicated matter. Men who were enslaved were subject to their masters. An adult man was subject to the authority of his father, the *paterfamilias*. Elites were subject to the authority of the emperor. The emperor was subject to the authority of the gods. From this perspective, it may be worthwhile to define self-control with greater complexity. A more comprehensive definition of self-control would help us exegete the ways in which Cornelius the centurion interacts with Judean civilians, his military superiors, and the God of Israel.

At the same time, Acts 10 invites a reading that is relevant to empire studies. Cornelius' affiliation with the empire allows the interpreter to compare and contrast his portrayal with that of other representatives of the empire. While scholars have for some time investigated how Luke negotiates imperial issues, in recent years scholars have begun to interpret Luke's story as a challenge to or critique of Roman sovereignty. Conway alludes to such a challenge of Roman sovereignty when she details how Luke characterizes Jesus in ways that link Jesus and the emperor.[29] This dissertation stands in line with Conway's perspective, and further suggests that the προσκυνεῖν gesture indicates Roman submission to the God of the Judeans. This study also interacts and concurs with the scholarship of Gary Gilbert, whose two articles interpret Luke-Acts as a challenge of Roman sovereignty.[30] More studies of Luke-Acts and empire will likely be published, perhaps from a perspective similar to this study, and future publications could enrich the argument made here.

More could be done with the portrait of Cornelius in light of Jewish masculinity. Early rabbinic texts and rabbinic understandings of good men may shed some light on the masculinity of Cornelius, and how he may have been perceived among Jewish men. This would be appropriate given the continuity between the Way and Judaism. According to Martin Goodman, "in early rabbinic texts, the ideal male is depicted as subservient to God, reliant on divine help for success and prepared to suffer

---

29. These commonalities between Jesus and the emperor include the references to Jesus as "savior" and "bringer of salvation" in Luke's infancy narratives and the ascension scene at the end of Luke's Gospel. Conway states: "Given the frequency with which other powerful men were named as saviors and bearers of salvation, this statement stands out as a bold challenge to imperial authority." Conway, *Behold the Man*, 130; see also 129–32, 135–39.

30. Gilbert, "Luke-Acts and Negotiation of Authority"; Gilbert, "Roman Propaganda and Christian Identity," both noted above.

martyrdom rather than fight like a warrior."³¹ Likewise, Daniel Boyarin argues that rabbinic culture "defined ideal men as gentle, peaceful, and nurturing,"³² while "substantial segments of the rabbinic tradition delineated the essence of the rabbinic Jewish male as he who does not beat his wife . . ."³³ Cornelius' submission to the God of the Judeans and his lack of brutality toward Judean subjects may be more in line with Jewish masculinity than Roman masculinity. The concept of "rabbinic culture," itself, however, is a broad one, and the rabbis continued to influence Jewish practice for several centuries beyond the time period of the New Testament. The pursuit of cultural specificity as well as specificity with regard to era, may help the study of masculinity develop the necessary nuance to envision Cornelius not only as a Roman man but also as a Jewish one.³⁴

The question about Jewish masculinity and the portrait of Cornelius leads to a larger question about whether the Way, as Luke envisions it, is Judaism. Scholars have different opinions about this issue. Some argue that the Way is largely Gentile Christianity, and that Luke is portraying a movement that has already broken away from Judaism. The movement in Acts can no longer be considered Judaism because it has left behind traditional markers of Jewish identity, such as circumcision, food laws, and Sabbath observance. Gentiles are integrated in large numbers and the movement now consists more of Gentiles than of Jews. However,

---

31. Goodman, *Rome and Jerusalem*, 292. Goodman could have been more precise about which early rabbinic texts are relevant.

32. Boyarin, *Unheroic Conduct*, 162.

33. Ibid. Boyarin here refers to the Ashkenazic tradition, during the medieval period. Early rabbinic texts (from second or third century CE onward) may suggest something similar. More research needs to be done along this line.

34. Gleason, "By Whose Standards," 327. One could also ask more specific questions about how a Roman centurion could adhere to Judaism and successfully fulfill his duties as a centurion. The Jewish understanding of the Sabbath, food regulations and concerns about purity would likely make military duty difficult. An interpreter could conclude that military duty and Judaism were incompatible, not only because of the practices themselves but also because of the different sovereignties inherent in Roman military duty and Judaism. An interpreter could also conclude that in order to keep his job as a centurion, a man would have to choose which Jewish practices to adopt, and which to leave behind. The removal of purity concerns with regard to food in Acts 10 would have made military duty easier, to some extent, although the observance of Sabbath would still be a major barrier. In light of this and other barriers, perhaps some military men remained God-fearers and did not fully convert to Judaism.

other scholars argue the opposite.³⁵ From this perspective, the Way is Luke's vision of an inclusive Judaism. The emphasis on Hebrew Bible prophecy in Luke-Acts and the agreement about minimum requirements in Acts 15 suggest that the Gentiles now belong to the people of Israel. A key question is, "When does the Way stop becoming Judaism and start becoming something else?" While the debate surrounding this question is beyond the scope of this study, I suggest that in Acts 10, Luke is not creating something entirely new. Luke takes pains to show continuity with Judaism, despite his departures from strict Torah observance.

AVENUES TO EXPLORE: MASCULINITY IN THE NEW TESTAMENT

Further investigation can also be pursued with other male characters in the New Testament. When male characters are considered gendered rather than a neutral standard or a homogenous unisex representative, the field of analysis becomes wide open. The question will then be where to stop, rather than where to start. New Testament texts give us a variety of men to analyze. Any male character can be studied, compared, and contrasted to what we know about masculinity in the first and second centuries CE, and those characters can be analyzed as rhetorical fodder within their respective contexts.

Characters in Acts, besides Cornelius, could provide fodder for a hermeneutic of masculinity. Peter and Paul would be included in this cast of characters. Barnabas also presents a challenge to interpreters who are interested in masculinity and the construction of gender. Barnabas sells his land and gives the money to the apostles (Acts 4). He defends Paul when others are skeptical about Paul's sincerity (Acts 9) but later splits from Paul and sails to Cyprus (Acts 15). Barnabas is the only man in Acts whom Luke describes as "a good man" (ἀνὴρ ἀγαθός, 11:24). Danker identifies this phrase as an indicator of benefaction in ancient inscriptions,³⁶ but one could explore more fully how masculinity was linked to benefaction, as well as the relationship between a good man and a good benefactor. These characters could also be compared to Cornelius, and their traits put alongside one another as ways in which Luke comments on masculinity.

---

35. Jervell, *Luke and the People of God*, noted above; Tiede, *Prophecy and History*.
36. Danker, *Benefactor*, 318–19.

Colleen Conway has advanced the study of masculinity in New Testament texts by writing about the portrayals of Jesus and other men in the canonical Gospels, the Pauline letters, and Revelation. This way of reading New Testament texts is only beginning to develop. In addition to and with respect toward her pioneering work, one could study in greater detail some portrayals of men in the Gospels. These interpretive opportunities include the disparaging portraits of the disciples in Mark, the obedient disciples in Matthew, and the contrasts between the authority of Jesus and the authority of Jewish and Roman leaders in the Gospels. The portraits of all of these men may shed light on the rhetorical agendas of the authors of their respective stories.

One could also study Paul's portrayal of himself in his letters, and how he interacts with the communities to whom he writes. As noted above, Beverly Roberts Gaventa has considered Paul's maternal imagery. Brigitte Kahl and Jennifer Larson, however, have analyzed Paul's masculinity and masculine imagery.[37] In 1 Corinthians 4:15, Paul describes himself as the father of the people; this may lead the interpreter to ask what a father does, and how Paul uses the authority associated with a father figure to make his point. In 2 Corinthians 6:3–10, Paul describes how he has suffered physically for his work, including "beatings, imprisonments, riots, labors, sleepless nights, hunger . . ." (2 Cor 6:5). From an elite Roman perspective, this physical suffering and lack of protection would signal something less than manliness. Ironically, Paul seems to describe these sufferings as badges of honor, or as signs that he has continued to work despite great hardship (6:4). An alternative understanding of manliness may underlie this portrayal.

Some characters in Revelation may also present opportunities for a hermeneutic of masculinity. Much has been written on the portrayals of women in Revelation, from such scholars as Barbara Rossing,[38] Elisabeth Schüssler Fiorenza,[39] and Tina Pippin.[40] The portrayal of Jesus as a man may be a place to begin to think critically about the characterizations of men in Revelation. John of Patmos describes the physical appearance of Jesus on several occasions.[41] Conway has begun to think

37. Larson, "Paul's Masculinity"; Kahl, "'No Longer Male.'"
38. Rossing, *Choice between Two Cities*.
39. Schüssler Fiorenza, *Book of Revelation*.
40. Pippin, *Death and Desire*.
41. Rev 1:12–16.

along these lines in her book *Behold the Man*.[42] Given the importance of physical appearance for some constructions of masculinity, these descriptions may provide some indication of how they were to be perceived with regard to gender. The manly warrior in Revelation 19 gives some indication of military masculinity, yet the Lamb proposes an alternative to military might.[43] The virgins in Revelation 14 propose a sort of ascetic masculinity that does not "defile" itself with women (14:4). The archangel Michael protects the woman clothed with the sun and fights the dragon that was about to devour her child (12:1–9). In Revelation, the portrayals of men are saturated with the activities of war, of success and defeat, of battle and blood. In the end, Jerusalem is a female figure, "like a bride adorned for her husband" (21:2). That husband may be God. Overall, masculinity comes in a variety of shapes and sizes in Revelation, and further analysis could reveal the rhetorical angles that these shapes and sizes might contain.

CONCLUSION

Although more avenues could be pursued, this study has been informed by and attempts to contribute to a variety of scholarly approaches and topics. This study is a step toward assessing critically the portraits of men in the New Testament, using what we know from history. As such, this book could be included in the category of gender studies. The method employed here is narrative criticism, and therefore it is one of many narrative analyses. Finally, an interdisciplinary approach was used to establish the historical background in this study, gleaning insights from classics, philosophy, archaeology, the history of Judaism, and scholarship about the Roman military. I hope that it is a step in the right direction, especially for scholars who wish to explore masculinity as a historical and textual phenomenon.

---

42. Conway argues that Revelation presents multiple images of Jesus the man: "the angelic Son of Man," "the warrior rider," and "the Lamb." Conway, *Behold the Man*, 159–74.

43. Frilingos, "Sexing the Lamb."

Bibliography

Alston, Richard. "Arms and the Man: Soldiers, Masculinity, and Power in Republican and Imperial Rome." In *When Men Were Men: Masculinity, Power, and Identity in Classical Antiquity*, edited by Lin Foxhall and John Salmon, 205–23. Leicester-Nottingham Studies in Ancient Society 8. London: Routledge, 1998.

Aristotle. *The Nicomachean Ethics*. Translated by H. Rackham. LCL. Cambridge, MA: Harvard University Press, 1926.

———. *The Poetics*. Translated by W. Hamilton Fyfe. LCL. London: W. Heinemann, 1927.

Bach, Alice. "Signs of the Flesh: Observations on Characterization and the Bible." In *Characterization in Biblical Literature*, edited by Elizabeth Struthers Malbon and Adele Berlin, 61–79. Semeia 63. Atlanta: Scholars, 1993.

Barton, Carlin A. "All Things Beseem the Victor: Paradoxes of Masculinity in Early Imperial Rome." In *Gender Rhetorics: Postures of Dominance and Submission in History*, edited by Richard Trexler, 83–92. Medieval and Renaissance Texts & Studies 113. Binghamton, NY: Medieval & Renaissance Studies, 1994.

———. "The Roman Blush: The Delicate Matter of Self-Control." In *Constructions of the Classical Body*, edited by James Porter, 212–34. Body, in Theory. Ann Arbor: University of Michigan Press, 1999.

———. *Roman Honor: The Fire in the Bones*. Berkeley: University of California Press, 2001.

Beard, Mary, John A. North, and Simon R. F. Price. *Religions of Rome*. 2 vols. Cambridge: Cambridge University Press, 1998.

Booth, Wayne C. *The Rhetoric of Fiction*. Chicago: University of Chicago Press, 1961.

Boyarin, Daniel. *Unheroic Conduct: The Rise of Heterosexuality and the Invention of the Jewish Man*. Contraversions 8. Berkeley: University of California Press, 1997.

Brent, Allen. *The Imperial Cult and the Development of Church Order: Concepts and Images of Authority in Paganism and Early Christianity before the Age of Cyprian*. Supplements to Vigiliae Christianae 45. Leiden: Brill, 1999.

Burnett, Fred. "Characterization and Reader Construction: Characters in the Gospels." In *Characterization in Biblical Literature*, edited by Elizabeth Struthers Malbon and Adele Berlin, 3–28. Semeia 63. Atlanta: Scholars, 1993.

Burrus, Virginia. "Mapping as Metamorphosis: Initial Reflections on Gender in Ancient Religious Discourses." In *Mapping Gender in Ancient Religious Discourses*, edited by Todd Penner and Caroline Vander Stichele, 1–10. BIS 84. Leiden: Brill, 2007.

Campbell, J. B. *The Emperor and the Roman Army: 31 BC–AD 235*. Oxford: Clarendon, 1984.
Carroll, John. "Luke's Portrayal of the Pharisees." *CBQ* 50 (1988) 604–21.
Cassius Dio Cocceianus. *Dio's Roman History*. Translated by Earnest Cary. 9 vols. LCL. 9 vols. LCL. London: W. Heinemann, 1914–27.
Charlesworth, James H., editor. *The Old Testament Pseudepigrapha*, vol. 1 (*Apocalyptic Literature and Testaments*). Garden City, NY: Doubleday, 1983.
Chatman, Seymour Benjamin. *Story and Discourse: Narrative Structure in Fiction and Film*. Ithaca, NY: Cornell University Press, 1978.
Cohen, Shaye J. D. *The Beginnings of Jewishness: Boundaries, Varieties, and Uncertainties*. Hellenistic Culture and Society 31. Berkeley: University of California Press, 1999.
———. *From the Maccabees to the Mishnah*. Library of Early Christianity 7. Philadelphia: Westminster, 1987.
———. "Respect for Judaism by Gentiles according to Josephus." *HTR* 80.4 (1987) 409–30.
Conway, Colleen M. *Behold the Man: Jesus and Greco-Roman Masculinity*. Oxford: Oxford University Press, 2008.
———. "Gender and Divine Relativity in Philo of Alexandria." *Journal for the Study of Judaism* 34.4 (2003) 471–91.
Cotter, Wendy. "Cornelius, the Roman Army, and Religion." In *Religious Rivalries and the Struggle for Success in Caesarea Maritima*, edited by Terence L. Donaldson, 279–301. SCJ 8. Waterloo, ON: Wilfrid Laurier, 2000.
Culpepper, Alan R. *Anatomy of the Fourth Gospel: A Study in Literary Design*. Foundations and Facets: New Testament. Philadelphia: Fortress, 1983.
D'Angelo, Mary Rose. "The ΑΝΗΡ Question in Luke-Acts: Imperial Masculinity and the Deployment of Women in the Early Second Century." In *A Feminist Companion to Luke*, edited by Amy-Jill Levine with Marianne Blickenstaff, 44–69. Cleveland: Pilgrim, 2001.
———. "Εὐσεβεία: Roman Imperial Family Values and the Sexual Politics of 4 Maccabees and the Pastorals." *BibInt* 11.2 (2003) 139–65.
———. "Gender and Geopolitics in the Work of Philo of Alexandria: Jewish Piety and Imperial Family Values." In *Mapping Gender in Ancient Religious Discourses*, edited by Todd Penner and Caroline Vander Stichele, 63–88. Biblical Interpretation 84. Leiden: Brill, 2007.
———. "'Knowing How to Preside over His Own Household.'" In *New Testament Masculinities*, edited by Stephen D. Moore and Janice Capel Anderson, 265–96. Semeia 45. Atlanta: Society of Biblical Literature, 2003.
Damon, Cynthia. *Res Gestae Divi Augusti*. Bryn Mawr Latin Commentaries. Bryn Mawr, PA: Bryn Mawr College, 1995.
Danker, Frederick W. *Benefactor: Epigraphic Study of a Graeco-Roman and New Testament Semantic Field*. St. Louis: Clayton, 1982.
Danker, Frederick W., Walter Bauer, William F. Arndt, and F. W. Gingrich. *A Greek-English Lexicon of the New Testament and Other Early Christian Literature*. 3rd ed. Chicago: University of Chicago Press, 2000.
Darr, John A. *Herod the Fox: Audience Criticism and Lukan Characterization*. JSNTSS 163. Sheffield: Sheffield Academic, 1998.
———. "Irenic or Ironic? Another Look at Gamaliel before the Sanhedrin (Acts 5:33–42)." In *Literary Studies in Luke-Acts: Essays in Honor of Joseph B. Tyson*, edited

by Richard P. Thompson and Thomas E. Phillips, 121–40. Macon, GA: Mercer University Press, 1998.

———. "Narrator as Character: Mapping a Reader-Oriented Approach to Narration in Luke-Acts." In *Characterization in Biblical Literature*, edited by Elizabeth Struthers Malbon and Adele Berlin, 43–60. Semeia 63. Atlanta: Scholars, 1993.

———. *On Character Building: The Reader and the Rhetoric of Characterization in Luke-Acts*. Literary Currents in Bibical Interpretation. Louisville: Westminster John Knox, 1992.

———. "'Watch How You Listen' (Luke 8:18): Jesus and the Rhetoric of Perception in Luke-Acts." In *The New Literary Criticism and the New Testament*, edited by Elizabeth Struthers Malbon and Edgar V. McKnight, 87–107. JSNTSS 109. Sheffield: Sheffield Academic, 1994.

Davies, Roy William. "The Daily Life of the Roman Soldier under the Roman Principate." In *Aufstieg und Niedergang der römischen Welt: Geschicht und Kultur Roms im Spiegel der neuren Forschung*, 2.1, edited by Hildegard Temporini, 299–338. Berlin: de Gruyter, 1974.

Dessau, Hermann. *Inscriptiones Latinae Selectae*. 3 vols. Berlin: Weidmann, 1892.

Dio Chrysostom. Translated by J. W. Cohoon and H. Lamar Crosby. 5 vols. LCL. London: W. Heinemann, 1932–51.

Dionysius of Halicarnassus. *The Roman Antiquities of Dionysius of Halicarnassus*. Translated by Earnest Cary. 7 vols. LCL. Cambridge, MA: Harvard University Press, 1937–50.

Dittenberger, William, editor. *Orientis Graeci Inscriptiones Selectae: Supplementum Sylloges inscriptionum graecarum*. 2 vols. Leipzig: S. Hirzel, 1903–5.

———. *Sylloge Inscriptionum Graecarum*. 4 vols. 3rd. ed. Leipzig: S. Hirzel, 1915–24.

Dobson, Brian. "The Significance of the Centurion and the '*Primi Pilaris*' in the Roman Army and Administration." In *Aufstieg und Niedergang der römischen Welt: Geschicht und Kultur Roms im Spiegel der neuren Forschung* 2.26.3, edited by Wolfgang Haase, 392–434. Berlin: de Gruyter, 1996.

Feldman, Louis H. *Jew and Gentile in the Ancient World: Attitudes and Interactions from Alexander to Justinian*. Princeton, NJ: Princeton University Press, 2001.

———. *Philo's Portrayal of Moses in the Context of Ancient Judaism*. Christianity and Judaism in Antiquity 15. Notre Dame, IN: University of Notre Dame Press, 2007.

Feldman, Louis H., and Meyer Reinhold, editors. *Jewish Life and Thought among Greeks and Romans: Primary Readings*. Minneapolis: Fortress, 1996.

Ferguson, Everett. *Backgrounds of Early Christianity*. 3rd ed. Grand Rapids: Eerdmans, 2003.

Finn, Thomas. "The God-Fearers Reconsidered." *CBQ* 47.1 (1985) 75–84.

Fisher, Nick. "Violence, Masculinity, and the Law in Classical Antiquity." In *When Men Were Men: Masculinity, Power, and Identity in Classical Antiquity*, edited by Lin Foxhall and John Salmon, 68–97. Leicester-Nottingham Studies in Ancient Society 8. London: Routledge, 1998.

Frilingos, Chris. "Sexing the Lamb." In *New Testament Masculinities*, edited by Stephen D. Moore and Janice Capel Anderson, 297–317. Semeia 45. Atlanta: Society of Biblical Literaure, 2003.

Fowler, Robert. "Characterizing Character in Biblical Narrative." In *Characterization in Biblical Literature*, edited by Elizabeth Struthers Malbon and Adele Berlin, 97–104. Semeia 63. Atlanta: Scholars, 1993.

Fox, Matthew. "The Constrained Man." In *Thinking Men: Masculinity and Its Self-Representation in the Classical Tradition*, edited by Lin Foxhall and John Salmon, 6–22. Leicester-Nottingham Studies in Ancient Society 7. London: Routledge, 1998.

Galinsky, Karl. *Augustan Culture: An Interpretive Introduction*. Princeton, NJ: Princeton University Press, 1996.

Gamel, Mary Kay. "Reading as a Man: Performance and Gender in Roman Elegy." *Helios* 23.1 (1998) 79–95.

Gaventa, Beverly Roberts. *The Acts of the Apostles*. Abingdon New Testament Commentaries. Nashville: Abingdon, 2003.

———. *From Darkness to Light: Aspects of Conversion in the New Testament*. Overtures to Biblical Theology 20. Philadelphia: Fortress, 1986.

———. *Our Mother Saint Paul*. Louisville: Westminster John Knox, 2007.

German Academy of Sciences. *Corpus Inscriptionum Latinarum*. 16 vols. Berlin: Reiner, 1862.

Gilbert, Gary. "Luke-Acts and Negotiation of Authority and Identity in the Roman World." In *The Multivalence of Biblical Texts and Theological Meanings*, edited by Christine Helmer with Charlene T. Higbe, 83–104. Society of Biblical Literature Symposium Series 37. Atlanta: Society of Biblical Literature, 2006.

———. "Roman Propaganda and Christian Identity in the Worldview of Luke-Acts." In *Contextualizing Acts: Lukan Narrative and Greco-Roman Discourse*, edited by Todd Penner and Caroline Vander Stichele, 233–56. Society of Biblical Literature Symposium Series 20. Atlanta: Society of Biblical Literature, 2003.

Glancy, Jennifer. "Protocols of Masculinity in the Pastoral Epistles." In *New Testament Masculinities*, edited by Stephen D. Moore and Janice Capel Anderson, 235–64. Semeia 45. Atlanta: Society of Biblical Literature, 2003.

Gleason, Maud W. "By Whose Standards (If Anybody's) Was Jesus a Real Man?" In *New Testament Masculinities*, edited by Stephen D. Moore and Janice Capel Anderson, 325–27. Semeia 45. Atlanta: Society of Biblical Literature, 2003.

———. "Elite Male Identity in the Roman Empire." In *Life, Death, and Entertainment in the Roman Empire*, edited by D. S. Potter and D. J. Mattingly, 67–84. Ann Arbor: University of Michigan Press, 1999.

———. *Making Men: Sophists and Self-Presentation in Ancient Rome*. Princeton, NJ: Princeton University Press, 1995.

———. "The Semiotics of Gender: Physiognomy and Self-Fashioning in the Second Century CE." In *Before Sexuality: The Construction of Erotic Experience in the Ancient Greek World*, edited by David M. Halperin, John J. Winkler, and Froma I. Zeitlin, 389–415. Princeton, NJ: Princeton University Press, 1990.

Goodman, Martin. *Judaism in the Roman World: Collected Essays*. Ancient Judaism and Early Christianity 66. Leiden: Brill, 1007.

———. *Rome and Jerusalem: The Clash of Ancient Civilizations*. London: Allen Lane, 2007.

Gowler, David. *Host, Guest, Enemy, and Friend: Portraits of the Pharisees in Luke and Acts*. Emory Studies in Early Christianity 2. New York: P. Lang, 1991.

Graver, Margaret. "The Manhandling of Maecenas: Senecan Abstractions of Masculinity." *American Journal of Philology* 119.4 (1998) 607–32.

Haenchen, Ernst. *The Acts of the Apostles: A Commentary*. Translated by Bernard Noble and Gerald Shinn. Philadelphia: Westminster, 1971.

Hanson, Ann. "The Roman Family." In *Life, Death, and Entertainment in the Roman Empire*, edited by D. S. Potter and D. J. Mattingly, 19–66. Ann Arbor: University of Michigan Press, 1999.
Helgeland, John. "Roman Army Religion." In *ANRW* 2.16.2, edited by Hildegard Temporini and Wolfgang Haase, 1470–1505. Berlin: de Gruyter, 1978.
Hornblower, Simon, and Antony Spawforth, editors. *Oxford Classical Dictionary*. 3rd ed. Oxford: Oxford University Press, 1996.
Howell, Justin. "The Imperial Authority and Benefaction of Centurions in Acts 10:34–43: A Response to C. Kavin Rowe." *JSNT* 31.1 (2008) 25–51.
Ilan, Tal. *Integrating Women into Second Temple History*. Texts and Studies in Ancient Judaism 76. Tübingen: Mohr/Siebeck, 1999.
Ivarsson, Fredrick. "Vice Lists and Deviant Masculinity: The Rhetorical Function of 1 Corinthians 5:10–11 and 6:9–11." In *Mapping Gender in Ancient Religious Discourses*, edited by Todd Penner and Caroline Vander Stichele, 163–84. BIS 84. Leiden: Brill, 2007.
Jennings, Theodore W., Jr., and Tat-Siong Benny Liew. "Mistaken Identities but Model Faith: Rereading the Centurion, the Chap, and the Christ in Matthew 8:5–13." *JBL* 123.3 (2004) 467–94.
Jervell, Jacob. *Luke and the People of God: A New Look at Luke-Acts*. Minneapolis: Augsburg, 1972.
Johnson, Lee. A. "A Literary Guide to Caesarea Maritima." In *Religious Rivalries and the Struggle for Success in Caesarea Maritima*, edited by Terence L. Donaldson, 35–56. SCJ 8. Waterloo, ON: W. Laurier, 2000.
Jones, John Melville. *A Dictionary of Ancient Coins*. London: Seaby, 1990.
Josephus. Translated by H. St. J. Thackeray et al. 10 vols. LCL. Cambridge, MA: Harvard University Press, 1926–65.
Joubert, Stephen. "One Form of Social Exchange or Two: Euergetism, Patronage, and Testament Studies—Roman and Greek Ideas of Patronage." *BTB* 31.1 (2001) 17–25.
Juvenal and Persius. Translated by G. G. Ramsay. LCL. Cambridge, MA: Harvard University Press, 1961.
Kahl, Brigitte. "'No Longer Male': Masculinity Struggles behind Galatians 3:28?" *JSNT* 23.79 (2001) 37–49.
Kampen, Natalie Boymel. "Gender Theory in Roman Art." In *I, Claudia: Women in Ancient Rome*, edited by Diana E. E. Kleiner and Susan B. Matheson, 14–25. New Haven, CT: Yale University Art Gallery, 1996.
———. "What Is a Man?" In *What Is a Man?: Changing Images of Masculinity in Late Antique Art*, edited by Natalie Boymel Kampen, Elizabeth Marlowe, and Robecca M. Molholt, 3–15. Portland, OR: Trustees of the Reed Institute and the Douglas F. Colley Memorial Art Gallery, Reed College, 2002.
Kim, Kyoung-Jin. *Stewardship and Almsgiving in Luke's Theology*. JSNTSS 155. Sheffield: Sheffield Academic, 1998.
Kittel, Gerhard, and Gerhard Friedrich. *Theological Dictionary of the New Testament*. Translated by Geoffrey W. Bromiley. 10 vols. Grand Rapids: Eerdmans, 1964–76.
Klauck, Hans-Josef. *Magic and Paganism in Early Christianity: The World of the Acts of the Apostles*. Translated by Brian McNeil. Minneapolis: Fortress, 2003.
Kraabel, A. Thomas. "The Disappearance of the 'God-Fearers.'" *Numen* 28.2 (1981) 113–26.
Kraemer, Ross Shepard, and Mary Rose D'Angelo, editors. *Women & Christian Origins*. Oxford: Oxford University Press, 1999.

Kuefler, Mathew. *The Manly Eunuch: Masculinity, Gender Ambiguity, and Christian Ideology in Late Antiquity*. Chicago Series on Sexuality, History, and Society. Chicago: University of Chicago Press, 2001.

Larson, Jennifer. "Paul's Masculinity." *JBL* 123.1 (2004) 85–97.

Le Bohec, Yann. *The Imperial Roman Army*. London: B. T. Batsford, 1994.

Lehtipuu, Outi. "Characterization and Persuasion: Rich Man/Poor Man in Luke 16." In *Characterization in the Gospels: Reconceiving Narrative Criticism*, edited by David M. Rhoads and Kari Syreeni, 73–105. JSNTSS 184. Sheffield: Sheffield Academic, 1999.

Lehmann, Clayton Miles. "The City and the Text." In *Caesarea Maritima: A Retrospective after Two Millennia*, edited by Avner Raban and Kenneth G. Holum, 381–91. Documenta et monumenta Orientis antiqui 21. Leiden: Brill, 1996.

Lehmann, Clayton Miles, and Kenneth G. Holum. *The Greek and Latin Inscriptions of Caesarea Maritima*. The Joint Expedition to Caesarea Maritima Excavation Reports 5. Boston: American Schools of Oriental Research, 2000.

Lepper, F. A., and Sheppard Sunderland Frere. *Trajan's Column: A New Edition of the Cichorius Plates*. Gloucester: A. Sutton, 1988.

Leroux, Ernest. *Bulletin Archéologique du Comité des Travaux Historiques et Scientifiques*. Paris: National Printers, 1928–29.

Leutzsch, Martin. "Konstructionen von Männlichkeit in Urchristentum." In *Dem Tod nicht Glauben: Sozialgeschichte der Bibel: Festschrift für Luise Schottroff zum 70*, edited by Frank Crüsemann et al., 600–618. Gütersloh: Gütersloher, 2004.

Levinskaya, Irina. "The Inscription from Aphrodisias and the Problem of God-Fearers." *Tyndale Bulletin* 41.2 (1990) 312–18.

Lewis, Naphtali, editor. *The Documents from the Bar Kokhba Period in the Cave of Letters: Greek Papyri*. Judean Desert Studies 2. Jerusalem: Israel Exploration Society, 1989.

Liew, Tat-Siong Benny. "Re-Mark-able Masculinities: Jesus, the Son of Man, and the (Sad) Sum of Manhood?" In *New Testament Masculinities*, edited by Stephen D. Moore and Janice Capel Anderson, 93–136. Semeia 45. Atlanta: Society of Biblical Literature, 2003.

Livy. Translated by Benjamin Oliver Foster, Evan Taylor Sage, Frank Gardner Moore, and Alfred Carey Schlesinger. 14 vols. LCL. London: W. Heinemann, 1919–59.

Lopez, Davina C. *Apostle to the Conquered: Reimagining Paul's Mission*. Paul in Critical Contexts. Minneapolis: Fortress, 2008.

———. "Before Your Very Eyes: Roman Imperial Ideology, Gender Constructs, and Paul's Inter-Nationalism." In *Mapping Gender in Ancient Religious Discourses*, edited by Todd Penner and Caroline Vander Stichele, 115–62. BIS 84. Leiden: Brill, 2007.

MacMullen, Ramsay. *Soldier and Civilian in the Later Roman Empire*. Harvard Historical Monographs 52. Cambridge, MA: Harvard University Press, 1963.

Matthews, Shelly. *First Converts: Rich Pagan Women and the Rhetoric of Mission in Early Judaism and Christianity*. Contraversions. Stanford, CA: Stanford University Press, 2001.

Malina, Bruce J. *The New Testament World: Insights from Cultural Anthropology*. 3rd ed. Louisville: Westminster John Knox, 2001.

Malina, Bruce J., and Jerome H. Neyrey. *Portraits of Paul: An Archaeology of Ancient Personality*. Louisville: Westminster John Knox, 1996.

Martin, Dale. "Contradictions of Masculinity: Ascetic Inseminators and Menstruating Men in Greco-Roman Culture." In *Generation and Degeneration: Tropes of Reproduction in Literature and History from Antiquity to Early Modern Europe*, edited by Valeria Finucci and Kevin Brownlee, 81–108. Durham, NC: Duke University Press, 2001.

Mattingly, Harold. *Coins of the Roman Empire in the British Museum.* 6 vols. London: Longmans, 1923.

Menander. Edited and translated by W. G. Arnott. 3 vols. LCL. Cambridge, MA: Harvard University Press, 1979–2000.

Merenlahti, Petri. "Characters in the Making: Individuality and Ideology in the Gospels." In *Characterization in the Gospels: Reconceiving Narrative Criticism*, edited by David M. Rhoads and Kari Syreeni, 49–72. JSNTSS 184. Sheffield: Sheffield Academic, 1999.

Merenlahti, Petri, and Raimo Hakola. "Reconceiving Narrative Criticism." In *Characterization in the Gospels: Reconceiving Narrative Criticism*, edited by David M. Rhoads and Kari Syreeni, 13–48. JSNTSS 184. Sheffield: Sheffield Academic, 1999.

Metzger, James A. *Consumption and Wealth in Luke's Travel Narrative.* BIS 88. Leiden: Brill, 2007.

Moloney, Francis. "Narrative Criticism of the Gospels." *Pacifica* 4 (1991) 181–201.

Moore, Stephen D. *God's Beauty Parlor: And Other Queer Spaces in and around the Bible.* Contraversions. Stanford, CA: Stanford University Press, 2001.

———. *Literary Criticism and the Gospels: The Theoretical Challenge.* New Haven, CT: Yale University Press, 1989.

———. "Matthew and Masculinity." In *New Testament Masculinities*, edited by Stephen D. Moore and Janice Capel Anderson, 67–92. Semeia 45. Atlanta: Society of Biblical Literature, 2003.

———. "'O Man Who Art Thou . . .': Masculinity Studies and New Testament Studies." In *New Testament Masculinities*, edited by Stephen D. Moore and Janice Capel Anderson, 1–22. Semeia 45. Atlanta: Society of Biblical Literature, 2003.

Moore, Stephen D., and Janice Capel Anderson. "Taking It Like a Man: Masculinity in 4 Maccabees." *JBL* 117.2 (1998) 249–73.

Moxnes, Halvor. "Conventional Values in the Hellenistic World: Masculinity." In *Conventional Values of the Hellenistic Greeks*, edited by Per Bilde et al., 263–84 Studies in Hellenistic Civilization 8. Aarhus: Aarhus University Press, 1997.

Murray, Michele. "Jews and Judaism in Caesarea Maritima." In *Religious Rivalries and the Struggle for Success in Caesarea Maritima*, edited by Terence L. Donaldson, 127–52. SCJ 8. Waterloo, ON: W. Laurier, 2000.

Noreña, Carlos. "The Communication of the Emperor's Virtues." *JRS* 41 (2001) 146–68.

Neusner, Jacob, editor and translator. *The Tosefta.* Division 2: *Moed (The Order of Appointed Times).* New York: Ktav, 1981.

Neyrey, Jerome H. "Jesus, Gender, and the Gospel of Matthew." In *New Testament Masculinities*, edited by Stephen D. Moore and Janice Capel Anderson, 43–66. Semeia 45. Atlanta: Society of Biblical Literature, 2003.

Osborne, Robin. "Sculpted Men of Athens: Masculinity and Power in the Field of Vision." In *Thinking Men: Masculinity and Its Self-Representation in the Classical Tradition*, edited by Lin Foxhall and John Salmon, 23–42. Leicester-Nottingham Studies in Ancient Society 7. London: Routledge, 1998.

Painter, R. Jackson. "Greco-Roman Religion in Caesarea Maritima." In *Religious Rivalries and the Struggle for Success in Caesarea Maritima*, edited by Terence L. Donaldson, 105–25. SCJ 8. Waterloo, ON: W. Laurier, 2000.

———. "The Origins and Social Context of Mithraism at Caesarea Maritima." In *Religious Rivalries and the Struggle for Success in Caesarea Maritima*, edited by Terence L. Donaldson, 205–25. SCJ 8. Waterloo, ON: W. Laurier, 2000.

Penner, Todd, and Caroline Vander Stichele. "'All the World's a Stage': The Rhetoric of Gender in Acts." In *Luke and His Readers: Festschrift for A. Denaux*, edited by R. Bieringer, et. al., 373–96. Bibliotheca Ephemeridum Theologicarium Lovaniensium 182. Leuven: Leuven University, 2005.

———."Gendering Violence: Patterns of Power and Constructs of Masculinity in the Acts of the Apostles." In *A Feminist Companion to the Acts of the Apostles*, edited by Amy-Jill Levine with Marianne Blickenstaff, 193–209. Cleveland, OH: Pilgrim Press, 2004.

Petronius. *Satyricon*. Translated by Michael Heseltine and W. H. D. Rouse. LCL. Cambridge: Harvard University Press, 1969.

Philo. Translated by F. H. Colson and Rev. G. H. Whitaker. 12 vols. LCL. London: William Heinemann, 1929–1962.

Pierce, Karen. "Ideals of Masculinity in New Comedy." In *Thinking Men: Masculinity and Its Self-Representation in the Classical Tradition*, edited by Lin Foxhall and John Salmon, 130–47. Leicester-Nottingham Studies in Ancient Society 7. London: Routledge, 1998.

Pilch, John. "'Beat His Ribs While He Is Young' (Sir. 30:12): A Window on the Mediterranean World." *BTB* 23.3 (1993) 101–13.

Pippin, Tina. *Death and Desire: The Rhetoric of Gender in the Apocalypse of John*. Literary Currents in Biblical Interpretation. Louisville: Westminster John Knox, 1992.

Plato. Translated by Harold North Fowler, W. R. M. Lamb, and Robert Gregg Bury. 10 vols. LCL. London: W. Heinemann, 1914–29.

Plautus, Titus Maccius. Translated by Paul Nixon. 5 vols. LCL. London: William Heinemann, 1916.

Potter, David. "Introduction." In *Life, Death, and Entertainment in the Roman Empire*, edited by D. S. Potter and D. J. Mattingly, 1–16. Ann Arbor: University of Michigan Press, 1999.

Powell, Mark Allan. *What Is Narrative Criticism?* Guides to Biblical Scholarship: New Testament Series. Minneapolis: Fortress, 1990.

Resseguie, James L. *Narrative Criticism of the New Testament: An Introduction*. Grand Rapids: Baker, 2005.

Rhoads, David M. *Israel in Revolution, 6–74 C.E.: A Political History Based on the Writings of Josephus*. Philadelphia: Fortress, 1976.

———. "Narrative Criticism: Practices and Prospects." In *Characterization in the Gospels: Reconceiving Narrative Criticism*, edited by David M. Rhoads and Kari Syreeni, 264–85. JSNTSS 184. Sheffield: Sheffield Academic, 1999.

———. "Performance Criticism: An Emerging Methodology in Second Testament Studies—Part I." *BTB* 36.3 (2006) 118–33.

———. *Reading Mark: Engaging the Gospel*. Minneapolis: Fortress, 2004.

Rhoads, David M., Joanna Dewey, and Donald Michie. *Mark as Story: An Introduction to the Narrative of a Gospel*. 2nd ed. Minneapolis: Fortress, 1999.

Rossing, Barbara R. *The Choice between Two Cities: Whore, Bride, and Empire in the Apocalypse.* Harvard Theological Studies 48. Harrisburg, PA: Trinity, 1999.
Richlin, Amy. "Gender and Rhetoric: Producing Manhood in the Schools." In *Roman Eloquence: Rhetoric in Society and Literature*, edited by William J. Dominik, 90–110. London: Routledge, 1997.
Rimmon-Kenan, Schlomith. *Narrative Fiction: Contemporary Poetics.* New Accents. London: Methuen, 1983.
Russell, Brigette Ford. "The Emasculation of Antony: The Construction of Gender in Plutarch's *Life of Antony*." *Helios* 25.2 (1998) 121–37.
Saddington, D. B. "The Centurion in Matthew 8:5–13: Consideration of the Proposal of Theodore W. Jennings, Jr., and Tat-Siong Benny Liew." *JBL* 125.1 (2006) 140–42.
———. "Military and Administrative Personnel in the New Testament." In *ANRW* 2.26.3, edited by Wolfgang Haase, 2409–35. Berlin: de Gruyter, 1996.
Saller, Richard P. *Personal Patronage under the Early Empire.* Cambridge: Cambridge University Press, 1982.
Satlow, Michael. "'Try to Be a Man':The Rabbinic Construction of Masculinity." *HTR* 89.1 (1996) 19–40.
Schüssler Fiorenza, Elisabeth. *The Book of Revelation: Justice and Judgment.* 2nd ed. Minneapolis: Fortress, 1998.
Seneca. *Moral Essays.* Translated by John W. Basore. 3 vols. LCL. London: W. Heinemann, 1928–35.
Skinner, Marilyn. "Zeus and Leda: The Sexuality Wars in Contemporary Classical Scholarship." *Thamyris* 3.1 (1996) 103–23.
Smallwood, E. Mary, editor. *Documents Illustrating the Principates of Gaius, Claudius, and Nero.* London: Cambridge University Press, 1967.
———. *The Jews under Roman Rule: From Pompey to Diocletian.* Studies in Judaism in Late Antiquity 20. Leiden: Brill, 1976.
Smith, Abraham. "'Full of Spirit and Wisdom': Luke's Portrait of Stephen (Acts 6:1–8:1a) as a Man of Self Mastery." In *Asceticism and the New Testament*, edited by Leif E. Vaage and Vincent L. Wimbush, 97–114. New York: Routledge, 1999.
Speidel, Michael. "Bithynian Gravestones of Roman Legionaries." In *Roman Army Studies*, edited by Michael Speidel, 2:180–87. Mavors Roman Army Researches 8. Stuttgart: F. Steiner, 1992.
———. "Furlough in the Roman Army." In *Roman Army Studies*, edited by Michael Speidel, 2:330–41. Mavors Roman Army Researches 8. Stuttgart: F. Steiner, 1992.
———. "The Centurion's Titles." In *Roman Army Studies*, edited by Michael Speidel, 2:21–39. Mavors Roman Army Researches 8. Stuttgart: F. Steiner, 1992.
———. "The Roman Army in Judea under the Procurators: The Italian and Augustan Cohort in the Acts of the Apostles." In *Roman Army Studies*, edited by Michael Speidel, 2:224–32. Mavors Roman Army Researches 8. Stuttgart: F. Steiner, 1992.
Spencer, F. Scott. "'Women of 'the Cloth' in Acts: Sewing the Word." In *A Feminist Companion to the Acts of the Apostles*, edited by Amy-Jill Levine with Marianne Blickenstaff, 134–54. Cleveland: Pilgrim, 2004.
Swancutt, Diana. "'The Disease of Effemination': The Change of Effeminacy and the Verdict of God (Romans 1:18—2:16)." In *New Testament Masculinities*, edited by Stephen D. Moore and Janice Capel Anderson, 193–233. Semeia 45. Atlanta: Society of Biblical Literature, 2003.

———. "Still before Sexuality: 'Greek' Androgyny, the Roman Imperial Politics of Masculinity, and the Roman Invention of the TRIBAS." In *Mapping Gender in Ancient Religious Discourses*, edited by Todd Penner and Caroline Vander Stichele, 11–61. BIS 84. Leiden: Brill, 2007.
Suetonius. *Lives of the Caesars.* Translated by J. C. Rolfs. 2 vols. LCL. London: W. Heinemann, 1914.
Tacitus. *The Histories*. Translated by Clifford H. Moore. *The Annals*. Translated by John Jackson. 4 vols. LCL. Cambridge, MA: Harvard University Press, 1925–37.
Tannehill, Robert C. *The Narrative Unity of Luke-Acts: A Literary Interpretation*. 2 vols. Foundations and Facets. Minneapolis: Fortress, 1994.
Taylor, Joan. "Pontius Pilate and the Imperial Cult in Roman Judaea." *New Testament Studies* 52.4 (2006) 555–82.
Thomas, Michael. "The World Turned Upside-Down: Carnivalesque and Satiric Elements in Acts." *Perspectives in Religious Studies* 31.4 (2004) 453–65.
Thompson, Marianne Meye. "'God's Voice You Have Never Heard, God's Form You Have Never Seen': The Characterization of God in the Gospel of John." In *Characterization in Biblical Literature*, edited by Elizabeth Struthers Malbon and Adele Berlin, 177–204. Semeia 63. Atlanta: Scholars, 1993.
Thompson, Richard. "Believers and Religious Leaders in Jerusalem: Contrasting Portraits of Jews in Acts 1–7." In *Characterization in Biblical Literature*, edited by Elizabeth Struthers Malbon and Adele Berlin, 327–44. Semeia 63. Atlanta: Scholars, 1993.
———. "Subtlety as a Literary Technique in Luke's Characterization of Jews and Judaism." In *Literary Studies in Luke-Acts: Essays in Honor of Joseph B. Tyson*, edited by Richard P. Thompson and Thomas E. Phillips, 313–26. Macon, GA: Mercer University Press, 1998.
Thurman, Eric. "Looking for a Few Good Men: Mark and Masculinity." In *New Testament Masculinities*, edited by Stephen D. Moore and Janice Capel Anderson, 137–62. Semeia 45. Atlanta: Society of Biblical Literature, 2003.
———. "Novel Men: Masculinity and Empire in Mark's Gospel and Xenophon's *An Ephesian Tale*." In *Mapping Gender in Ancient Religious Discourses*, edited by Todd Penner and Caroline Vander Stichele, 185–229. BIS 84. Leiden: Brill, 2007.
Tiede, David Lenz. *Prophecy and History in Luke-Acts*. Minneapolis: Fortress, 1980.
Valerius Maximus. *Memorable Doings and Sayings*. Edited and translated by D. R. Shackleton Bailey. LCL. Cambridge, MA: Harvard University Press, 2000.
Velleius Paterculus. *Compendium of Roman History: Res Gestae divi Augusti*. Translated by Frederick W. Shipley. LCL. London: W. Heinemann, 1924.
Walters, Jonathan. "Invading the Roman Body: Manliness and Impenetrability in Roman Thought." In *Roman Sexualities*, edited by Judith P. Hallett and Marilyn B. Skinner, 29–43. Princeton, NJ: Princeton University Press, 1997.
———. "'No More Than a Boy': The Shifting Construction of Masculinity from Ancient Greece to the Middle Ages." *Gender & History* 5.1 (1993) 20–33.
Walton, Steve. "The State They Were In: Luke's View of the Roman Empire." In *Rome in the Bible and the Early Church*, edited by Peter Oakes, 1–41. Grand Rapids: Baker, 2002.
Watson, George Ronald. "Documentation in the Roman Army." In *ANRW* 2.26.3, edited by Wolfgang Haase, 493–507. Berlin: de Gruyter, 1996.
Webster, Graham. *The Roman Imperial Army of the First and Second Centuries A.D.* London: Black, 1969.

Wilcox, Max. "The 'God-Fearers' in Acts—A Reconsideration." *JSNT* 4.13 (1981) 102–22.
Williams, Craig A. *Roman Homosexuality: Ideologies of Masculinity in Classical Antiquity.* Ideologies of Desire. Oxford: Oxford University Press, 1999.
Witherup, Ronald D. "Cornelius Over and Over and Over Again: 'Functional Redundancy' in the Acts of the Apostles." *JSNT* 15.49 (1993) 45–66.
Young, Steve. "Being a Man: The Pursuit of Manliness in *The Shepherd of Hermas*." *Journal of Early Christian Studies* 2.3 (1994) 237–55.
Zanker, Paul. *The Power of Images in the Age of Augustus.* Translated by Alan Shapiro. Jerome Lectures, 16th ser. Ann Arbor: University of Michigan Press, 1988.

Subject and Name Index

almsgiving
  angel, 34
  Barnabas, 31
  benefaction, 81–83
  Cornelius, 3, 8, 66, 83–85, 105, 112, 159
  fidelity, 103
  God-fearers, 96, 97
  reciprocity, 80
  rhetoric, 29
  temple, 108–9
Alston, Richard, 71–72, 144–45, 147, 161
alternative masculinities, 38, 61–67, 116, 167
Anderson, Janice Capel, 18, 62, 64
Augustan Cohort, 129–30
Augustus, emperor
  coinage, 150
  Caesarea, 153–54
  generosity, 81–82
  imperial cult, 103
  Judaism, 95
  physical appearance, 47
  piety, 73, 74
  reign, 91, 92, 133
  Res gest. divi Aug., 86, 116–17, 146–47
  soldiers, 119, 144
  virtues, 69, 78, 79

Bach, Alice, 12–13
baptism, 34, 35, 102–3, 128, 143
Barnabas, the evangelist, 30, 31, 32, 35, 170
Barton, Carlin
  blushing, 51
  elite Greco-Roman masculinity, 4, 39, 65
  physical appearance, 45–47
  politics, 38, 63
  shame, 54
Beard, Mary, 73, 90
benefaction
  Greco-Roman, 80–85, 99, 170
Booth, Wayne, 12
Borg, Marcus, 166
Boyarin, Daniel, 169
Burnett, Fred, 9
Caesarea
  Cornelius, 32, 135, 159
  coinage, 150n155
  Luke's strategy, 144, 153–56
  military inscriptions, 90, 131
  pre-war conflict, 123–24
Campbell, J.B., 89, 122, 146
centurion, *primus pilus*, 91, 92, 114, 121, 126
characterization
  ancient, 7–10
  Luke-Acts, 13–17, 26–29

modern, 10–13
circumcision
    Cornelius, 111
    Luke-Acts, 98, 101, 105, 169
    purity, 102
    Roman attitude, 151n161
Cohen, Shaye, 4, 93, 95, 97, 100, 109–10
coinage
    gender, 150
    Judea Capta, 86–87, 149–50
    piety, 74
    reminder of war, 125
    virtues, 74
Conway, Colleen
    Augustus, 116
    belief in Jesus, 141, 160
    gender categories, 68
    Jesus and emperor, 168
    literary reading, 4
    Moses, 106–7
    overview, 59–61
    recent work, 5, 38, 171–72
    Roman empire, 142
    self control, 153
    virtues, 71, 72
Cotter, Wendy, 92, 97–98
Culpepper, Alan, 24
D'Angelo, Mary Rose, 18–19, 38, 55–57, 61, 72
Danker, Frederick
    generosity, 80n51
    key words, 70
    Paul, 76
    piety, 74, 75
    rewards, 53–54
Darr, John, 7, 12, 13, 14–15
Davies, Roy, 131
Dewey, Joanna, 24, 29
Domitian, emperor, 86–87, 91, 101, 150
Ethiopian eunuch, 17, 30, 32, 35

Feldman, Louis, 106, 108
feminist hermeneutics, 13, 17–18, 20–22, 62, 158
Finn, Thomas, 96–97
Fiorenza, Elisabeth Schüssler, 171
food laws
    Cornelius, 111
    Luke-Acts, 98, 101, 105, 169
    military life, 94
    purity, 102
    Roman attitude, 151n161
Fowler, Robert, 10–11
Fox, Matthew, 49n67
Galinsky, Karl, 4, 71, 79, 116–17, 149–50
Garrison, Roman, 81
Gaventa, Beverly Roberts, 13, 16–17, 102, 165, 171
Gentiles
    Christianity, 169
    cleansing, 104
    Cornelius, 2, 5, 34, 35, 109, 157
    4 Maccabees, 62–63
    God-fearers, 96–97
    integration, 26, 99, 101, 102, 103, 111, 128, 159
    kings, 112
    military men, 100
    mission, 32
    prayer, 110
Gilbert, Gary, 98, 168
Gleason, Maud
    Conway, 59–60
    D'Angelo, 56, 57
    elite Greco-Roman masculinity, 4, 39
    Latin words, 167n12
    men in baths, 41
    New Testament scholarship, 38, 55, 65
    Polemo as exception, 53n84
    public speaking, 19, 42, 43–45

Subject and Name Index 187

sculptures, 50, 163
God-fearer
    Conway, 60
    historical evidence, 96–97
    Judaism, 159
    military life, 95–96, 98, 169n34
    Moses, 70
    piety, 5, 9, 35, 101, 105
    Roman, 2, 25
Goodman, Martin
    Caesarea, 155
    dehumanization, 145
    ideal male, 168–69
    pre-war climate, 123, 124
    reciprocity, 81
    Romans and Judeans, 4, 101, 151n161
    Titus, 86
Gowler, David, 7, 10, 11, 12, 13–14
Hadrian, emperor, 44, 131
Helgeland, Richard, 89
hermeneutic of masculinity
    fusion, 4, 158
    concerns, 20–23
    contributors, 55, 58, 62
    candidates, 170
Herod
    architecture, 154
    characterization, 14
    as foil, 6, 153
    generosity, 81, 82
    piety, 73, 77
Holy Spirit
    Acts 11 and 15, 99–100
    baptism, 102
    Cornelius, 9, 34, 67, 103, 137–38, 152
    falls upon Peter, 110, 111
    God of Israel, 135–36, men in Acts, 2, 27, 29, 35, 118
    Paul, 33
    Peter, 30
    Peter and Cornelius, 99
    poured out, 105, 142–43
    Stephen, 31, 32
    Tannehill, 15, 16
Howell, Justin, 90, 91, 98–100, 103
Ilan, Tal, 166
images, ancient
    Aphrodisias, 21–22
    centurions, 103
    coinage, 149–50
    elite men, 86
    emperors, 74
    piety, 69
    usefulness, 4, 50, 61, 149, 162
imperial cult, 98–100, 101, 103, 104, 105
inscriptions, ancient
    generosity, 81–82
    God-fearers, 96
    military, 90, 114, 129, 131, 132
    piety, 75
    recognition, 53
    Roman rulers, 73–74, 86
    shame, 54n88
    usefulness, 4, 61, 115, 116
    virtues, 78
Italian Cohort, 128–29
Jesus
    centurion, 141
    Cornelius, 101
    emperor, 105, 168
    feminine imagery, 165, 166
    Luke-Acts, 60, 84–85, 152, 160
    the man, 49n66, 59, 64
    righteousness, 79–80
Jewish masculinity, 57, 62–64, 168–69
John the Baptist, 100, 104–5
Johnson, Lee, 155
Julius Caesar, 45–47, 78, 94
Kahl, Brigitte, 171
Kampen, Natalie Boymel, 149, 162
Kenan, Schlomith Rimmon, 7, 10–11, 27, 28

188 Subject and Name Index

Kraabel, A.T., 96–97
Kraemer, Ross Shepard, 166
Kuefler, Mathew, 37
Larson, Jennifer, 171
LeBohec, Yann
  army as workforce, 120
  centurions, 91, 121
  emperor, 90
  function of army, 119
  Judea, 130–31, 132
  military history, 4
  obedience, 136
Lehmann, Clayton, 74
Lehtipuu, Outi, 28
Liew, Tat-siong Benny, 38, 55, 57–59, 61
Lopez, Davina, 21–22, 149–50
MacMullen, Ramsay, 121, 131–32
Malina, Bruce, 9–10, 22–23
Martin, Dale, 39, 40, 41, 51, 53
Matthews, Shelly, 19
Michie, Donald, 24, 29
Moloney, Francis, 24–25
Moore, Stephen
  alternative masculinity, 66
  4 Maccabees, 61–63, 64
  literary criticism, 15n33
  literary reading, 4
  narrative criticism, 24, 28
  recent work, 5, 38
  Williams, 48
Moses, patriarch, 70, 101, 102, 105–9, 111
Murray, Michele, 154
Nero, emperor, 69, 73, 132, 155, 163
Noreña, Carlos, 69, 71, 74, 78, 162
narrative criticism, 3, 4, 14–15, 24–29,
Painter, R. Jackson, 86, 131, 150
Paul, the evangelist
  Acts as a whole, 30, 32, 35, 118, 170
  almsgiving, 108–9

centurions, 129, 134, 141, 152
Christian, 23n59
feminine imagery, 165
Malina, 9
masculine imagery, 171
piety, 76–77
speech, 29
Penner, Todd, 52n77, 77n34, 153n167
Pentecost, 30, 99
Peter, the evangelist
  Acts as a whole, 30, 32, 67, 118, 143, 170
  baptism, 102–3, 110, 128
  Cornelius episode, 34, 87, 111, 113, 134, 144, 151
  gesture at feet, 3, 11, 135, 138–41, 152, 157
  obedience, 137
  piety, 76, 77, 79
  purity, 104
  recognition, 85
  righteousness, 80
  speech, 29, 35
  visions, 27, 99, 101–2
Philip, the evangelist, 27n79, 118
physiognomy, 43–45, 60n113
Pilate, 6, 123, 153
Pippin, Tina, 171
Potter, David, 132, 145–46
prayer, 96, 97, 98, 109–112
reader response criticism, 14n33, 29
Resseguie, James, 26
Rhoads, David
  characterization, 28
  forms of criticism, 15n33
  ideal reader, 29n89
  narrative criticism, 24, 25
  narrator, 26
  obstacles, 101
  repetition, 84
  toleration, 123

Richlin, Amy, 39, 42
Roman-Jewish war
   backdrop, 109, 115–6, 135, 151, 157
   Caesarea, 154–5
   Judaism, 93–94
   material remains, 86–87
   occupation, 131
   overview, 122–25
   physical force, 144
   temple, 108
Roman military
   calendar, 89, 94
   oath, 89–90, 94
   structure, 119–22
Rossing, Barbara, 171
Russell, Brigette, 42
Sabbath
   Luke-Acts, 95–96, 98, 105, 169
   military, 94
   purity, 102, Roman attitude, 151n161
Saddington, D. B., 59n111, 130, 131
Saller, Richard, 81
sexual behavior
   anti-Greek discourse, 42
   biology, 40–41
   domination, 38, 47–50
   as key, 39, 49n67
   New Testament characters, 57–59, 66–67, 167
   penetration, 43, 53
Skinner, Marilyn, 48
slaves, 34, 128
Smallwood, E. Mary, 94, 95
Speidel, M. P., 128–29
standards of judgment, 26, 30, 33, 101–2, 158
Stephen, the evangelist, 30, 31–32, 35, 118
Swancutt, Diana, 40, 41
Tannehill, Robert, 13, 15–16, 24
Taylor, Joan, 74
Thomas, Michael, 140
Tiberius, emperor, 91, 95n122, 125
Thompson, Richard, 8
Thurman, Eric, 61, 63–65, 66
Torah, 94, 95, 110, 170
Titus, emperor, 124, 150, 155
Trajan, emperor
   coinage, 86, 150
   generosity, 81, 82
   piety, 69, 74, 90
   victory, 163
Vander Stichele, Caroline, 52n77, 77n34, 153n167
Vespasian, emperor
   coinage, 71, 150, 155
   military, 131, 133
   siege, 124, 147
Walters, Jonathan, 47, 48, 49–50
Walton, Steve, 152
Williams, Craig
   domination, 160
   effeminacy, 52n81
   elite Greco-Roman masculinity, 4, 39
   New Testament, 55, 58–59, 65
   physical appearance, 47
   sex, 38, 48–49
Witherup, Ronald, 13, 17
Zanker, Paul, 117, 162

Ancient Documents Index

APOCRYPHA

4 Maccabees

5:22–23	63

PSEUDEPIGRAPHA

Sibylline Oracles

5:165–68	164

NEW TESTAMENT

Matthew

8:5–13	58, 59

Luke

1	87
1:51–52	140
1:52	6, 67, 118
3	100, 160
3:8	104
3:14	100, 103, 104
4	139
4:7	139
4:8	139
6:35	81
6:36	84
7	100, 129, 134, 141, 160
7:1–10	100
7:5	134
7:8	128
16	28, 87
22	84
22:24–30	112
22:24–27	80
22:25–27	85
22:25	112
22:26	112
22:27	81

Acts

1–10	35
1–9	4, 30, 31, 32, 35
1:8	142
1:13	30, 31
2	99, 101, 142, 159
2:1–4	143
2:14	30
2:17	105

Acts (continued)

2:38	30
2:43–47	31
3	85
3:12	76
3:16	76
4	170
4:7	30
4:8	30
4:13	11, 30, 140
4:29	30
4:31	30
4:32–35	31
4:35–37	31
5:3	30
5:9	30
6:1–6	31
6:3	31
6:5	31
6:8	31
7:55	32
7:58	33
7:60	32
8	159
8:1–3	33
8:14–17	142
8:26–40	17
8:26–28	31
8:30	31
9	31, 85, 170
9:1	33
9:10	33
9:17–19	33
9:19b–25	33
9:26–29	33
9:32–43	30
10–11	15, 16, 17, 27, 152
10	2, 3, 4, 6, 12, 13, 16, 18, 22, 30, 34, 60, 62, 67, 69, 71, 72, 83, 87, 95, 97, 98, 99, 102, 105, 107, 112, 113, 114, 119, 128, 138, 139, 140, 156, 159, 168, 170
10:2	11, 35, 72, 75, 83, 84, 85, 98, 103, 107
10:3	138
10:4	84, 85, 87, 98, 103, 109, 110
10:5	128
10:7–8	34, 128, 134
10:7	76, 138
10:9	34
10:15	104
10:22	35, 78, 79, 98, 107, 109, 111, 138
10:23–24	27
10:23	34
10:24	34, 134
10:25	138, 139, 140
10:25–26	140
10:26	139
10:27	34
10:28	104
10:30–33	138
10:30	34
10:31	87, 98, 109, 110
10:34–35	102
10:38	80, 105
10:42	105
10:44–48	110
10:44–46	99
10:44	113, 143
10:47	102, 143
10:48	34, 143
11	99
11:1–3	27
11:12	34, 103
11:15	34, 143
11:24	170
11:26	23
12	77
12:19	156
12:20	77

Acts (*continued*)

12:21–22	77
12:23	77
15	14, 99, 101, 105, 159, 170
15:7	102
15:9	103, 159
15:14–21	26
15:16–17	105
15:19–21	102, 159
15:19	102, 159
15:23–29	159
17:21	77
17:23	76
22	111
23	141
23:17–18	141
24	108
24:17	109
24:24–27	155
24:25	156
24:26	156
24:27	156
25:9	156
26:28	23
27	134, 141
27:3	129
27:11	129
27:31–32	134, 141
27:42–44	129, 134
27:42	129
28:25	142

1 Corinthians

3:1	165
4:15	171

2 Corinthians

6:3–10	171
6:4	171
6:5	171

Galatians

1:15	165
4:4	165
4:19	165

1 Thessalonians

2:7	165

1 Peter

4:16	23

Revelation

12:1–9	172
14	172
14:4	172
19	172
21:2	172

RABBINIC WRITINGS

Tosefta, *Pisha*

7.14.182L	93–94

GRECO-ROMAN WRITINGS

Aristotle, *Poetics*

15:2	8

Aristotle, *Nicomachean Ethics*

2:15	71

Augustus, *Res Gestae divi Augusti*

1:7	73
3	119
3:19–21	73
4:20	81
5:29	146
8	116
8:5	116

Dio Cassius, *Roman History*

37:17	101
56:34	146–47
67:14	101

Dio Chrysostom, *On Concord with Apamea*

3	82
8	83

Dio Chrysostom, *Protest against Mistreatment*

3	83
6	83
8	83
9	83

Dionysius of Halicarnassus, *Roman Antiquities*

1:5	117–18

Josephus, *Against Apion*

2:181	106
2:293	106

Josephus, *Antiquities of the Jews*

1:6.240	138
2:66	107
2:67	107
6:263–65	107
14:204	94
16:153–55	82
18:60–62	123
19:343	154
20:32–48	96
20:105–12	123

Josephus, *Jewish War*

1:149	148
1:351	148
2:175–77	123
2:223–27	123
2:262	122
2:409–10	124
2:450–54	93
2:457	155
2:487–98	124
3:329–35	133
4:37	125
4:440–42	133
4:560–61	164
6:8	148
6:175–76	148–49
6:262	122
7:142–44	147

Juvenal, *Satire*

16	148

Livy, *Histories*

8:14	91
22:60	117

Philo, *On Dreams*

124	108

Philo, *Embassy to Gaius*

156–57	108
157	81–82

Philo, *On the Life of Moses*

1:54–55	164–65
1:151	108

Plato, *Laws*

3:694–96	146

Plautus, *Braggart Warrior*

2:90	127

Seneca, *Moral Epistles*, "De Providentia"

6:3	117

Suetonius, *Deified Augustus*

26:1	133
31:5	117

Suetonius, *Tiberius*

36	95

Suetonius, *Vespasian*

8:1	147

Tacitus, *Annals*

1:23	147

Tacitus, *Histories*

1:56	136
1:59	136
1:43	137
1:54	137
5:5	101

Valerius Maximus, *Memorable Sayings and Doings*

6:ext. 2	133
6:10	126